The Novels of Evelyn Waugh

Series in English Literature

Fictional Theories and Three English Novels
Asha Kanwar

Kipling's Vision
Sukeshi Kamra

The Novels of Graham Greene
P.N. Pandit

The Novels of Virginia Woolf
B. Sudipta

Virginia Woolf and Anita Desai: A Comparative Study
Asha Kanwar

Nayantara Sahgal and Doris Lessing: A Feminist Study in Comparison
Neena Arora

The Novels of Evelyn Waugh

A Study in the Quest-Motif

A. CLEMENT

PRESTIGE

Published by
Prestige Books International
New Delhi 110 060

1994
ISBN: 81-85218-89-7

Phototypesetting by
Pivot Computers
Delhi 110 006
Phone 2918404

Printed at
Mehra Offset Press
Delhi 110 006

Contents

Preface

Evelyn Arthur St. John Waugh is one of the major twentieth-century novelists. I was encouraged in the idea of writing this book by the fact that there has not been a full-length study of Evelyn Waugh yet in our country. In his own country, namely Britain, Waugh was for a long time, regarded as a mere period-writer whose novels reflected accurately the moral confusion of the age. Reception of Waugh's novels in India has been slow. Given his inflexible "Englishness" and religious exclusiveness, it is not surprising that he has not been popular with the Indian fiction-reading public as his contemporary and admirer Graham Greene is. But the television series of *Brideshead Revisited* and *A Handful of Dust* in recent times has generated such enormous interest in the public that Evelyn Waugh has been recognised for what he is – a superb stylist and a remarkable literary craftsman. It is hoped that the publication of the present book will stimulate Waugh studies in our country.

I wish to thank Professor D.D. Baskiyar (Ranchi University, Bihar) and Professor Paul M. Doyle (Nassau Community College, New York, and Editor, *Evelyn Waugh Newsletter*) for their help and guidance in the present project. I also want to place on record my gratitude to Prestige Books for bringing out this book elegantly and expeditiously.

New Delhi **A. Clement**

Preface

[illegible]

[illegible] present book will stimulate further studies in our country.

[illegible]

[illegible]

Introduction

Fiction, whether in prose or verse, is an ordered restructuring of reality by means of which the bewildering multiplicity of life is reduced into an artistic integral unity. The movement of the creative process in fiction is from disorder to order, from the particular to the general and from matter to form. What the novelist or, for that matter, any writer of imaginative literature attempts to do, is to introduce, to adapt Waugh, "a little order into this chaos" of experiential existence. The writer has accepted as axiomatic that art is an imitation of life, or to use the classical term, "mimesis." However his job is not the drab and uninspired reportage of the teeming, throbbing life around us but a revealing imitation. Fiction can never be a lucid one-to-one mimesis but an imaginative interpretation of the riddle of life. The fiction writer sets out to express his own vision of life and give us an imitation of his own inner reality. What we are dealing here is with approximations, for as Leon Surmelian points out, "reality itself is beyond our grasp when we try to express in words."[1] Engaged as he is in a constant struggle with the chaos of life, apparently meaningless, the novelist is always fighting through a fog to make his meaning clear. The reader's novel-reading experience is, or ought to be, an experience of a living sensuous picture of life. Only a person with a special sensitivity for words can attempt at an aesthetic re-creation of life.

Evelyn Waugh whose literary career spanned a little over three decades following the instantly popular *Decline and Fall* in 1928 was a writer with such imaginative and expressive gifts. A born writer with an extraordinary sensory equipment, Waugh could not avoid his vocation that was his since his childhood. As he was to recall later in life in his slim volume of autobiography which he called, with an apparent humility not unmixed with irony, *A Little Learning*, his education seemed to provide him with the preparation for the unique trade of an English prose writer. Style, he maintained throughout his career was what distinguished literature from trash. Waugh's vision of life is embodied in a style which is characterized by lucidity, elegance and individuality—the three qualities which he thought combined "to form a preservative which ensures the nearest approximation to permanence in the fugitive art of letters."[2] Style to him was not a seductive decoration added to a functional structure; it was of the essence of his work of art. Among his early influences may be mentioned Ernest Hemingway, T.S. Eliot and Ronald Firbank. To the last mentioned he owned an allusive and cinematic style to which Waugh was to add the elegance and polish of a classicist. Despite his rare stylistic gifts however, Waugh was for a long time ignored, as Martin Stannard suggests,[3] as one of the foremost writers who was responsible for perfecting certain technical innovations of the English novel. The source of this neglect was largely Waugh himself. Like his own creations Apthorpe and Ben Ritchie-Hook in his war-trilogy, Waugh was an enfant terrible of the world of English letters. His idiosyncratic toryism and uncompromisingly rigid views on religion won him more enemies than friends. He enjoyed teasing those hostile to him by sudden and unexpected shifts in his critical and fictional positions which led his enemies commit grave and bizarre biographical fallacies. Waugh has given an accurate self-portrait in his novel *The Ordeal of Gilbert Pinfold* (1957), written directly after his recovery from an attack of temporary insanity. The tone is confessional:

> Among [the] novelists Mr. Gilbert Pinfold stood quite high. At the time of his adventure, at the age of fifty, he had written a dozen books all of which were still bought and read. They were translated into most languages and in the United States of America enjoyed intermittent but lucrative seasons of favour. Foreign students often chose them as the subject for their theses but those who sought to detect cosmic significance in Mr. Pinfold's work, to relate it to fashions in philosophy, social predicaments or psychological tensions were baffled by his frank curt replies to their questionnaires . . . Mr. Pinfold gave nothing away.[4]

Critics of Waugh, like those of his fictional persona, were baffled and angered by the intrusion into his works, especially after his *Brideshead*, of his intransigent views on politics and religion. However, they were fascinated by the complexity of his personality and since his death in 1966, there has been renewed interest in his works, thanks largely to the publication of his biography by his friend and co-religionist Christopher Sykes in 1975 and of Waugh's *Diaries* (ed. Michael Davie, 1976) and his *Letters* (ed. Mark Amory, 1980). The claim of Pinfold, who is Waugh's spokesman, that his novels are subjects of theses by foreign students is less fanciful than it may first appear. American and British research on Evelyn Waugh has been greatly stimulated in recent years. Two very valuable books of reference exclusively on Waugh—*Evelyn Waugh, A Reference Guide* (ed. Margaret Moriss and D.J. Dooley, 1984) and *A Bibliography of Evelyn Waugh* (ed. R.M. Davies et al, 1986) – together with *Evelyn Waugh, The Critical Heritage* (ed. Martin Stannard, 1984) attest to the growing popularity and literary stature of Evelyn Waugh. The *Evelyn Waugh Newsletter* begun in 1966 by Paul A. Doyle (working at present in the English Department at Naussau College, N.Y.) designed to stimulate research and continue interest in the life and writings of Evelyn Waugh, is published three times a year. The newsletter provides a running bibliography of scholarship on Waugh. Of the full-length studies on Waugh, Frederick J. Stopp's *Evelyn Waugh: Portrait of an Artist* seems most outstanding. Although written in 1958, before the last volume of the trilogy, Stopp's analysis of Waugh shows rare critical insights and vast sympathy for the author.

A study of Waugh criticism reveals a whole gamut of critical responses – from the insensitive indignation of Ernest Oldmeadow in his review of *Black Mischief* to Jerome Meckier's assertion that it is impossible not to love Waugh a little and admiration of Waugh's allusiveness and use of symbols. Waugh's other admirers include such figures as Anthony Powell, Anthony Burgess, Angus Wilson, his friend and co-religionist Graham Greene, Henry Green, Frank Kermode, David Lodge and Muriel Spark. Few of the reviewers of Waugh's own time detected his subtlety of approach to the dauntingly chaotic raw materials of life which he tried to reduce to order and meaningful coherence. Misunderstandings of his perceptions persisted late into his career but a gradual change in critical direction was noticeable in the late fifties. Present-day writers on Waugh have demonstrated sobriety and technical sophistication in their approach to his fiction, coupled with the ability to distinguish between the man who suffered and the mind which created some of the memorable characters and scenes in English fiction. The earlier critics praised Waugh often for the wrong reasons and tended to focus attention on certain aspects of his art to the near-total exclusion of the other aspects. They did not have at their disposal the critical tools of our own day which have helped us to see the ironic perspective of the author. What they failed to see was the seriousness of purpose behind the 'lightest' comedies of Waugh's youth.

Brideshead Revisited (1945) threw the critics into further disarray. Those, who like Edmund Wilson and Kingsley Amis, were admirers of the early Waugh deplored what they saw as extravagant romanticism of the novel's language and the intrusion of the author's militant Catholicism into the narrative. The novel seemed to signal the author's departure from his customary satiric vein. On the other hand, those who hailed *Brideshead* as Waugh's magnum opus began to make a serious reappraisal of the earlier novels and wondered whether Waugh had not been a serious writer from the very beginning of his novelistic career. Although Waugh himself regretted the cloying luxuriance of style of the novel and revised it in 1959, he did not regret the mystical element of the novel and made it explicit in his 'Fan Rare' article that in his future books he would be concerned with two things: style and man's relation to God, in other words, throwing off his disguise as a light-hearted satirist which hid his real purpose. Despite the fact that Waugh lost his prestige as an entertainer, with some of the critics, *Brideshead* became a best-seller and made him a celebrity in America. Waugh's rejection of the Hollywood proposal to turn the novel into a film on the grounds that the script-writers of the projected film missed the novel's theological meaning is now well-known. It was a question which involved the author's aesthetic principle. Several literary journals which at first ignored Waugh began to take notice of him with the publication of *Brideshead*. Even Leavis's *Scrutiny* which consistently ignored Waugh, referred to his *Loved One* (1948) in one of its articles. With the publication of *Unconditional Surrender* (1961), the last volume of the war-trilogy, Waugh's stature as a major novelist who could grapple with life's issues was firmly established.

In over-emphasising the satire the critics have also misinterpreted the element of fantasy and grotesque in the early novels. Critics who have acclaimed Waugh's early novels have not demonstrated adequate sensitivity to the function of the grotesques in the Waugh universe. As in Flannery O'Connor, the American "Southern" Catholic writer, there is nothing gratuitous in the use of the grotesque. It is meant to highlight the distortion in life that is in desperate need of spiritual redemption. The pervasive presence of the grotesque in Waugh suggests their basic sense of irrationality of human experience where fixed values have ceased to exist. It is the sensuous expression of the irresolvable paradox of existence in a world that defies logical understanding. The idea of the grotesque is inextricably intertwined with that of the 'absurd.' 'Absurd' denotes something that is out of harmony or incongruous or ridiculous. But the word has wider connotation than its dictionary meaning when it is used by writers like Camus or Sartre or any of the existentialist writers. In an essay on Kafka, Ionesco defined his understanding of the term as follows: "Absurd is that which is devoid of purpose. . . . Cut off from his religious metaphysical and transcendental roots, man is lost; all his actions become senseless, absurd, useless."[5]

A sense of the senselessness of life, of the inevitable devaluation of ideals, purity and purpose is, in a way of speaking, the theme of much of the work of Evelyn Waugh and Flannery O'Connor. Albert Camus who once told a group of churchmen that while he shared their concern for the human condition even if he did not share their hope, said nearly the same thing. In *The Myth of Sisyphus*, one of the great, seminal examinations of the human situation in a world of shattered beliefs, Camus said: "A world that can be explained by reasoning, however faulty, is a familiar world. But in a universe that is suddenly deprived of illusions and of light man feels a stranger. He is an irremediable exile, because he is deprived of memories of a lost homeland as much as he lacks the hope of a promised land to come. This divorce between man and his life, the actor and his setting, truly constitutes the feeling of Absurdity."[6]

Whereas Camus viewed the human predicament from the secular-agnostic standpoint, Waugh and Flannery O'Connor viewed the same situation from a religious perspective. Art, with writers of Christian concern such as Waugh and O'Connor must point beyond itself to transcendent values which alone can give meaning to the lives of the characters. Cut off from grace, the early Waugh heroes move through an utterly alienated world. In such a confused world governed by irrationality where nothing can be predicted, man becomes a willing victim and plaything of frightening coincidences and chance.

This brings us to the question of the nature of Waugh's satire. When Waugh was asked if his books were meant to be satirical, he replied: "No. Satire is a matter of period. It flourishes in a stable society and presupposes homogeneous moral standards – the early Roman Empire and 18th century Europe. It is aimed at inconsistency and hypocrisy. It exposes polite cruelty and folly by exaggerating them. It seeks to produce shame. All this has no place in the Century of the Common Man where vice no longer pays lip service to virtue."[7] This quotation is taken from the article headed "Fan-Fare" which appeared in *Life* in 1946, not long after the publication of *Brideshead Revisited* which won Waugh international fame. But as critics have noted, the tone of the article suggests that Waugh has not been entirely serious in his description of the nature of satire. As James W. Nichols has observed, as far as the novel is concerned, a "satire . . . is a novel so constructed and so written as to embody a point of view which adversely criticises the manners and morals of its characters – and often the society to which they belong. Even a casual reading will make plain that most of Waugh's early novels are intended to be satire as well as comic."[8] Nichols expands the idea further and argues that most great satire has been written at times when there was great agreement about what constituted right moral standards. The modern satirist cannot count upon homogeneous standards in his audience. Therefore he has to establish within the satire a moral norm which the audience will accept.

In contrast to irony where the reader is not sure of what the author's attitude is or what his own is supposed to be, the moral norms of satire are clear and it assumes standards against which the grotesque and the absurd are to be measured. Satire, as Northrop Frye defines it, is "militant irony," which by its very nature demands "a token fantasy a content which the reader recognises as grotesque and at least an implicit moral standard, the later being essential in a militant attitude to experience."[9] Thus the very act of selection of the satirist's "absurdities" is a moral act. The act of satire is structurally close to the comic, for what is involved in satire is a comic struggle of two societies. One normal and moral and the other absurd, irrational and defiant of the moral law. So his own disavowal to the contrary notwithstanding, Waugh was a satirist throughout his career – scathing in tone in the early novels and somewhat subdued in the later ones. His satire has two essential things common to all that genre, namely humour founded on a sense of the grotesque or the absurd and the object of attack with which, from Waugh's moral standpoint, he has little in common. Taking a high moral line, Waugh exposes the futility and smugness of the people living in a world full of anomalies, injustices, follies and crimes.

Critics who complain that the early novels of Waugh lack a stable moral centre have misunderstood the tone of these novels and in fact the purpose of Waugh's satire as a whole. Even such critics as Malcolm Bradbury, Graham Martin and James F. Carens have maintained that not until *Brideshead Revisited* has Waugh shown responsibility as a serious writer. *Decline and Fall, Vile Bodies, Black Mischief* and *A Handful of Dust*, are in their view negative and cruelly destructive. But as Jeffrey Heath[10] has argued, far from being cruel for the sake of being cruel the early novels demonstrate what Waugh was to make more explicit in *Brideshead* and after, that no writer worth his name can create a heterocosm to the total exclusion of God and his design in creation. In his letter of 13 Oct. 1961 to the editor of *The Spectator* he expresses one of his credal tenets as a writer: "writing is an expression of thought. There is no abstract writing. All literature implies moral standards and criticism – the less explicit the better."[11] Nearly fifteen years earlier he had said the same thing in "Fan-Fare" in which he said that only by leaving out God can a writer make his characters "pure abstractions" and taxed some of the modern writers with committing the error: "The failure of modern novelists since and including James Joyce is one of presumption and exorbitance. They are not content with artificial figures which hitherto passed so gracefully as men and women. They try to represent the whole human mind and soul and yet omit its determining character – that of being God's creature with a defined purpose."[12]

Waugh's satires had a profounder moral and religious purpose than his detractors suspected. Like the satirists of the eighteenth century England, Waugh exposed "his target as corrupt as a means of positing the mode of its redemption."[13] The fate of the characters in the early Waugh novels who are indeed caricatures, is the fate of the men and women of an age which is reeling from the collapse of traditional values and institutions. Waugh uses the physical activities of these zany amoralists to suggest their spiritual needs. His growing conservatism in religion and politics is linked to his growing scepticism about man's ability to answer ultimate questions for himself. The fates of Paul Pennyfeather, Grimes and Prendergast in *Decline and Fall*, of Agatha Runcible who meets with violently raving death in *Vile Bodies* and Prudence who is "eaten" by her lover at a cannibal's feast in *Black Mischief* graphically dramatise the spiritual deprivation of a whole generation. Their spiritual affliction, Waugh wants his readers to infer, is the inevitable and unimprovable consequence of the Fall of Man. And unless he seeks to owe allegiance to an authority or tradition outside himself, modern man has little or no chance to redeem himself. Waugh's satires are attempts at "persuasions." Although he, as satirists do, distances himself from his characters, he makes himself felt throughout by means of the measured style, at once allusive and evocative, of a self-confessed classicist. Waugh's own normal standard is to be implied in the Palladian elegance of language in which is rendered the chaos and moral collapse of the world of his characters. They are victims not of the author's rage, but rather of their own ignorance. In attacking what he sees as the corrupt and quantitative values of his times, Waugh implies a set of values which have religious and moral orientations. Thus in a paradoxical way Waugh's presence is most pervasive in his satires. This is true of *The Loved One* (1948) which critics hailed as a perfect little masterpiece in the Waughian manner by which they meant Waugh's cool indifference to his "victims." On the contrary *The Loved One* is one of Waugh's most religious novels in which he examines, although not overtly, the theological implications of death and the need for human identity. By the same token, his *Scoop* (1938) in which he lampooned devious and unprofessional journalism implies, by contrast, the author's unswerving moral assumptions. Waugh valued equally moral and aesthetic disciplines.

As far back as 1956, A.A. DeVitis in his *Roman Holiday: The Catholic Novels of Evelyn Waugh* suggested that Waugh's position as a novelist can be fully assessed only if his novels are put in the context of modern agnostic literature. DeVitis was one of the first writers on Waugh who argued that the latter's moral stance informed his entire corpus. Jerome Meckier in his insightful review article "Evelyn Waugh" in *Contemporary Literature* (1977) speaks of Waugh's "Apollonian Christianity" underlying even his pessimistic comedies and of his Catholicism being latent in his early fiction. Critics who have begun to see the unity in Waugh's fictional oeuvre will readily assent to the view that Waugh was from the beginning a Christian writer who respected the classical or rather neo-classical virtues of order and appeal to authority. "Waugh believed," says Meckier, "in the rationality of Catholicism as an adjunct to the reasonable man's desire for meaningfulness, order and restraint."[14] Calvin W. Lane in his *Evelyn Waugh* (1981) taking a similar view on the religious element in Waugh's fiction strongly asserts that Waugh's Catholicism is manifest in his early works by his implied condemnation of Protestant ethos. One may infer from Lane's argument that the demarcation of Waugh's comic and Catholic novels may after all be an artificial one. Further support to the argument that Waugh had a religious temperament from the beginning, may prove redundant.

In his Christian perspective from which he views contemporary disillusionment and the exceptional discipline which his art reflects, Waugh resembles T.S. Eliot to whom he was drawn while young and for whom he retained admiration throughout his career. Rebecca West in her review of *Vile Bodies* in 1930 was among the first critics to notice this literary affinity. Cecchim Giovanni who in his article in 1963 accused Waugh's critics of not paying adequate attention to his literary methods maintained that his works deserved as close a study as T.S. Eliot's, for the writings of the two writers represented a gradual process of clarification. Eliotean echoes are heard not only in *A Handful of Dust* (the title is itself a quotation from Eliot's *Waste Land*) but in *Brideshead* and the war-trilogy. It was however left to Peter E. Firchow in 1971 to make a scholarly research into Waugh's literary borrowings from T.S. Eliot, Tennyson, Dickens and others. Edward McAleer in his article on *Decline and Fall* in *Evelyn Waugh Newsletter* for Winter 1973, called attention to Waugh's technique of imitation of passages form the Bible, Shakespeare, Pater and other writers—an allusive technique usually associated with Eliot. *Decline and Fall* is a prose *Waste Land* in which like his great poetic predecessor, Waugh summons up the past by allusions to the great masterpiece to expose the trivialisation of the modern age.

Having identical moral concerns in their writings, Waugh and Eliot wondered whether the values of the world in which they lived could withstand the onslaught of barbarism. The characters in Waugh's novels were wastelanders who in Eliot's words in "The Dry Salvages," the third of the latter's Quartets, "had experience but missed the meaning."[15] Nowhere is the similarity more apparent than in Waugh's treatment of the recurring narrative motif—the quest—and the images with which the quest motif is fleshed out in the novels. The recurrence of the quest motif in Waugh's novels in terms of the quest shows distinct stages of Waugh's imaginative vision and the rich diversity of his theme. An interpretation of Waugh's novels in terms of the quest shows distinct stages of Waugh's own career as a novelist—"an early period of waste land frustration resulting in destructive satire from *Decline and Fall* through *A Handful of Dust*, then conversion proclaimed in *Brideshead Revisited* and afterwards total allegiance to Roman Catholic tradition as a rock in the midst of social and moral decay"[16]—a progression closely parallel to T.S. Eliot's from his *Waste Land* through *Ash Wednesday* to the *Four Quartets*.

The word 'quest' as used by Sir James Frazer in his *The Golden Bough* and Jessie Weston in her *From Ritual to Romance* may be defined as a search for someone or for something which can restore a former healthy state. But as Peter Revell in his book *Quest in Modern American Poetry* points out, the word "seems to imply (though the standard dictionaries do not support the view) something different from a search—the searcher knows what he is looking for, can often describe it in considerable detail, while the quester seeks to find something not completely known, or imperfectly understood. The most rewarding quest is one which continues indefinitely."[17] The "quest," this definition implies, is a ceaseless exploration of the self, a search for existential meaning, sometimes mysterious and terrifying, and an endless process of growth in maturity and wisdom. By its very nature therefore a quest has a spiritual or metaphysical dimension but in which the knowledge of the self is one of its essential aspects. A completely successful quest leads to the discovery of several truths about the individuals who undertake the voyage of exploration—truths about themselves, of the societies they are alienated from and of the need for integration. In no other way can enlightenment which comes in the wake of a new awareness of self and others and an awareness of human interrelationships, be achieved than through the process of questing.

Since the virtual re-discovery of the Arthurian legend (as B. Taylor and E. Brewer have argued in their book *The Return of King Arthur*[18]), writers have become aware of the potential of the myth of the Holy Grail as a new source of the symbolism of the quest. The myth has such a strong hold on man's imagination even today that writers of the twentieth century have found in it the means of expressing something of the attitudes, ideals and anxieties of their times. The Holy Grail has come to signify the unceasing human aspiration towards something more than human gratification. Each age thought that the Grail gave new and symbolic expression to its own experience. As Charles Kingsley the nineteenth century novelist aptly remarked, "Each of us has a Golden Fleece to seek and dragons to slay before we win it."[19] It is a type of quest which demanded personal valour and self-sacrifice, but a sacrifice which is worth while, for even if one fails in the quest, it still consoles us with the thought that the attempt is its own reward. The myth of the Holy Grail, like that of Perseus with the winged sandals, is concerned with self-realisation and with the processes of individuation. As with most symbolic stories, inner meanings are apprehended through the outer events. Writers like Charles Williams and C.S. Lewis have found the Grail episodes suitable vehicle of transcendent religious experience that goes beyond the comprehension of expectations of conventional, every-day religion. The dedicated quest of Galahad provided admirable subjects for psychological exploration, through the medium of dramatic monologue and poetic drama. The First World War helped those who lived through its horrors to direct attention to an aspect of the Arthurian legend not previously found significant – the Waste Land. The term struck T.S. Eliot as most appropriate as a metaphor for the spiritual desolation and barrenness of the western society in the nineteen twenties. There were other writers as well who freely used the motifs and symbols and also the structure of the Grail myth to represent the states of mind and spirit, both of the individual and the community.

More than any other writer in the twentieth century, it was T.S. Eliot who while emphasising the image of the Waste Land, the spiritual poverty and moral decadence, at the same time conceived of the Grail quest as the means for achieving spiritual renewal in an evil time. Writers of the nineteenth century saw the legend merely as a basis of allegory, but with the publication of Eliot's poem in 1922, writers of the twenties and after began to see beneath the narrative surface of the Grail stories new and startling meanings for an age which seemed to have lost its moral centre. The single most important literary cause was the publication of Jessie Weston's *From Ritual to Romance* in 1920. Eliot himself suggested the importance and value of Weston's book in his 'Notes on the Waste Land':

> Not only the title but the plan and a good deal of the incidental symbolism of the poem were suggested by Miss Jessie L. Weston's book on the Grail Legend. . . . Weston's book will elucidate the difficulties of the poem much better than my notes can do; and I recommend it (apart from the great interest on the book itself) to any who think such elucidation of the poem worth the trouble.[20]

Jessie Weston gave new authenticity to the grail stories by interpreting them anthropologically, applying the methodology of Sir James Frazer's *The Golden Bough*, another important book on the study of the quest. Weston asserted that far from being a product of imagination, literary or popular, the Grail story had at its root, the record more or less distorted, of an ancient Ritual having for its ultimate object the initiation into the secret of life, physical or spiritual. With Weston's interpretation of the myth, the images of the Grail story acquired newer connotations and symbolic resonances.

The central theme of Eliot's poem is man's need for spiritual rebirth, for which the symbolism of the grail was an excellent vehicle. From the legend Eliot took two major images, the Waste Land and the Fisher King. But in the poem, as Taylor and Brewer remark, "though the Grail chapel appears there is no quest, no Grail city or castle, no lance or cup. It is the devastation rather than the means of revitalisation with which the poem is concerned."[21] Although Eliot's poem runs counter to the vegetation myth of Weston which suggests that the land will experience regeneration, the myth of the Grail becomes in Eliot's hands, a potent instrument of exploration, making possible an analysis of his own experience, at the same time that it illuminates our understanding of the sickness of our times. Even while admitting that Eliot's allusive method involved a wide range of reference drawing upon recondite material, pagan and Christian as well as upon several different literatures, yet without Jessie Weston's *From Ritual to Romance* there would probably have been no such poem for no other single source could have provided him with the plan and symbol of the Grail myth.

All legends are facets of a timeless reality. The Holy Grail of the Arthurian legend has been looked upon as an aid as well as a standard to be achieved. It brings sustenance and healing to the sinful and has always been in some form or other adapted at each stage of the imitations of the consciousness of man. Thus, according to Gareth Knight, to the tribal Celts it was a "magical, regenerating, bountiful, inspirational cauldron long before it became one of the implements of Christ's passion to medieval man."[22] Its role throughout the ages has been to awaken man's self-consciousness.

There can be little doubt that Evelyn Waugh was influenced both in the technique and theme by T.S. Eliot. In the satiric world of *Decline and Fall, Vile Bodies* and *Black Mischief* the adventures of an ingenu or anti-hero or a rogue parody the quest pattern of the hero of the romantic world, in which the hero's adventures take the form of a quest or voyage dealing with his triumphant return and a happy marriage. The quests of Paul Pennyfeather, of Adam Fenwick and Basil Seal, in different ways reflect the chaos of the debased world by becoming aimless themselves. This picaresque pattern moves us to recognition of the chaos of our own times. The dull canal in "The Fire Sermon," the third section of Eliot's poem, which offers little hope of spiritual growth, makes its appearance in Waugh's *Vile Bodies*. Tony Last in *A Handful of Dust* is a quester who has failed, for he does not put the right questions which will release Todd from his spiritual dungeon. Instead he becomes a prisoner in the latter's hands. *A Handful of Dust* most fully echoes the quest for the Grail and Eliot's *Waste Land.*

Northrop Frye's discussion of the quest-motif and his three-fold classification may be a further critical aid in the interpretation of Waugh's fiction:

> The complete form of the romance is clearly the successful quest and such a completed form has three main stages: the stage of the perilous journey and the preliminary minor adventures; the crucial struggle, usually some kind of battle in which either the hero or his foe or both must die; and the exaltation of the hero. We may call these three stages respectively, using Greek terms, the *agon* or conflict, the *pathos* or death-struggle and the *anagnorisis* or discovery, the recognition of the hero, who has clearly proved himself to be a hero even if he does not survive the conflict.[23]

Broadly speaking, Frye's description of the quest puts Waugh's novels into two categories: the early satiric ones and the later romantic ones. The characters in the fiction of the early Waugh are naive, who, without either developing or aging, go through one adventure after another aimlessly. With *Brideshead Revisited*, there is a beginning of what Frye terms "romance" in which the minor adventures of the hero leads up to a major climacteric adventure of which hints are thrown early on in the story. We may call this major adventure, according to Frye, the element that gives the literary form to the romance, the quest. It is after a series of adventures or rather misadventures that Charles Ryder in *Brideshead* and Guy Crouchback in the war-trilogy discover themselves.

According to Frye, a quest involving conflict assumes two main characters, a protagonist or hero and an antagonist or an enemy, thus making the central form of the quest of romance dialectical: everything focused on a conflict between the hero and the enemy and all the reader's values bound up with the hero. The enemy is associated with winter, darkness, confusion, sterility, moribund life and old age while the hero with spring, dawn, order, fertility, vigour and youth. As examples, Frye cites the stories of St. George and Perseus, heroes who slay dragons. Perseus arrives when the land is laid waste by a sea monster who has devoured one young person after another until it is now the turn of the king's own daughter. The hero after performing such preliminary feats as beheading the ugly Medusa, undertakes the major adventure of killing the awful monster and marrying the king's daughter. The ritual analogies of the myth suggest that the sterility of the land is present in the age and impotence of the king. His position is that of Adonis overcome by the boar of winter. Adonis's wound is suggestive of symbolic castration. Further examples are provided by the Bible. The leviathan, the sea-monster is diametrically opposed to the plans of the Messiah and is the source of social sterility. Described in the Book of Job as the "king over all the children of pride," leviathan is equally associated with the natural sterility of the fallen order of nature, a world of struggle, poverty and disease. An elaborate dragon-killing metaphor in Christian symbolism in which the leviathan, Satan and the Edenic serpent are all identified in the Book of Revelation where the hero is Christ and the rescued bride the Church. Frye concludes his argument on the quest by saying that translated into ritual terms, the quest-romance is the victory of fertility over the waste-land.[24]

There is no direct confrontation between the hero and the dragon in Waugh as in the myth of Perseus and the Bible stories. Paul Pennyfeather in *Decline and Fall* does not go in search of adventure but allows himself to become a victim of chance. The world of the early satires is a world governed by Fortune rather than by Christian Providence. And yet the duality of good and evil, of the Apollonian and the Dionysiac, underlines the themes of the satires. Although Waugh does not explicitly express his own values, through recurrent imagery and lucidity of style, he lets the reader know what those values are. For him the Apollonian meant Christian order and rationality while the Dionysiac meant chaos and irrationality. At a crucial point in the adventures of his hero in *Decline and Fall,* Waugh describes him as the "shadow that has fitted about this narrative under the name of Paul Pennyfeather" which

> materialized into the solid figure of an intelligence, well-educated, well conducted young man, a man who could be trusted to use his vote at a general election with discretion and proper detachment, whose opinion or a *ballet* or a crucial essay was rather better than most people's, who could order a dinner without embarrassment and in a critical French accent, who could be trusted to see to luggage at foreign railway-stations and might be expected to acquit himself with decision and decorum in all emergencies of civilized life.[25]

Paul Pennyfeather is several things at the same time; a student, a bridegroom, a convict and finally a minister. These several roles reflect the lack of stable identity. Identity for Waugh, as Heath has said, is a result of "affiliation with enduring institutions."[26] The characters in *Vile Bodies* and *Black Mischief* and even Tony Last in *A Handful of Dust* for all his high-mindedness suffer a similar fate. They are creatures of chaos. Their selves fragmented, these characters do not understand the nature of the world and the tasks they set out to perform. Unlike Perseus or St. George, they are unaware of the dangers that await them. The Dionysiac forces outside are arrayed against them and stop them from achieving individuation or growth. Because of their own spiritual blindness, these picaroons do not comprehend the nature of evil. Salvation in Waugh is predicated upon an acute sense of discrimination between good and evil. Unless like Theseus and Perseus and other mythical heroes, they confront evil or Hell, "the toothed gullet of an aged shark," and not allow the forces of evil to destroy them, the characters in Waugh satires can never attain Christian redemption. The car race in *Vile Bodies* is a similar case of unprecedented speed without specific goals. Miss Agatha Runcible as a representative of the modern men who are motivated in their actions by no other desire than that of a strong death-wish.

It is in the later Catholic novels that the journey, as in the classical examples cited by Frye, becomes a metaphor as the heroes begin to comprehend its nature and meaning. In proportion as they grow, the protagonists are confronted with the essential meaning of reality. Helena is the supreme exemplar of a clear-eyed quester who setting aside all the airy speculations of theologians belonging to different doxies, goes in search of the True Cross which alone will help men to face up to the answers of meaninglessness of their absurd condition. *The Ordeal of Gilbert Pinfold* which Waugh wrote in 1957, in the years between the second and final instalments of his war-trilogy is Waugh's most successful fictional dramatisation of his own confrontation with and control of the forces of evil. As Anthony Cronin in his "Portrait of Artist" in *Sunday Times* observed, the novel celebrates the author's triumph over malevolent spirits by means of courage, stubbornness and adroitness.[27] The ship on which Pinfold travels is significantly called "Caliban," the savage and deformed slave in Shakespeare's *Tempest.* Caliban is an image of un-god-like aspects of human nature, which often set themselves up as God. He stands for a force or power which lead men to diabolism or perversion. In psychological terms Caliban may be identified with the "shadow." If such a figure is understood and brought into proper relation with the other figures, it becomes an essential prerequisite for the deliverance of the ego from the false belief in its own goodness or spiritual pride which the Greeks called "hubris." One cannot rise to spiritual heights without confronting the "shadow" and coming to terms with it.

The evil that the heroes in Waugh's Christian novels have to wrestle with is not only the "dragon" external to them but more often the anarchic, beastly impulses that emanate from within. They cannot ignore the demonic forces which may reside within them as in the case of Pinfold or exist outside them as Guy Crouchback is to experience during the war. To ensure our sense of mystery of God and the universe we need a sense of evil.

In the "committed" Catholic novels—*Brideshead Revisited, Helena*, the war-trilogy and *The Ordeal of Gilbert Pinfold*—the quest motif suggests that life is a journey with a goal. The journey has however been an archetype since the classical times; it furnishes the framework for *The Odyssey, The Aeneid* and *The Divine Comedy*. In all these works, the journey takes on the significance of a quest in which the protagonist searches for a goal of some importance to himself and his society. The principal characters in Waugh's Catholic novels are all loners who by their uniqueness represent the latent spiritual impulses of a society which however debased can yet be redeemed. Their progression is not merely a geographically linear one. The inward nature of the quest is increasingly emphasised in these novels, as they probe the psyches of not only the protagonists but of their societies. The waste lands of the *Inferno*, and the Arthurian romances are similar to the sterile landscapes that the heroes of Waugh's Catholic novels have to cross. And as in Dante, Charles Ryder, Helena, Guy Crouchback and Pinfold have to traverse the meaningless terrains in order to reach a green world where they can find new life and spiritual rejuvenation. These heroes of a spiritual odyssey have another similarity: they are rootless and homeless. Charles Ryder, the narrator, describes himself in the epilogue of *Brideshead*, as "homeless, childless, middle aged, loveless." Like Ryder his friend Sebastian desires only solitude. The recurring image of the "shadows" in the novel strongly reinforces the sense of utter lostness. Helena's journey to the Middle East, in her advancing old age is a typically lone quest for a spiritual ideal. Guy Crouchback in the war-trilogy fulfils all the classical conditions of a quester. His asceticism, homelessness, womanlessness, his dedication to an ideal and repudiation of the seductions of the world—all these class Guy with the heroes of the Arthurian and pagan legends. In these novels, the protagonists, unlike those in the early Waugh, move step by painful step towards blessedness. Except Helena, the other heroes are only dimly aware, if at all, of the blessedness that lies ahead. But throughout their journey, hints and symbols of Divine life are thrown in their way. In the years between *A Handful of Dust* and *Brideshead Revisited*, Waugh wrote three novels: *Scoop* (1938), *Work Suspended* (1942) and *Put Out More Flags* (1942). These books mark the start of Waugh's literary transition, in which Waugh experimented with first-person writing and interior monologue. But they are equally important from the point of view of theme. For all its resemblance to the earlier satiric manner, *Scoop* explores the contrast between the inauthentic secularity with the permanence authenticated by religion. Stylistically, *Work Suspended* makes a complete departure from Waugh's earlier books. Written in the first person narrative and in a language highly metaphorical *Work Suspended* treats the theme of the maturation of the artist. It tells the story of John Plant, disagreeable, deceitful and aesthetical who shows signs of growth. From an unsuccessful artist who loves the second-rate and the shoddy, and cut off from his fellow human beings, Plant, through the influence of the young Lucy who is open and unselfish, comes to true nature of artistic vocation. The birth of Lucy's child symbolises Plant's own growth, from that of the "petrified egg" that his dead father had made him into a mature, well-rounded human being. Like Paul Pennyfeather, Adam Symes and other earlier heroes, John Plant lacks precise identity and is in constant flight, for he feels ever threatened. He is immature and has to go a long way to learn the value of self-sacrifice:

> There was the rub. It was precisely this fear that had been working in my mind for days, the fear of making myself a sitting shot to the world. It lay at the root of the problem of privacy; the choice which torments to the verge of mania between perpetual flight and perpetual siege; and the unresolved universal paradox of losing things in order to find them.[28]

John Plant is literally and metaphorically, a homeless artist and the search for the right sort of house for him to live in, on which he embarks in the company of Lucy, become the quest which becomes at once the structure of genuine friendship between the two individuals and the symbol of the search for permanence, order and sustaining stability. Martin Stannard in his article "*Work Suspended*: Waugh's Climacteric" argues that Waugh left the novel incomplete because it lacked a supernatural dimension.[29] He disliked reverting to the method of the earlier writings which working within a humanist framework described behaviour and asserted Catholic values by negative suggestion. But Waugh does seem to have reverted to the style of the thirties in *Put Out More Flags*. Outrageously funny like the earlier Mayfair pieces, *Put Out More Flags* is at the same time, a serious examination of the destructiveness generated by the Second World War and many of the themes central to the later war-trilogy. This absurdist energy which negates all the contemplative values of religion is embodied in Basil Seal who is even more seasoned in his roguery than when we saw him last in *Black Mischief*. By making this rascal and man of action which "the country needs"[30] during the war triumph over insubstantial aestheticism represented by Ambrose Silk,

Waugh exposes the folly and cupidity of the war-time generation. Waugh is to suggest in the Catholic novels that are to follow—*Brideshead Revisited*, *Helena* and the war-trilogy—that religion alone can offer the requisite balm for the human corruption of *Put Out More Flags*.

The marked change in tone and style in *Brideshead Revisited* and the other Catholic novels signals the changed nature of the quest of the protagonists. *Brideshead* is the first of the novels in which the principal and some of the peripheral characters achieve successful maturation. The wholeness that these characters attain is made to depend upon a discernment of the divine scheme in the life of each individual. These novels portray the pain that accompanies the quester's pilgrimage without which participation in the divine life is impossible. The characters in the novels of the early and transitional periods are balked of authentic self-realisation precisely because they are misguided and uninformed. Ambrose, the "cenobitic" aesthete in *Put Out More Flags* with his wish for limbo, where there is "no communal order but wine and conversation and imperfect various humanity"[31] is the spokesman for all spiritually blind questers.

Waugh's protagonists progressively move ever close to a mysterious sense of blessedness. The "still point" of T.S. Eliot parodied in the amusement park ride in *Decline and Fall* and seemed elusive is no longer imaginary but is actual. Charles Ryder, Guy Crouchback and Helena move from the profane to the sacred, from the City of Man to the City of God, only because they allow Divine Grace to operate upon their wills. The little red flame in Brideshead and Broome stirs in the protagonists thoughts that are too deep for ordinary language to convey.

Waugh did not consider his works as mere aesthetic achievement which had private meanings turning in upon themselves centripetally. Religion was a master sentiment at the root of his creative act and it permeated his works as a structural dynamic. In works such as Waugh's which are strongly marked by a religious dynamic, polysemous symbols with potential meanings move outwards towards the world centrifugally. Jerome Meckier's assertion that symbols are the key to Waugh's art imparting as they do in the reader's mind the essence of his vision does not come amiss.[32] An analysis of the symbols and imagery apart from establishing his moral seriousness and artistic commitment is bound to enhance our understanding and appreciation of the text. The implicit functional religious dynamic of Waugh's early novels can be reconstructed by following the evolution of some of the persistent themes such as the quest-motif from one work to another. The traditional four-fold schematisation of Dante seems a valid approach to extend the meaning of Waugh's novels beyond the literal or even metaphoric levels. Such an approach helps the reader along in his own quest for the religious centre and the dynamic idea unfolded in the author's work. The chart of Waugh's mind can be detected in the recurrence of themes, situations, images and definite character-types.

Dante expounds his four-fold scheme of interpretation in *The Banquet* and in the letter to his friend and patron Can Grande della Scala. The schematisation follows that of Thomas Acquinas and the early Christian predecessors. For Dante and others "the allegorical mode was not merely a matter of cleverness; it was part and parcel of their way of thinking about the world, which was itself considered full of symbolic meaning—like a work of art, we might say today."[33] In his *The Banquet* Dante says:

> it should be known that writings can be understood and ought to be expounded chiefly in four senses. The first is called the literal and this is that sense which does not go beyond the strict limits of the letter; the second is called allegorical and this is disguised under the cloak of such stories, and is a truth hidden under a beautiful fiction. . . . The third sense is called moral; and this sense is that for which teachers ought as they go through writings intently to watch for their own profit and that of their hearers; . . . The fourth sense is called anagogic, that is above the senses; and this occurs when a writing is spiritually expounded which even in the literal sense by the things signified likewise gives intimation of higher matters belonging to eternal glory; as can be seen in that song of the prophet which says that Israel went up out of Egypt, Judea was made holy and free. And although it be plain that this is true according to the letter, that which is spiritually understood is not less true, namely that the soul issues forth from sin she is made holy and free as mistress of herself.[34]

In his discussion of the four-fold interpretation in his letter to Can Grande, Dante chooses the text from Psalm 114 ("When Israel came out of Egypt and the House of Jacob from among the people, Judah was his sanctuary and Israel his dominion") as his illustrative example which, he maintains, while asserting a historical fact, can yet be interpreted allegorically on three different levels. Glossing on the Dantean hierarchy of meanings, Flannery O'Connor has pointed out that writers whose point of view is Catholic in the widest sense of the term read nature the same way the medieval commentators read Scriptures. They found the three levels of meaning in the literal level of the sacred text—the allegorical, in which one stands for another; the moral which has to do with what should be done; and the anagogical, which has to do with the Divine life, and our participation in it, the level of grace.[35] The discovery of the interrelationship of meaning in the Catholic novels of Waugh enriches and deepens our understanding of the author's world-view and the metaphysic that governs his oeuvre. It is however on the level of grace or the anagogical level that the quest-motif in *Brideshead Revisited, Helena* and the war-trilogy is seen to yield the most complex and aesthetically satisfying interpretations. At the heart of these novels lies the struggle of the human soul for Redemption. "An attempt to trace the workings of divine grace in the pagan world"—Waugh's statement in the first edition of *Brideshead Revisited*—is the theme that runs through all the Catholic novels. And since only grace can make man's participation in the Divine possible, the "anagogic" suggests the soul's relation to the Divine grace and the soul's ultimate destiny. The return of the human soul to the reality which man lost through fall is the central thematic concern of the novels. While this view is implicit in the early satires, Waugh makes no apology for it in the novels written after 1945. Illumination aided by grace assists the characters in seeing the barriers such as secularism, selfishness and intellectual rationalism that they have erected for themselves in the way of their salvation. Their whole physical environment and their relationships with the other beings undergo a transformation once the anagogic sense is aroused in the characters. As in Francis Thompson's poem *The Hound of Heaven* the characters are overwhelmed with the consciousness of a significant presence in their lives and in the world outside. In different ways, Charles Ryder, Helena and Guy Crouchback who spend their lives, Ixion-like, embracing phantoms and do not refer back their "quest of the exquisite" to some ethical centre, are, by an act of God, twitched back to that overwhelming presence. Although Waugh has been himself faulted for the excessively romantic prose in his *Brideshead Revisited* his own purpose in that novel and those following it has been to attack the romantic melancholy of the characters, which is the source of their incapacitating sense of nostalgia for the past. Charles Ryder, Sebastian Flyte and Guy Crouchback, like Dennis Barlow in *The Loved One* are victims of *taedium vitae*, one of the main traits which goads these men onto an exasperated quest of novelty. This sense of ennui which derives from the victim's private and personal illusions invariably results in spiritual inertia and ultimately in moral despair. Lacking in ethical centre these romantics are cut off from normal contact with their fellowmen and are thrown back more and more on themselves, consumed by inexplicable secret ardours and are incapable of self-guidance. It was one of the firm convictions of Waugh that the remoteness from other men and the sense of isolation is the severe penalty that has visited on men for ignoring traditional religious values. To be ethically efficient one should seek to unite with God but to achieve this one must undergo religious conversion like

Charles Ryder or experience spiritual reorientation like Guy Crouchback. Waugh's statement on the need for deference to an order higher than that of the human law is a reformulation in modern terms what the medieval men tirelessly insisted upon. According to the medieval Christian the man who looked upon himself as cut off from God and therefore ceased to strive, was the victim of acedia. Irving Babbit in his analysis of the causes of the romantic melancholy points out that acedia or the sluggishness and slackness of spirit, "the mere drifting and abdication of will, may, as Chaucer's parson suggests be the crime against the Holy Ghost."[36] To Waugh's mind the Church which has sternly and veraciously wrestled with the facts of human nature has aided men in their self-transcendence and has perceived clearly how men through his supreme spiritual effort can move towards true happiness and how in the absence of such striving is doomed to the supreme danger of spiritual sloth.

Thomas Merton, the Cistercian monk whom Waugh held in high respect and whose books Waugh cordially reviewed, asserts in *The Ascent to Truth* that grace is granted to us in proportion as we dispose ourselves to receive it by the interior activity of the theological virtues of faith, hope and charity[37] – virtues which require full and constant exercise of will and intelligence, although man in his fallen state is blinded by the meaningless and destructive external forces. Ryder and Sebastian who would have seemed at first two of the most unlikely candidates for blessedness, are yet granted this supernatural gift by which they are assisted in achieving eternal salvation and their vocations, unique to each of them. With their will and understanding suddenly illuminated and their vision enlarged by the power of grace, the characters are able to appreciate the true nature of God and Christ's relationship to Him. It stirs Julia and Sebastian to reflection of their helpless state and prepares the way for illumination. It causes upheavals and inner violence in Lord Marchmain and Charles Ryder, so that at the end they merely acquiesce in its irresistible and sweeping power. Their conversion also effects a change in their view of the world and of human nature. What seemed so long fragmented and out of joint appear to be part of a coherent, harmonious whole. Helena is imparted such insight while she is at the Cave of Nativity for the Feast of Epiphany. The response of the characters in these cases determines the final outcome of their quest. Hooper in the 'Epilogue' in *Brideshead Revisited* does not fail to notice a marked change in Ryder after the latter's visit to the Blessed Sacrament in the dilapidated chapel. The image of the avalanche in the novel illustrates the catastrophic yet creative energy of grace. Homeless and childless Ryder may be, but in the place of a wife and home, he is rewarded with the assurance of spiritual redemption and a secure place in the City of God. Tony Last in *A Hand-*

ful of Dust is incapable of responding to grace and hence he not only does not achieve his quest but is even destroyed.

The present work attempts through close textual analysis of the major works of Waugh's fiction, to illustrate the purpose and variety of the quest in them. A chronological study of the novels exemplifies the various techniques in Waugh's fictional writing and reveals the depth and complexity of his art as well as the range of his imagination.

NOTES

1. Leon Surmelian, *Techniques of Fiction Writing: Measure and Madness* (New York: Doubleday, 1969), p. 3.
2. *Evelyn Waugh, A Little Order*, ed. Donat Gallagher (London: Eyre Methuen, 1970), p. 107.
3. *Great Writers of English Language: Novelists and Prose Writers*, ed. James Vinson (New York: Macmillan Press, 1979), p. 1267.
4. Evelyn Waugh, *The Ordeal of Gilbert Pinfold* (UK: Penguin, 1962), p. 9.
5. Martin Esslin, *The Theatre of the Absurd* (UK: Penguin, 1961; rpt. 1980), p. 23.
6. *Ibid.*
7. *A Little Order*, p. 33.
8. James W. Nichols, "Romantic and Realistic; The Tone of Evelyn Waugh's Early Novels," *College English,* 21 (October 1962), p. 46.
9. Northrop Frye, *Anatomy of Criticism: Four Essays* (Princeton: 1957), pp. 223-24.
10. Jeffrey Heath, *The Picturesque Prison: Evelyn Waugh and His Writing* (Kingston and Montreal: McGill Queen's University Press, 1982), pp. 55-62.
11. *The Letters of Evelyn Waugh*, ed. Mark Amory (UK: Penguin, 1992), p. 274.
12. *A Little Order*, p. 31.
13. *Eighteenth Century English Literature*, ed. Geoffrey Tillotson et al (New York: Harcourt Brace Jovanovich, 1969), p. 9.
14. Jerome Meckier, "Evelyn Waugh," *Contemporary Literature* (University of Wisconsin Press, 1977), p. 100.
15. *The Complete Poems and Plays of T.S. Eliot* (London: Faber and Faber, 1969), p. 186.
16. Paul Wiley, "Evelyn Waugh," *Contemporary Literature*, 1988, p. 263.

17. Peter Revell, *Quest in Modern American Poetry* (USA: Vision and Barnes and Noble, 1981), p. 2.
18. Beverly Taylor and Elisabeth Brewer, *The Return of King Arthur* (UK: Barnes and Noble, 1983), p. 382.
19. *Ibid.*, p. 6.
20. *The Complete Poems and Plays of T.S. Eliot*, p. 76.
21. *The Return of King Arthur*, p. 238.
22. Gareth Knight, *The Secret Tradition in Arthurian Legend* (Northamptonshire: The Aquarian Press, 1983), p. 322.
23. Northrop Frye, *Anatomy of Criticism: Four Essays* (New Jersey: Princeton University Press, 1957), p. 187.
24. *Ibid*. p. 193.
25. Evelyn Waugh, *Decline and Fall* (London: Heinemann Educational Books, 1966), p. 122.
26. *The Picturesque Prison*, p. 26.
27. *Sunday Times*, London, 21 July 1957.
28. Evelyn Waugh, *Work Suspended and Other Stories* (UK: Penguin, 1967; rpt. 1982), p. 133.
29. Martin Stannard, "*Work Suspended*: Waugh's Climacteric," *Essays in Criticism*, No. 2, 1978, p. 319.
30. Evelyn Waugh, *Put Out More Flags* (Boston, MA: Little, Brown, 1977), pp. 51-52.
31. *Ibid*. p. 72.
32. Jerome Meckier, "Cycle, Symbols and Parody in Evelyn Waugh's *Decline and Fall*," *Contemporary Literature*, vol. 20, no. 1, Winter 1979, pp. 57-75.
33. *Critical Theory Since Plato*, ed. Hazard Adams (San Diego: Harcourt Brace Jovanovich, 1971), p. 120.
34. *Ibid*., p. 121.
35. Mattie Daniels Thomas, "The Quest Motif in Flannery O'Connor's Short Stories." Diss. Purdue, 1982, p. 8.
36. *Critical Theory Since Plato*, p. 802.
37. Thomas Merton, *The Ascent to Truth* (New York: Harcourt, Brace, 1951), p. 6. Waugh's letters to Merton contain some of his incisive critical statements on literary writing. *The Letters of Evelyn Waugh*, pp. 308-9; *Evelyn Waugh Newsletter* (Spring 1969), pp. 1-4.

A Journey Without a Goal: *Decline and Fall*

Informed critics have noted that Evelyn Waugh is not only a major writer of English prose but a serious novelist who wrestles with some of the intellectual problems of his age. Waugh's entire fictional oeuvre is coming to be increasingly recognised as one "block" (rather than as independent pieces of work with little connection with one another) which makes a decisive aesthetic statement on the nature of man. Waugh's career as a novelist is often compared to that of T.S. Eliot whose themes and techniques Waugh has undoubtedly admired. Just as the medley of themes of *Four Quartets* are anticipated in *The Love Song of J. Alfred Prufrock* the characters of Waugh's war-trilogy may be seen as extensions of the ingenus of his first novels. Guy Crouchback, the protagnoist of the trilogy (emotionally close to his creator), bears a familial relationship to Paul Pennyfeather of *Decline and Fall*. Their pilgrimages expose the corruption of their surroundings, and the absence of meanings and values in the public sphere. At thirty-six, Guy is an "innocent" like Paul and like him, self-estranged. They are both at odds with the world in which they find themselves.

Differences in emphasis and authorial attitudes notwithstanding, there is a marked thematic continuity in Waugh's writings. Broadly speaking, all his novels portray the disintegration, the ennui, and moral confusion of the human race. Of these the 'quest' is one of the most insistently recurring motifs in Waugh's canon. The term "quest," as has been noted earlier, implies not merely a search for something already known to the searcher but often a search not fully understood. Passive and morally weak, the heroes of *Decline and Fall* and *Vile Bodies* can have little claim to the title of "quester" in its conventional usage. Yet these two novels treat in a satirically negative way the themes of alienation, identity and self-realisation – themes which have traditionally been associated with the idea of quest and issues which are central to the novelists of the twentieth century. The World of Paul Pennyfeather (*Decline and Fall*) and Adam Fenwick-Symes (*Vile Bodies*) is a 'thin' world and the characters are 'shadows,' not full-blooded enough to have a sense of evil. Having no sense of the past or hope for the future and moving in a world of meaninglessness and chaos, the characters look like spectres of the classical pagan underworld. Such an anarchic world has laws of its own: governed by Unreason, everything happens according to chance or fortune. Sudden shifts of situations and loyalty and exchange of roles are common (predictable!) occurrences. Mismatch and duplicity have displaced human integrity and substantiality. The characters undergo a surprising series of misadventures. Puppets as these characters may seem, Waugh's detachment enables him to reveal the reality of their plight

By 1928, the year of publication of the first novel, Waugh had matured as a great writer of fiction who had already discovered stylistic and narrative techniques by means of which he could convincingly present moral dilemmas. In some of Waugh's immature but still precocious literary attempts before *Decline and Fall* may be detected germs of future greatness. Waugh tells us in his autobiography that as a small boy he wrote parodies of the masters of the past. His early acquaintance with the great masterpieces sharpened his sensibilities and made him aware of the need for craftsmanship. Mere mastery of technique would have made Waugh little more than a virtuoso but he at the same time, possessed in an unusual degree, keenness of observation of men and manners and acute perception of the human situation. "Balance," a short story written before *Decline and Fall* demonstrates his concern for some of the serious life-issues. The story's title is happily apposite, balancing as it does an understanding between life and death. Palpably autobiographical, "Balance" explores the human appetite which determines whether a man wishes to live or die. A similar serious vein may be detected in the first two novels.

Decline and Fall was Evelyn Waugh's first novel. It was an instant success and has ever since been regarded as the author's major achievement. The novel earned Waugh the reputation of the gretest satirist of modern times; it has not however, earned him the title of a major novelist. Nearly forty years after its publication, James F. Carens called him a "modern satirist" and wrote casually thus: "Waugh's career as a satirical novelist began in 1928."[1] The initial response to the novel which established the young author as an accomplished satirical virtuoso has seriously restricted unbiased criticism of the author's later works, and, as William Cook has argued, this "has consequently lessened the critical esteem with which these works might have otherwise been favoured."[2] The status of Waugh's fiction has thus been affected by an exclusive attention to his satirical skill. The majority of critics long after the publication of *Decline and Fall* have dismissed him as a satirist, – a brilliant one, who writes the unique sort of lambast typified by this first novel.

Early reviewers saw this book as a genuinely comic work and a story of the vicissitudes of an ingenuous young man, a victim of the most shocking trupitudes and betrayals. Rose Macaulay recognised the sparkle of the author's wit and the book's baroque detail, and the ease and coherence with which the story is told. The sphere of the novel however, was that of irreverent and anarchic fantasy.[3] Even Frederick J. Stopp who was one of Waugh's most sympathetic critics saw the work as the hero's "static romanticism."[4] John Willet's review of the novel for the "Times" in March 1966 was a genuine appreciation of the author's merit: Willet described the dominant themes of the book as the boy's boarding school, so dear to the twentieth century British heart. The institution of the boarding school, had been attempted many times before, but Willet claimed, that Evelyn Waugh was the very first novelist who turned his attention to its "submerged depths." One of Waugh's revelations, said Willet, was Captain Grimes: "There are not many very durable characters in the modern English novel, let alone immortals, like Don Juan or Jeeves, but Grimes is part of our heritage; his language and values, his reflections on the public schools and the honour of the regiment are marvellous glimpses of a suppressed rich underworld of English life. As a result, he is the mainstay of the novel, even though the space given him hardly suggests it."[5] Willet was among the first critics to notice the symmetry of the novel's structure. The novelist's device in bringing the school staff in the prison stresses the craziness of the two regimes. Willet recognised that the author's seriousness of moral purpose was evident in the hero's meditations on the relativity of honour: "There are interesting anticipations here of the author's later writings. Honour, much more subtly handled, is the theme of his war-trilogy."[6] Willet thus sees a unity in Waugh's works, although he somewhat patronizingly calls it as mere "juvenilia." Perceptive modern critics have recognised in Waugh's oeuvre a seriousness of purpose and of design and have begun to looking upon the works of Waugh as one whole block, the early novels each contributing to its meaning: Ian Littlewood, for instance, detects in all Waugh's works an element of sadness: "Waugh's temperament is not sunny, nor are his books – even the funniest of them. From *Decline and Fall* to *Unconditional Surrender* they are shot through with an awareness of most of the things that tempt men to despair: whatever lies between social boredom and concentration camp, disappointment in love and the decline of civilization."[7]

Waugh's *Decline and Fall* has been described by critics as the prose equivalent to T.S. Eliot's *The Waste Land* which gave quintessential expression to the poet's despair in the world of modern decline and decadence. T.S. Eliot was among Waugh's favourites and Éliotean echoes can be heard in many of Waugh's fiction. The disillusionment and despair, the lack of spiritual and metaphysical dimension to modern man's life and its utter futility is the theme common to both Eliot's first great poem and Waugh's first great novel. The 'waste-land' imagery of futility is seen "in the context of Eliot's notions about the decay of western culture and the fundamental importance of 'tradition.'"[8] Stylistically, Waugh has affinities with T.S. Eliot. Waugh's *Decline and Fall* and Eliot's *The Waste Land* have shored up literary fragments against their ruins. The two writers subscribe to the traditional view that each new work should be a fresh focus of power through which former streams of beauty, emotion and reflection are directed. Like Eliot's poems, Waugh's novel is not only a close web of quotations and adaptations but also a purposeful parody of some of the well-known masterpieces of the past. Waugh and Eliot were Augustan in their critical taste and the idea of "originality" with the implication that the reminiscence of other writers is a defect in the work seemed ludicrous to them as it would have sounded ludicrous to the poets of the Augustan age.[9]

The characters in *Decline and Fall*, like the people in *The Waste Land* are exiles in the arid plains. That man is in exile is one of the dominant ideas in Waugh's writings: "Man is by nature an exile, haunted, even at the height of his prosperity, by nostalgia for Eden: individually and collectively he is always in search of an oppressor who will take responsibility for his ills."[10] Paradise for Waugh, as Littlewood remarks, is Paradise Lost.[11] Behind the hilarity of the book lurks a sense of deep distress of the oppressiveness of modern times and of modern society. Modern man, of whom Waugh's ingenue hero Paul Pennyfeather is a representative, is an exile from Eden, a scene of unsullied innocence and bliss. The bitterness of the pain of exile is progressively illustrated in Paul's unenviable career through life. *Decline and Fall* marks the inauguration of Waugh's 'myth of decline' a catalogue of change and decay. Man's gradual and irretrievable alienation from his "home" is told with ruthless relish.

Paul, a theological student at Oxford, is drawn through no fault of his own, into a fantastic world which he cannot fully comprehend. The butt of a practical joke, he is sent down from Oxford for indecent behaviour. He is then hired by Dr. Fagan, an incompetent headmaster of a shady establishment called Llanaaba Castle. A number of grotesque characters people the place: Fagan's daughters, Captain Grimes, Prendergast, and Philbrick. While here, he is seduced by Margot Beste-Chetwynde, mother of one of Paul's students. He is about to marry Margot, when he is arrested while unknowingly trying to arrange for her the transportation of a group of prostitutes. He is imprisoned and is again the victim of the Lucas-Dockery experiments in criminal rehabilitation. He is rescued from gaol by Margot who has arranged a fake release and a change of identity for him. Under a new name, he returns to college and resumes studies. The novel is "geometrically arranged so that each of the three parts explores one of these segments of modern civilization."[12] Paul passes through three different worlds: the effete school systems at Scone and Llanabba, the corrupt upper-class society of the Beste-Chetwyndes, and the pretensions and ineffective penal system of Lucas-Dockery. The hero's life is a voyage through and a comment on diverse but commonly decadent societies. His story is thus an exploration of the values or of their loss, in the several elements of modern society. Such a "picture of a society is irredeemable futility,"[13] comparable to the land of spiritual malaise and infertility of Eliot. The landscape of both the artists suffers from a dearth of love and faith. The hero in Waugh's book, like the inhabitant of Eliot's wasteland, is passive and incapable of deliberate action, and equally incapable of distinction between the apparent and the real.

In a sense, both T.S. Eliot's *The Waste Land* and Waugh's *Decline and Fall* are parodies of the quest-motif. The quest has ever been regarded as a symbol which expresses the purest desire and best attainment of the human spirit, an objective correlative of man's search for an ideal and true religion. Eliot's poem however has often been interpreted as a kind of narrative history of the wanderings of the quester in the unrestored wastelands. Eliot not only describes the conditions of the wasteland of his own time but in an oblique way, informs the reader that the happenings in the poem are wastelands of one kind or other, both ancient and modern. In Eliot's wasteland the orders of the natural world, and its cycles of seasons are reversed. In the vegetation myths, the seasons of the year are seen as reflecting the life-cycle of a god who dies and is resurrected. Adonis spends half the days with the goddess of the underworld Persephone and half with Goddess of love Aphrodite. Such a myth accounts for the demise and resurrection of the god and with him the death and revival of the vegetation. The poem abounds in symbols which recall directly or by allusive association the quest of the Grail legend. Like *Gerontion*, Eliot's earlier poem, the victims of the wasteland wait for deliverance in vain. The sterility of the quester, who is the representative of the inhabitants, come from spiritual failure. Modern man is unable to achieve cultural and spiritual healing, on account of his failure of "mystical initiation" of the Grail legend; the traditional initiation which enabled the hero to attain maturity. Consequently the land is like Dante's inferno inhabited by the inculpably secular and spiritually ignorant men and women. All spiritual values have been overturned. The shadow of the rock, the hyacinth girl, the chapel, the Wheel of Fortune in Madame

Sosatris's pack of cards are among several symbols which establish the hideous loss of values in Eliot's world. Waugh's *Decline and Fall* is a parody of the conventional *Bildungsroman*. The protagonist does not grow and his quest is futile and circular. Waugh's hero resembles Eliot's Prufrock and Tiresias, who as Ronald Paulson points out, are not "different in kind from the feigned speakers of many of Swift's and Pope's satires."[14] In the vegetation ceremonies, the seasons of the year are seen reflecting the life-cycle of a god who dies and is resurrected, who is wounded and cured of his hurt, or who descends to the nether world and returns again. The myth of Adonis accounts for the demise and resurrection of the god and with him the death and revival of the vegetation. In Waugh's *Decline and Fall* such a life-cycle is parodied. The fortunes of the hero follow a sterile circular course rather than fruitful cyclical one. In symbolic terms, the hero and the other characters prefer the barrenness of the dead season to the fruitfulness of the soil or the return of spring.

The flowering of Grail scholarship and the quest-myth has enrolled not only such authors as T.S. Eliot, T.H. White and Charles Williams but also Faulkner, Camus and Pasternak among others, and the circle is ever-expanding. One of the main preoccupations of these writers is to explore the "Grail impulse," as the quest for self-realization through insight into the human condition has come to be termed. The modern search for identity is a thematic equivalent of the medieval leitmotif of the quest for the chalice or the talismanic stone. The writings of the present century feature modern man as involved in an examination of the possible personal, social and religious affiliations by means of which he can define himself. A great deal of post-war British fiction, as James Girdin[15] points out confronts the problem of identity. The hero of the modern novel longs for the security that a specific affiliation can give him and he often finds that his own complexity as well as that of the world in which he lives cannot be adequately expressed through any definable affiliation.

Waugh's *Decline and Fall* is a masterpiece of a mock-picaresque in which the affiliations are too easily made ludicrous. In the world of the novels, none of the identities and definitions provide any meaningful satisfaction. The protagonist and other characters alike are too apathetic to perceive the absence of meaningful relationships which results in alienation.

The reader is left with the unmistakable impression that the individual in the modern world is too drained of the capacity to deal with the crises or specific needs with which he is beset. Such an incapacity produces dissociation in the meaningfulness of the life of the individual. His loss of control over social or natural forces is experienced as disfunction between the self and important aspects of the world. Alienation is thus potential in the human condition. In Waugh's novel, however, it is not only the modern individual who is the butt of his satire but the whole society which fails to produce what human beings perceive as satisfactions of legitimate human goals, comes in for severe criticism.

Waugh's vision of the modern secular world is pessimistic but his pessimism is brilliantly encapsulated in symbols which are Eliotean in range and tone. Besides providing a concrescence of structural pattern, these symbols perform a further function of giving the author the needed aesthetic distance.

The symbols, in the main, summarise the loss of identity of the characters. An abandonment of identity issues in mismatch and madness and a general inversion of traditional norms and accepted values. In the logic or "illogic" of the inane and anarchic world of *Decline and Fall* the innocents bear the blame while the guilty go unpunished. The characters in the novel have no sense of direction; the hero ends as he began and everyone is groping towards an elusive "still point."

The central imagery of the book is contained in the passage on the chestnut trees which Paul contemplates enroute to King's Thursday, the country home of the enormously rich and beautiful Margot Beste-Chetwynde:

> The temperate April sunlight fell through the budding chestnuts and revealed between their trunks green glimpses of parkland and the distant radiance of a lake. 'English spring' thought Paul, 'in the dreaming ancestral beauty of the English country.' Surely, he thought, these great chestnuts in the morning sun stood for something enduring the serene in a world that had lost its reason and would so stand when the chaos and confusion were forgotten? And surely it was the spirit of William Morris that whispered to him in Margot Beste-Chetwynde's motor car about seed-time and harvest, the superb succession of the seasons, the harmonious interdependence of rich and poor, or dignity, innocence and tradition?[16]

Far from being a purple patch, the description has a serious satiric function. Apart from the implied Platonic contrast between the perishability of earthly objects with an invisible spiritual reality, the passage explores the further antithesis between the purposeful cycle and fruitful succession of seasons of the chestnuts and the fruitless circularity of lives in the modern wasteland. Waugh's treatment of the themes of identity and rebirth is parodic and subversive. Placed as it is in the central part of the novel's design, the passage prefigures the hero's own "death" and "rebirth" at the end of the book. Paul's new identity and secularised renewal is to be set against the recurrence and rebirth of the natural order symbolised by the chestnut trees. No renewal or resurrection can be conceived without a spiritual dimension. Paul's faked death and assumption of a new name is not a commencement of a new cycle as in the chestnut tree 'the great-rooted blossomer' but a fruitless circularity. As Jerome Meckier puts it: "The chestnuts reveal Paul's bottomless innocence. He, not they, is ripe for a fall."[17] Paul Pennyfeather is thus made to appear as the legendary wandering Jew, a restless soul who is for ever balked of the assurance of salvific renewal. Paul's career is very unlike that of Coleridge's mariner whose sterile remorse is to be succeeded by a fruitful repentance and ultimate salvation.

It is not Paul alone who feels the need to adopt a new identity but practically everybody in the novel undergoes farcical transformation. Captain Grimes, Prendergast, Philbrick, and Augustus Fagan – all these lack an essential self and as a consequence are able to change their personalities with an amazing Protean ease. Captain Grimes heads the list of these ebullient Dionysian personages. He is among the "immortals," Waugh's parodic "resurrection man," and, as is often described a parodic embodiment of Shavian life-force. Like Dickens' Micawber he has an absurd and over-weening confidence in himself just because he is a "public school man." Seemingly destructible Grimes undergoes a series of "deaths" but re-emerges with a new identity. Grimes has already a long and chequered career when Paul meets him at Llanabaa Castle. He tells Paul about his "false" leg which he says he lost in the war but is not sure. He makes a lasting impression on Paul (and on the reader) with his powers of invention and bravado resminiscent of Shakespeare's Falstaff: "'This looks like being the first end of term I've seen for two years' he said dreamily. 'Funny thing, I can always get on all right for about six weeks, and then I land in the soup. I don't believe I was ever meant by Nature to be a school master.'" (18) Here is the first hint that Grimes is foot loose. His adventures began, he tells Paul, when he was only sixteen but it is the Public School system that has saved him from court-martial. "'I've been in the soup pretty often since then but never quite so badly. Some one always turns up and says, "I can't see a public-school man down and out. Let me put you on your feet again." I should think' said Grimes 'I've been put on my feet more often than any living man.'"(20) No medieval knight-errant imbued with burning chivalric ideals of love and honour, Grimes looks upon his bigamous union with Florence, the headmaster's daughter as fetters on his free spirits and decides to leave her without qualm:

> 'There she is waiting for me,' said Grimes. 'Now it might be a very romantic sight to some chaps, a light burning in a tower window. I knew a poem about a thing like that once. Forget it now, though. . . . I was no end of a one for poetry when I was a kid – love and all that. Castle towers came in quite a lot. Funny thing one grows out of that sort of thing.' (84)

The pile of clothes found on the sea-shore are identified as Grimes's and he is presumed dead. The irony in his "resurrection" at Egdon Heath Penal Settlement is deadly for he is for ever a prisoner of life. Caught in the temporal order of life, he never grows or matures. He disappears into the impenetrable white mist of Egdon Heath. In Paul's reflections on his "second death," Grimes's parodic identification with Christ is complete:

> But later, thinking things over as he ate peacefully . . . Paul knew that Grimes was not dead. Lord Tangent was dead; Mr Prendergast was dead; the time would even come for Paul Pennyfeather; but Grimes, Paul at last realised, was of the immortals. He was a life-force. Sentenced to death in Flanders, he popped up in Wales; drowned in Wales he emerged in South America; engulfed in the dark of Egdon mire, he would rise again somewhere at some time, shaking from his limbs the musty integuments of the tomb. (170)

In the Gospel story of the rising of Lazarus from the grave to which reference is made in the passage, Christ declares himself as "the resurrection and the life."[18] Grimes will rise again and again but his resurrection is devoid of genuine transcendence.

Prendergast the uncommitted modern churchman is "a parody of a spiritual man – an example of fervour without faith."[19] His wigs, like Grimes's false leg, is a symbol of the inauthenticity of modern living. Prendergast has come to Llanabba Castle after having been a clergyman for ten years. He is assailed with "Doubts" especially about "why God had made the world at all." "Perhaps," he tells Paul, "one day I shall see light and then I shall go back to the ministry." He does return to the ministry as a chaplain of the prison where Paul has been committed. He tells Paul with dignity: "I've only been at the job a week. I was very lucky to get it. My bishop said he thought there was an opening for a Modern Churchman in this kind of work than in the parishes. The Governor is very modern too."(141) Prendergast is content to draw full salary of a beneficed clergyman without committing himself to any belief. However, he is less adept at changing his identity and dies a "martyr" for the modern ministry he has come to serve. He is slain by a monomaniacal

Calvinist Zealot who believes that he is obeying the Lord's command. If Grimes is a parodic Christ, Prendergast is a parodic John the Baptist. Whereas John the Baptist was beheaded for daring and outspokenness born of fervour, Prendergast's death is as pointless as his whole life which was without aim or purpose. His head is a grotesque symbol of the worthlessness of modern religion which while pretending to offer the solaces of religion, is no religion at all, for it has no institutional sanction. Prendy's "resurrection" is as hollow as Grimes's.

Philbrick, who works as cook at Llanabba Castle has at least three identities. He represents himself as the former Sir Solomon Philbrick (the ship owner) to Prendy, as the novelist to Grimes and as the retired burglar to Paul. In the prison, he describes himself as the brother of the Governor. At the end of the story, he passes by Paul in an open Rolls-Royce but does not stop.

The transfiguration of Augustus Fagan Ph.D. into Dr. Augustus Fagan M.D. neither of which degree he holds is symbolic of the mobility in a society where aleatory relationships have replaced rational causes and effects. Fagan, a recognisably Dickensian character is at the beginning, seen as presiding over an outrageously fradulent educational establishment called Llanabba Castle and, at the end, as a doctor issuing fake certificates of death. He is one of the many memorable 'Waugh incompetents' and his description is strongly reminiscent of an underworld character in Dickens, notably Fagins in *Oliver Twist.*

> He was very tall and very old and very well dressed; he had sunken eyes and rather long white hair over jet black eyebrows. His head was very long and sways lightly as he spoke; his voice had a thousand modulations, as though at some remote time had taken lessons in elocution; the backs of his hands were hairy and his fingers were crooked like claws. (9)

In his unctuous insistence on "tone" and "vision" Fagan is a clearly distinguishable type of a sponge whose words do not match deeds.

Waugh locates the source of modern instability with its attendant moral confusion and loss of identity in the disappearance of traditional ethos and values. The process of decline and fall is illustrated by the image of the transformed country house of Margot Beste-Chewynde. King's Thursday which was once the Tudor glory is now a modern horror. The great house has been remodelled by the hypercivilised Professor Otto Silenus, the man of the future:

> It had been built in an age when twenty servants were not an unduly

> extravagant establishment and it was scarcely possible to live there with fewer. But servants, the Beste-Chetwyndes found were less responsive than their masters to the charms of Tudor simplicity. . . . Modern democracy called for lifts and labour-saving devices, for hot-water taps and cold-water taps and (horrible innovation!) drinking water taps for gas rings and electric ovens. (99)

This "finest piece of domestic Tudor in England" before it fell into the hands of Otto Silenus represented "a kind of Prelapsarian universe."[20] In talking about the decay of King's Thursday Waugh is thinking of Eden after the Fall. For the space of our adult lives, we exist in the consciousness of dispossession. As Waugh says: "To have been born into a world of beauty, to die amid ugliness, is a common fate of all as exiles."[21]

The characters in *Decline and Fall* are incapable of self-discovery and self-definition precisely because they have lost all consciousness of sin, living as they do in a century of homelessness and exile of nervous disorder and barbaric cruelty. All the characters in the book violate the order of endurance and serenity symbolised by the chestnut trees but the chief offender is Margot Beste-Chetwynde, who is the novel's "chaos merchant" as Meckier describes her. She is a soulless degenerate of the fallen world, who is almost everywhere triumphant and esteemed. Margot's position in this world where no moral scheme is observed or represented is unassailable. She is the cause at once of Paul's imprisonment and his later release and charge of identity.

In such an amoral universe of attenuation of emotion and moral confusion it will be naive to expect the characters to affirm the positive values of life. The "vitality and the generous impulse" that F.R. Leavis finds embodied in Sissy in Dickens' *Hard Times*[22] is totally absent. Such bleak, nihilistic attitude to life of Waugh's characters is not to be identified with Waugh's own. The tone of *Decline and Fall* is satiric and is that of contrast by which irony manifests itself. That irony presupposes a secure conviction about different and opposed realms of value.

Behind the image of exile lies the haunting memory of the lost Eden. Man is for ever in search of the lost empire or abode of happiness. This longing is parodied in Paul's willing retreat in the prison house which seems one of the few pockets of sanity in a world gone awry. He is truly happy in Blackstone Gaol:

> The next four weeks of solitary confinement were among the happiest in Paul's life. The physical comforts were certainly meagre but at the Ritz Paul had learned to appreciate the inadequacy of purely physical comfort. It was so exhilarating, he found, never to have to

> make any decision on any subject, to be wholly relieved from the smallest consideration of time, meals or clothes, to have no anxiety ever about what kind of impression he was making: in fact, to be free. (144)

To Paul, the shades of the prison house are infinitely preferable to the light of common day with its multiplicity of problems and ugly irritabilities. In some versions of the Grail quest, the visit of the wandering knight to a hidden temple or castle involved perilous adventures and privations which tested his character and courage. The hero of Waugh's novel, however, fails his test. His incarceration, contrary to what he would expect, does not bring him "an epiphany" but it merely blinds him more to the realities of life. Paul's meditations on the relativity of honour—which is one of the themes, incidentally, of the later novels, especially the war-trilogy—and on his defence of Margot reveal how blindly besotted with love he is with the temptress:

> In his six weeks of solitude and grave consideration he had failed to make up his mind about Margot Beste-Chetwynde: it was torn and distracted by two conflicting methods of thought. On one side was the dead weights of precept, inherited from generations of school masters and divines. . . . On the other hand, was the undeniable cogency of Peter Beste-Chetwynde's 'You cant see Mama in prison, can you?' . . . It was just that he saw the *impossibility* of Margot in prison: the bare connexion of vocables associating the ideas was obscene." (160)

In his idealization of his mistress and misperception of realities, Paul is a modern version of Cervantes's Don Quixote. He is ineducible in as far as he is unable to see that the prison which he looks upon as a "safe retreat" is in no way different from the world he has run away from: the roles are reversed in the prison as in the outside world. Those who ought to be in the strait-jacket are put in charge of criminals and monomaniacs. In her role of the saving providence who effects Paul's release, Margot parodies the delivering angel in the coloured windows of the prison chapel, who effects the escape of St. Peter and St. Paul from prison. The quotations from Lovelace's poem in the chapter headings become therefore terribly ironic. Noted for his cultivation and courtly manners the Cavalier poet Richard Lovelace (1618-57) was a steadfast supporter of the king for whose cause he was willing to undergo imprisonment gladly. A mind innocent and quiet such as his could regard prison as a hermitage, a liberty which is enjoyed only by angels. Paul Pennyfeather in the story is quite unlike Lovelace who not only typified the Cavalier spirit but also the graceful art that such a spirit could create.

Innvoation and novelty are the primary values which a modern spirit is ever in pursuit. "Progressivism" is the key word of the modern social science. Sir Wilfred Lucas-Dockery, the prison governor, with his theory that all crime is due to the repressed desire for the aesthetic is a Waugh grotesque who typifies the arrogant modern method of reproductive analysis. He gives the raving lunatic the carpenter's tools with which the latter saws off Prendy's head. The madman who looks "daily for the Second Coming" believes himself to be the Lord's appointed angel to kill Prendy.

Waugh uses certain striking symbols to implant in our mind the essence of his vision. The characters in *Decline and Fall* and the other early novels are thrown into a relativistic world in which nothing is certain. The result is confusion and meaningless activity. Waugh's images of the Castle, the Wheel and the Wall depict the vacuity of the characters who can't defend themselves against the forces of barbarism. In their grotesque antics which are a distortion of the cycle of the seasons, Waugh's characters resemble those of Anthony Powell who dance to the music of time.

In its circularity, the careers of Paul Pennyfeather and other characters resemble the Luna Park Wheel. Silenus, the architect of King's Thursday lectures Paul on life. He is the man of the future and he looks forward to the day when man will be as functional as machines and to him the Wheel of the Luna Park is the only image of life:

> It's like the big wheel at Luna Park. . . . You pay five francs and go into a room with tiers of seats all round and in the centre the floor is made of a great disc of polished wood that revolves quickly. At first you sit down and watch the others. They are all trying to sit in the wheel and they keep getting flung off, and that makes them laugh, and you laugh too . . . the nearer you can get to the hub of the wheel the slower it is moving and the easier it is to stay on. Of course at the very centre there's a point completely at rest, if one could only find it. . . . Lots of people just enjoy scrambling on again. . . . Then there are others . . . who sit as far out as they can hold on for dear life . . . the scrambling and excitement and bumps and the effort to get to the middle, and when we do get to the middle, it's just if we never started. It's so odd. (178)

To the smug and pompous Silenus the wheel is the apposite image of mechanism but to Waugh, it is the modern version of the Wheel of Fortune, an image that he puts to further use later in his *A Handful of Dust*. All movement is illusory because it is only circular. The polished wooden disc arbitrarily flings off all who board it in search of an elusive still point at the centre. "Only the fool, fixed in his folly" says Becket in T.S. Eliot's *Murder in the Cathedral* "may think he can turn the wheel on which he turns."[23] The circle has been the figure of perfection but, as Alvin Kernan points out, it has also been as in Dante's Inferno, "the figure of empty meaningless movement of eternal hunger."[24] Like the sinful lovers of Dante, the characters in Waugh's Waste Land are tossed for ever.

This loss of the fixed centre's stability in modern life has resulted in modern man's inability to cope with the forces of anarchy and barbarism. The walls of Llanabba Castle and the Scone College are symbols of vulnerability of contemporary civilization. Llanabba Castle, like the modernized King's Thursday, is an image of decline and decay. In his search for a living, Paul goes to the notorious Llanabba Castle run by the incompetent Fagan which presents two quite different aspects. (11-12) The main reason for the difference the author goes on, was that the Castle was built by unemployed mill workers in the cotton famine of the 1860s. The ladies held a charity bazaar to raise money for relief; the husband, a Lancashire mill owner influenced by the Liberal economists, was equally upset at having to give the money without due return. Sentimentality and "enlightened self interest" were both neatly satisfied by putting the men to work on the wall. A great deal of work was done cheaply and the taste for the romantic was combined with the neo-Gothic character of the blocks. The transformation of Llanabba House to Llanabba Castle was effected easily enough. The history of the Castle is indeed the history of decline of values, of equity and justice. The Annual School Supports at Llanabba Castle is a metaphor for material and moral disorder of the modern world. The stated purpose of the meet is to encourage the endurance of the pupils but its actual purpose is to impress the important visiting parents. The events are conducted in complete disregard of the ordinary rules of the game and sports. The high and low hurdles are not there and the tracks are not marked. The boys are asked to run round and round "until tea-time" and as a consequence there is shameless cheating. There is chaos when one of the school masters Mr Prendergast, serving as a starter, shoots one of the boys. Waugh's point is that once the boundaries, the rules and the markers are destroyed as in the Llanabba sports, then the "rational judgement no longer has a framework within which to locate and identify things and the purpose and human effort is lost."[25] To use Waugh's own phrase in *Robbery Under Law*, the moderns are all potential characters for anarchy.[26] With the obliteration of boundaries or border lines, goes order and discipline and complete wreckage sets in. The boys who run round and round the fields are being prepared for the giddy whirl of life where all rules are off and the markers gone and where there is no longer any clearly defined purpose.

Scone College which is the scene of rioting by the Bollinger Club at the beginning of the story is another symbol of vulnerability. Where one should expect decorum and sobriety of conduct, there is drunkenness and debagging. Two Oxford dons are seen cowering in their rooms anticipating with relish the fines they will impose on the rioting youngsters. One of them Mr. Sniggs is heard saying: "It'll be more if they attack the chapel. Oh, please God, make them attack the chapel." (2) The traditional or natural order is inverted: the huntsmen are turned into hounds and sacrilegeous prayers for attack on the house of God are offered. The walls of the college are unable to hold out the forces of barbarism.

In his lecture to Paul on the meaning of life, Professor Otto Silenus classifies people into two sorts – the "static" and "dynamic." Such a division he maintains, is better than the "absurd" distinction of the sexes. Margot Beste-Chetwynde in Silenus's classification belongs to the "dynamic" variety while Paul is "static." Through Silenus, who is the victim of his irony, Waugh directs his attack against the complacency of the age. As Donat Gallagher remarks in his introduction to Waugh's aestheticism in *A Little Order*, Waugh was a severe opponent of functional theories of art and in the Professor Silenus episodes he ridicules those theories hilariously.[27] Irony has been a potent means of poets and novelists of expressing the paradoxical nature of reality. Behind Waugh's ridicule of Silenus's theory of binary opposition, lies the author's own version of polarities: absolute vs relative, secular vs metaphysical. Silenus's complacent classification of reality into "dynamic" and "static" is a bleak reminder of the folly of seeking fulfilment inside time or history.

Waugh views history as a disintegrating proceeding, a movement from greater to lesser, from civilization to chaos. This is suggested by the book's title with its echo of Gibbon's 'Decline and Fall of the Roman Empire.' However, Waugh seems to have had a kind of negative identification with the eighteenth century historian. Where Gibbon blamed Christianity for the decline of the Western civilization, Waugh suggests the real collapse has been (to quote Meckier) "a gradual loss of formal, universally accepted belief."[28] To classicist Waugh, it is tradition embodied in social and religious institutions, morals and manners and aesthetic values that protects people from savagery and riot and assures them of meaningful existence. Written in 1928, two years before his conversion to the Roman faith, *Decline and Fall* presents an absurd secular world as a travesty of an earlier religious epoch. The novel is a satire and its movement as well as individual satiric passages on various contemporary systems such as education, the press and the prison, indicate a higher ethical purpose. *Decline and Fall* and the other early novels express a definite didactic purpose in a highly stylized, craftsman like prose. The circularity of the lives of characters corresponds to the secular laws of Gibbon and of Oswald Spengler whose *Decline of the West* became a rage in 1918, the year of its publication. Spengler argued that civilization experienced decline after "creative stages produced periods of comfort and reflection."[29] But Waugh discredits the secular view of these historians and exposes the futility inherent in their historical principles. The circularity of the characters' lives dramatize the cliche that history repeats itself and the same mistakes are remade. Such a view is possible in histories which are deprived of an extratemporal dimension. Waugh's characters in *Decline and Fall* lack such a dimension, as they live without the least eschatalogical anxiety. Waugh's own quest is not merely aesthetic, as some critics have argued,[30] but is a search for order and stability.

The lucidity and precision of Waugh's style emphasises the absurdity and chaos of the novel's world. It is the style of the eighteenth century which Waugh greatly admired. Language is thus the only depository of values in a confused world. The form admirably supports the theme – the theme of absurd quests and circularity. Language therefore is not an end in itself. The chestnut trees, the great houses, the prison and Egdon Mire – all perform a symbolic as well as a thematic function. Implicit also is the Catholic religion which Waugh was to accept two years later. The humanism of the great Victorians is no substitute for religion which alone can give direction to modern man. The description of Waugh as Dickensian is misleading for Waugh implies throughout the novel, especially in the prison scenes, that the virtues of humanism which Dickens espoused are hopelessly inadequate. Unless within a viable religious framework, temporal values are of no avail. In the crass materialism of post-war world, the quest of high ideals and identity of self is difficult of achievement.

NOTES

1. James F. Carens, *The Satiric Art of Evelyn Waugh* (Seattle: University of Washington Press, 1966), p. v.
2. William J. Cook, Jr., *Masks, Modes and Morals: The Art of Evelyn Waugh* (Rutherford: Fairleigh Dickinson University Press, 1971), p. 22.

3. *Evelyn Waugh, The Critical Heritage*, ed. Martin Stannard (London: Routledge and Kegan Paul, 1984), p. 92.
4. Frederick J. Stopp, *Evelyn Waugh: Portrait of an Artist* (London: Chapman and Hall, 1958), p. 70.
5. *The Critical Heritage*, p. 22.
6. *Ibid*., p. 23.
7. Ian Littlewood, *The Writings of Evelyn Waugh* (Oxford: Basil Blackwell, 1983), p. 3.
8. *The Critical Heritage*, p. 7.
9. The idea of literary allusion is discussed by Dorothy L. Sayers in *The Mind of the Maker*, Chapter VIII, 'Pentecost' (Connecticut: Greenwood, 1941).
10. Evelyn Waugh, *Robbery Under Law, The Mexican Object-Lesson* (London: Chapman and Hall, 1939), p. 109.
11. Ian Littlewood, p. 109.
12. William J. Cook, Jr., p. 65.
13. *Ibid*., p. 69.
14. Ronald Paulson in *Introduction to Satire: Modern Essays in Criticism* (Englewood Cliffs: Prentice Hall, 1971), p. xi.
15. James Gindin, *Post War British Fiction: New Accents and New Attitudes* (University of California, 1962; rpt. 1976), p. 226.
16. Evelyn Waugh, *Decline and Fall* (London: Heinemann Educational Books, 1966), pp. 104-5.
17. Jerome Meckier, "Cycle, Symbol and Parody in Evelyn Waugh's *Decline and Fall*," p. 54.
18. The Gospel according to St. John, Ch. 11: Vol. 25, *The Bible* (A.V).
19. Jerome Meckier, p. 57.
20. Malcolm Bradbury, *Evelyn Waugh* (London: Chapman and Hall, 1964), p. 38.
22. *Towards a Poetics of Fiction*, ed. Mark Spilka (Indiana University Press, 1977), p. 172.
23. T.S. Eliot, *Murder in the Cathedral* (New York: Harcourt, Brace, 1935), p. 24.
24. Alvin B. Kernan, "The Wall and the Jungle: The Early Novels of Evelyn Waugh," *The Yale Review*, 53 (Winter 1963), p. 208.
25. *Ibid*., p. 220.
26. *Robbery Under Law*, p. 2.
27. *A Little Order*, p. 33.
28. Jerome Meckier, p. 74.
29. *Loc. cit*.
30. Richard A. Long and Iva G. Jones, "Towards a Definition of the 'Decadent Novel'," *College English*, 22 (Jan. 1961), p. 249.

"A Vile Becoming:" *Vile Bodies*

Vile Bodies (1930) was Evelyn Waugh's second novel in which he continued to portray satirically the members of the upper and the upper middle classes of the late 20s and 30s. Contemporary reviews of the novel were mostly favourable but most of them regarded the book as just another brilliant satire after *Decline and Fall*. Richard Strauss called it "a masterpiece of inconsequence"[1] a most entertainingly ironical commentary on the juvenile absurdities of the day. L.P. Hartley praised Waugh's ability to prove that amusement could be derived from the most unpromising material, from people that is, whose one occupation in life was quest for amusement.[2] The characters in the novel belonged to the so-called smart set – pseudo-artistic, pseudo-literary and generally alcoholic; the set which was trying to run away from the shadow of its own stupidity.[3] Rebecca West thought that the novel had very considerable values as a further stage in the contemporary disillusionment which started with T.S. Eliot's *Waste Land*.[4] In their ape-like antics, the people in the *Vile Bodies* remind one of Aldous Huxley's characters. The group of youngsters in the novel are so madly and unmorally irresponsible that beside them Scott Fitzgerald's most defiant characters are staid and conservative.[5]

In their futile gyrations and in their sense of self-defeat and apathy, the characters seem absolutely devoid of any historical sense. Despite the volatility and uncertainty of the war years, British Society still retained a solid residue of custom, tradition and historical continuity. Writers like Elizabeth Bowen, L.P. Hartley and Evelyn Waugh regarded themselves as custodians of conservative virtues.[6] *Vile Bodies*, for all its surface frivolity, aims at exposing the loss of social stability which came from a sense of history, in the lives of the characters. Waugh is concerned with the people who in the meaningless pursuit of pleasures, were moving further and further away from the centre, the traditional middle. His humour and wit are really social weapons with which to decry the extremism and the raid on the extremes of his characters. The novelist cries for the need to fill the middle and for historical continuity. In the novel "things fall apart and the centre cannot hold," to adapt W.B. Yeats.

Where there is no centre as happens in the lives of the characters, events swirl as disaster, success and doom become routine circular processes. Waugh deplores the gradual slippage and fragmentation of the upper and the upper middle classes, who, one would have thought, would uphold the traditional values and virtues. The men and women in *Vile Bodies* are incomplete and are driven by frenetic urge to change the world order. They seek "the missing element" in endless quests which eventually prove to be obsessive and destructive. What is needed desperately is graduality and continuity. In their obsession for change, the giddy young people move from centres of true culture. Lack of faith, of ideology, and loss of community have all combined to create a vacuum which leads to isolation and non-entity. The characters in *Vile Bodies* do not search for inner meaning but flow like drift-wood with the temporal process. Craze for change has resulted in spiritual paralysis and the individual is ripped by doubts of self-definition.

As critics have remarked, *Vile Bodies* has practically no plot and there is no continuity of narrative. The scenes shift wildly from the stormy English channel to a party given to Mrs. Melrose Ape, the touring evangelist; from the intrigues of Father Rothschild, S.J. and Prime Minister Walter Outrage to the small talk of two middle class ladies on the train; from the drawing room of a great mansion to the dirt-tracks of the motor races. The disconnected and the seemingly irrelevant scenes are apparently meant to portray a world that is chaotic and out of joint, the technique employed by T.S. Eliot in his *Waste Land*. The protagonist (who is an anti-hero) Adam Fenwick-Symes and Nina Blount, the colonel's daughter Adam wishes to marry, are representative of the sickness of the entire inter-war generation. Their thwarted attempt to marry is a symbol of the frustrated search for values of all the Bright Young People, who are a bunch of sublimely uneducated, and gaily philistine moderns with minimum intelligence. Their gaiety and rebellion however, are symptomatic of a nagging sense of anxiety born of insecurity. Adam the protagonist is introduced in a tone which suggests his commonplaceness: "There was nothing particularly remarkable about his appearance. He looked exactly as young men like him look: he was carrying his own bag which was disagreeably heavy because he had no money left in francs and very little left in anything else."[7] The Jane Austen-like elegance of style is in sharp contrast to the triviality of the subject-matter. The amorality and the pseudo-literariness and the trivial nature of the quest of the protagonist are etched in with clarity. The casualness with which Adam gets engaged ("in the course of his correspondence") prefigures his later on-again, off-again engagements with Nina Blount, Adam's amoral counterpart in the novel. There is none of the innocence of the

Primal Adam before the fall. The shallowness of attitude to life and career of the hero of the present novel is immediately apparent.

Adam is a product of his age whose variety comes from the fact that it forgets two simple but essential things of life: the meaning of existence and the meaning of inwardness. It is an age which has rejected any form of *a priori* morality and which prides itself in an aggressive affirmation of total freedom from all sorts of constraints. As future events in the novel will demonstrate, Adam's alienation and loss of identity proceeds mainly from his failure to realise all the ontological potentialities and energies within him. Adam's "tragedy" is the tragedy of a generation in which the ego is divided and alienated from itself and is, to use Cardinal Newman's phrase "implicated in some aboriginal calamity."

Adam is constitutionally incapable of making a new and unique choice which moral situations demand. Imprisoned as he is in his own subjectivity he is cast in a world of irrevocable "absurdity" through which he thinks he can bungle his way. Devoid of all faculties of intelligence such as imagination, foresight and judgement he is unable to perceive any meaningful configuration in life-events. This process of integration which Carl Jung calls "individuation" is of critical importance to every individual. To be such an individual is to have overcome the fragmenting and alienating dimensions of existence.

Adam's loss of "identity" is symbolised by the confiscation of his memoirs by the customs officials. His autobiography which he has been writing in Paris was his only hope of livelihood and of marriage with Nina Blount. There is irony in the burning of Dante's *Purgatorio* by the customs officials at the same time they confiscate Adam's memoirs. The loss of identity is not of an individual but of an entire group. Not only is Adam deprived of his identity but another member of the smart set Hon. Miss Agatha Runcible who is mistaken for a well-known jewel smuggler and is stripped to the skin by two of the customs wardresses. The reaction of the young people is one of cool indifference. Agatha who has herself been disgraced by the officials pulls up Adam for complaining: "Adam, angel, don't fuss or we shall miss the train." (26) Like Paul Pennyfeather in *Decline and Fall* Adam is isolated even among the Bright Young Things. Like Paul, he recognises that the world is crazily mixed-up but unlike Paul he joins the chaos. However, he cannot establish community with other people, as he is slightly older now and cannot adequately perform an adolescent's role. The whole novel is an attempt of Adam to regain his lost identity. A drunken major (who is nameless!) cheats him out of a thousand pounds and successfully dodges Adam to the end. When he meets the drunken major on the noisy race track, the latter eludes him once more:

"It's no good – these infernal things make too much noise. What's your name? . . .;
"Adam Symes"
"Can't hear." . . . "I must know your name" he cried. All the drivers seemed to choose this moment to sound their horns; the woman cyclist at Adam's elbow rang her bell; the male cyclist tooted a little horn like a Paris taxi and the programme boy yelled in his car, "official programme-map of the course – all the drivers." "Adam Symes" he shouted desperately, but the Major threw up his hands in despair and he disappeared in the crowd. (232)

The absent-minded Colonel Blount, master of Doubting All, forgets Adam's identity more than once. When he does realise that he is the young man his daughter wishes to marry, he gives him a cheque for a thousand pounds signed "Charlie Chaplain." The plight of Adam is indeed that of a rudderless modern entity.

The heroes of the medieval legends of the Grail were inspired by motives of purity and piety and the end of their quest was entry to the eschatological banquet, to god's wedding feast. The quest of the characters in *Vile Bodies* on the other hand is of a perfectly mundane kind – that of money and an endless round of amusement. The bright young people reel from party to party, body to body, and binge to binge, racing faster and faster after an elusive something which always escapes them.[8] The party is a symbol of the new permissiveness. The hectic round of parties like the fatal auto-race near the end of the story reflects the empty circularity of the people in the novel. Adam who is otherwise impervious to the demands of higher life is himself sick of the endless parties that go round him:

Masked parties, Savage parties, Victorian parties, Greek parties, Wild West parties, Russian parties, Circus parties, where one had to dress as somebody else, almost naked parties in St. John's Wood, parties in flats and studios and houses and ships and hotels and night clubs, in wind mills and swimming baths, tea parties at school where one ate muffins and and meringues and tinned crab, parties at Oxford where one drank down sherry and smoked Turkish Cigarettes, dull dances in London and comic dances in Scotland and disgusting dances in Paris – all that succession and repetition of masked humanity. . . . Those vile bodies. . . . (170)

Critics have remarked that *Vile Bodies* is full of passages in parentheses which are intrusions of the authorial view. The reader is made continually aware of the immediate presence of the loquacious and knowledgeable narrator. As a detached analyst of the modern situation, Waugh decries the futility and rootlessness of the life not only of the bright young things but of the entire western civilization of the twenties. Waugh's keen powers of observation for the trivial and the peculiar and his artistry in catching the tone of the scene are immediately striking. He adapts his style to the endless succession of life's trivialities. Behind the facade of the gaiety of people's activities the author sees "the pathos of wasted lives."[9] The contrast between appearance and reality has been one of Waugh's preoccupations as of most serious writers. All parties turn out to be the same party where one hears the same vapid talk and sees the same dissipated faces. Stopp's assessment that the author is "disillusioned of the characters' disillusion" seems profoundly relevant.[10] The "Vile Bodies" of the book's title which occurs at the end of the passage is presumably taken from the Epistle of St. Paul to the Philippians 3:20-21 (Authorised Version):

> For our conservation is in heaven; from whence also we look for the Saviour, the Lord Jesus Christ:
> Who shall change our vile body, that it may be fashioned like unto his glorious body, according to the working whereby he is able even to subdue all things unto himself.

Waugh's intentions in the book are therefore clear. Beneath the satiric surface is a deep and religious sense of the tragic human predicament.

The bright young things carry their gaiety even into Number 10 Downing Street and implicate the Prime Minister's family. Miss Agatha Runcible who earlier in the novel vowed that she would publish the "outrage" of treatment of her by the customs officials, finds herself in grass skirt late in the night. When face to face with the Prime Minister early the next day, she panics and runs into the street to be photographed by newspaper men. The orgies of the bright set and the behaviour of Agatha Runcible especially, cause the Government of Sir James Brown, the Prime Minister, to fall.

It is not however only the young who are the offenders. The older generation is equally culpable. Mr. Outrage, the former Prime Minister plays the same game (as the younger set) with a Japanese baroness at the hotel. Colonel Blount's refusal to give the thousand pounds to Adam to enable him marry the Colonel's daughter is a reflection on the unwillingness of the older generation to view seriously the moral and financial problems of the younger people. Colonel Blount spends his days eating and sleeping and his eccentric interest in the "Silver Screen" is symbolic of his immaturity.

If the bankruptcy of politics is represented by Outrage, the bankruptcy of the modern populist religion is represented by the evangelist Mrs. Ape and her "fallen" angels. That would indeed be the religion in a fallen world, a religion without the consolations and the sturdy traditions of the church. The antics of Mrs. Ape's troupe of angels when they are left to their device, belongs to the species of a sub-human order true to the name of the leader. The fate of chastity is predictable: after a chequered career as a white slave she is finally seen with the drunken major on the battlefield.

In contrast to the vacuity and absence of values of the characters in the novel, Waugh's indirect comments throughout implicitly indicate a more conservative set of values. Sometimes, as James Nichols point out, Waugh establishes his point of view by juxtaposing two contrasting scenes.[11] The fantastic party of the bright young things in a captive dirigible is immediately followed by a description of a party given at Anchorage House, which is one of the last of London's great town houses. Like King's Thursday in *Decline and Fall* in its days of glory, Anchorage House stands as a symbol of all the best of conservatism and long tradition. The people who attended the reception are not the bloated great with their dubiously acquired fortunes but are honourable ones who cherish and uphold the virtues of a forgotten age. In contrast to the peers on the Yellow Press and bewildered Prime Ministers, these are staid men who care about their heritage: "their womenfolk well gowned in rich and durable stuffs, their menfolk ablaze with orders; people who had represented their country in foreign places and sent their sons to die for her in battle." (175)

The last survivor of London's noble houses, of august dimension, Lady Anchorage House has grace, dignity and other-worldliness redolent of a past elegant age. The ghosts of a concurrence of celebrities – of Pitt, Fox, Burke and Dr. Johnson – seem to lurk in the precincts. Waugh recalls in this splendid description the Pre-Raphaelite conception of Medievalism which stood for aesthetic and moral values. The medieval knight errant, very unlike his degenerate modern progeny, fought against materialism and quested for a just and noble order of life. Adam Fenwick, Nina Blount, Agatha Runcible and others are no knight errants glowing with high ideals but "vile bodies" who rape the great houses and all that they stand for. These vile bodies are the "anarchic elements" that Waugh talks about in his *Robbery Under Law*, these elements are so strong that it is a wholesome task to keep pace.

The thematic significance of Father Rothschild's remarks becomes apparent if they are placed alongside the passage about Lady Anchorage

House:

> 'Don't you think' said Father Rothschild gently, 'that perhaps it is all in some way historical? I don't think people ever *want* to lose their faith either in religion or anything else. I know very few young people, but it seems to me that they are all possessed with an almost fatal hunger for permanence.' (183)

The Jesuit is not a defender of the degenerate upper middle class youth but rather the voice of sanity and good sense. There are men, Waugh seems to hint, who seem to understand the youth and their follies. Few people like Rothschild know the secret of the youth's undoing—they have neglected the warnings of the Church, the citadel of clarity and order which alone can cope with the anarchy of the vile bodies of the modern world.

The casualness of the quest for money of the 'smart' set in order to pay for their amusement reveals their self-indulgent hedonism and the false bottom of their world. Money, in the novel, represents as Kernan remarks, "the support offered both by society to those who seek entrance to it and by the older generation to those who will share and perpetuate their values."[12] The parody of the quest for the kingdom of heaven with its entailment of sacrifice of money and material security, is implicit. Waugh's satire rests on his juxtaposition of the profane and divine worlds, the City of Man and the City of God. The only conceivable quest in the City of Man in which the vile bodies refuse to be transformed by the power of God and their only metamorphosis is the disguise they assume in their savage parties, is for money, the emblem of mundane support. The survival of the engagement of Adam Fenwick-Symes and Nina Blount depends upon the money that Adam is able to make in the world which worships Mammon. Adam first tries to earn the necessary money by writing his autobiography which the officious customs officials destroy as pornography. His identity destroyed with his autobiography, Adam can only trust to Fortune's Wheel. His first thousand pounds come quite easily in a childish bet he has with a rich young hard-drinking American at Lottie's hotel, by a simple trick with a few pennies. He however entrusts the thousand pounds to a drunk Major who is present at the hotel. The money is to be placed on a horse named Indian Runner. The horse wins but for the rest of the novel, the two chase each other to collect the money. Adam's pursuit of the drunk Major is symbolically suggestive of his search for the elusive meaning of existence: Adam catches glimpse of the Major who is bulky and elusive at the November handicap at Manchester where Adam has gone with Nina. They have the disheartening experience of seeing the Indian Runner come in as an easy winner and the drunk Major winning an enormous sum of money: "It was during the bottle-green bowler campaign and Adam was searching in vain for any sign of his influence when suddenly among the crowd, he saw the genial red face of the drunk major to whom he had entrusted his thousand pounds at Lottie's. . . . Adam was not sure whether the Major saw him, but in some mysterious way Adam's pursuit coincided with the Major's complete disappearance." (162) Adam sees the drunk Major face to face at the motor race when the latter admits to having made thirty thousand pounds on the Indian Runner but he gives Adam the slip once more. When the major does repay Adam the money it is on the enormous wasteland of the greatest battlefield in history. The thirty-five thousand pounds are however worth only a couple of drinks and a newspaper. The worthless cheque that the major is going to write out is a reminder of another fake cheque that Col. Blount gives Adam earlier in the novel.

In the world of *Vile Bodies* one man's failure means another man's happiness. Simon Balcairn, "Mr. Chatterbox" of the *Daily Excess* lives on his wits, as he churns out lies after lies in his columns until he is excluded from Lady Margot's party. He files a totally libellous story to the paper before killing himself in a gas oven. Adam who is offered his job, proves even more inventive than his predecessor. He runs a series on "Notable invalids" and "Titled eccentricities."

He invents archetypal characters who represent the ideals of his age. His inventions are indeed an improvement on the originals. His creations include Provna, the aristocratic Polish sculptor. Captain Angus Stuart-Kerr, the game hunter, and Mrs. Andrew Quest. His creations take on life: works of Provna appear on the market and Lord Monomark, Adam's publisher, tries to get a date with Mrs. Quest. Adam thus becomes, to quote James Hall, "the Basil Seal of London,"[13] sowing confusion, "by caricaturing ideals he considers himself past believing in." In Waugh's description of the imaginary Imogen Quest is implicit an ironic analogy to the unreality of the world of the 'smart set' of which Adam is an important member:

> Her character was a lovely harmony of contending virtues – she was witty and tender-hearted; passionate and serene, sensual and temperate, impulsive and discreet.
>
> Her set, the most intimate and brilliant in Europe, achieved a superb mean between those two poles of savagery Lady Circumstance and Lady Metroland. Soon Imogen Quest became a byword for social inaccessibility – the final goal for all climbers. (158-59)

Phrases such as "social inaccessibility," "the final goal" aptly sum up the nebulousness of the divided aims and purposes of the characters.

Adam's fame as a reporter does not last long. Nina who deputizes for him when he is away to see Nina's father about their wedding, goes a bit too far in her report on the Chatterbox page. Adam, as a consequence, is fired and Miles Malpractice becomes his successor on *Daily Excess*.

We next see Adam unemployed going to the motor races with Agatha Runcible, Miles and Archie Schwert. The loss of direction in the lives of Adam and others is emphasized and the future tragic events are foreshadowed: "Then Archie said he was too sleepy to drive any more, so Adam changed places with him and lost the way and they travelled miles in the wrong direction down a limitless bye-pass road." (215-16)

The randomness with which the young people look for their lodgings during the races is symbolic of their life-attitudes and the general randomness of contemporary life, lacking in a central point of faith or a goal of life. Miles who is the present "Mr. Chatterbox" is making up incredible stories for his paper on the races just as Adam would have done. The casual and the far from clear telegram that he sends Nina in the heat and bustle of the races, after spotting the drunken Major speaks for his misguided optimism. The passing reference to Agatha who is lost in her car is revealing. The plight of Adam is the plight of the modern man who suffers from an inervation of will. He is aware of his situation but lacks the moral strength to overcome vacuity and the flamboyant sensationalism which surrounds him. Adam is far from the cad he might appear. He shows enough sympathy for Agatha Runcible when she is in the nursing home after the gruesome motor accident. He spends a night with Nina who is engaged to be married to Ginger Littlejohn. His conversation with her is Waugh's commentary on him as a creature of Fortune and on the lack of human will in general: "I'd give anything in the world for something different. . . . Different from everything . . . only I've got nothing . . . what's the good of talking?" (272) But when pressed to explain what he means, Adam replies, "Nothing." Adam and others are incapable of understanding and defining this inescapable reality of meaninglessness. Such an understanding alone accounts for man's self-identity and his ability to define the "absurd" reality around him. Self-deprivation results from an inability to understand the chaos around and to bring a little order into it.

The way Adam settles Lottie's bill of seventy-eight pounds sixteen and two pence is less humorous than amoral. Adam proposes selling Nina to Ginger when the latter demands an explanation for staying out late with his fiancee, for the amount of money he owes Lottie. The idea is done and Nina is released. It is "an episode in which the themes of moral and economic anarchy neatly coincide."[14] Seen from an ethical perspective, Adam Fenwick-Symes, Ginger Littlejohn (the name suggestive of non-growth) Nina Blount and indeed the whole of the 'smart set' are inhabitants of a society devoid of axiological significance. Theirs is an alienation from moral and religious values. The result of such alienation is a lack of direction combined with a concomitant sense of meaninglessness of existence. In such a negative and atomized society which is bereft of meaningful relationships, men and women are mere commodities to be bought and sold in an open market. Adam's price on Nina is a symptom of a deep-seated malaise of the post World War I society. Their impoverishment is not so much material as moral. They are petulant children, dangerous and predatory. An obsessive quest for money has brought out all that is irrational in their nature while self-indulgence at any cost has made them increasingly inconsiderate and selfish. An undue and vulgar stress on sensations has accompanied a lowering of the general tone of the society and a loss of discrimination of values. An ideal of wisdom has been destroyed by uncontrolled experimentation and permissiveness.

Nina marries Ginger but when the latter is recalled to his regiment after the honeymoon, Adam with his usual audacity, impersonates Ginger and accompanies Nina to her parent's home for Christmas. The comedy of errors continues unabated with the old eccentric Colonel Blount having completely forgotten his earlier meeting with Adam. The question of money crops up again when Adam tells Nina of having given Ginger a worthless cheque in payment for Nina. Adam's temporary transformation into Ginger is indeed a species of Protean sociability and social mobility of Waugh's "motley society" that Virgil Nemoianu mentions.[15] The Rector who recognizes him is however confirmed in his suspicion that Adam is off his head and thinks that "it is a very bad look-out for the next generation." The Rector ranks with the old Colonel in his unperceptiveness of observation and gross misjudgement. The declaration of war at the end of the section is a symbolic premonition not only of the end of the gaiety of the bright young things but of an entire civilization bred on superficial optimism, crass materialism and love of luxury. The order of primordial innocence is beyond recovery, now more than ever. An age characterised by restiveness and cultural stultification cannot hope to retrieve the lost Eden.

The world of the Bright Young People is doomed to catastrophe. It is a futile world governed by no ideals but only such negative characteristics as sensationalism, lack of communications and cruelty. Adam the chief actor is seen in the final chapter of the book – entitled with bitter irony

"Happy Ending" – sitting on a splintered tree stump in "the biggest battle field in the history of the world," surrounded by desolation and destruction all round him. The chapter presents in the words of Kurt Bangert, "a complete picture of an anti-utopian society."[16] Waugh chooses the anti-Utopian vision of a war, anticipating some of the features of World War II which was to break out within ten years of the publication of the novel. Experience has not educated or transformed the central character in the book. He is seen reading a letter from Nina who, married to Ginger, has started her affair with Adam by whom she is going to have a child. He is spiritually unequipped to inaugurate a "brave new world," holding out a message of hope and rejuvenation. Confronted with the horror of the war, he is utterly exhausted and totally incapable of changing the world order either by the purity of his own motives or by acts of courage. Unillumined by vision of nobility, the modern knight-errant is lost in the chaos of the times.

As in the case of *Decline and Fall* major symbols dictate the circular design and the aimlessness of the characters in *Vile Bodies.* Like the Wheel in the Luna Park in the first novel, the auto-race in *Vile Bodies* serves as an analogue for the modern life-style. The dizzying circularity of movements of the novel's characters is objectified in the social gyrations in general and in the motor races in particular. The world of the novel is, in the words of Alvin Kernan, "a busy bustling one in which crowds of men race furiously about pursuing some *ignis fatuus.*"[17] The Odyssey-like return home is parodied in the brilliant opening of the book in which a cross-section of the world is seen making a bad crossing from France to England. The ship which sometimes pitched and sometimes rolled and sometimes stood quite still and shivered all over, poised above an abyss of dark water" (8) is certainly symbolic of the general instability of the world the characters occupy. The sea sickness of the Bright Young People while the ship makes a rough passage, is indicative of their spiritual state. Alone among the voyagers Father Rothschild thinks of the sufferings of the saints, the mutability of human nature and the Four Last Things. The captain and the chief officer are engrossed in a crossword puzzle on the bridge, indifferent to the fate of the passengers. The card game of the "commercial gents" may have some symbolic relevance to the entire situation of the novel.

Rebecca West finds an analogy between the cardgame and Waugh's apparently casual but actually intricate technique in the novel. The smooth glossy pieces of the card-pack are like the frivolous and fatuous men and women, fortune's fools all of them. The characters sort themselves out into suits: "There are the spades, the souls sad, however gay doomed to destruction, however much they wriggle with excess of vitality, such as the gossipwriters. . . . There are the clubs, not so fatal as the spades, but still low-priced and fatuous such as the wastrels who sit and drink with Lottie Crump in her frowsty Shepheard's house. . . . There are the diamonds . . . Lord Metroland, the circumferences, Mr. Outrage, Lord Monomark. There are the hearts, Adam and Nina."[18] Everything in the world of the characters is, in their own language, "too too bogus." They are easily bored however varied their amusements and with whatever speed they pursue their amusements. The author's two quotations from Lewis Carroll's fairy tale at the book's beginning set the tone of the book. The characters in Waugh's novel seem to reach their goal (whatever it may be) for there is a blurring of values and no difference between appearance and reality.

The auto-race in Chapter X of the book underpins the book's major theme of 'lostness' in the wilderness of modernity. Miss Agatha Runcible and her male companions who go to races look vainly for suitable lodgings and are driven from place to place. The bizarre male attire of Agatha symbolises her lack of femininity while Miles's touching up of his eyelids implies his inadequate maleness. The roles of sexes seem oddly reversed. It is Agatha Runcible, the brainless butterfly who takes over as the heroine in this most crucial part of the book.

The rain, which is one of the book's persistent symbols of bleakness, is beating on the window of Adam's bedroom which is itself strewed symbolically with odds and ends: "In his room stood a chest of drawers full of horrible broken fragments of stuff, a wash-hand stand with a highly coloured basin, an empty jug and an old tooth brush. There was also a rotund female bust covered in shiny red material and chopped off short, as in primitive martyrdoms, at neck, waist and elbows." (221) The heap of "broken images" within the room and of the stony rubbish outside it collectively emphasise man's spiritual exile from his pristine home of wholeness and purity. The "factory" and the "canal of shallow waters" outside stand for the deleterious effects of industrialization which has been one of the contributing causes of the decline of values in modern life. The description of the race-track and the conversation of the crowd are replete with suggestions of death and destruction. The "place to see the fun" is called "headlong corner," a veritable death-trap. Agatha is said to be "ready for anything." The dining room is crowded with speed-kings and reporters: "they were . . . eating what might prove their last meal on earth." (223)

The idea of death without hope and that actors are playthings of Fortune cannot be missed. The juxtaposition of a new-born child to be christened throws a starkly ironic contrast to the hopelessness of the race-fans: "There was a disconsolate family who had come to town for the christening of a niece. (No one had warned them there was motor race on: their hotel bill *was* a shock)." (223)

Spiritual rejuvenation clearly is out of the question in a world characterised by reckless speed. The staccato conversation which follows heighens the impression of dizziness. The point that modern human beings lack the capability of growth and fullness is emphasised in the passage on the two clearly differing types of car:

> The truth is that motor cars offer a very happy illustration of the metaphysical distinction between "being" and "becoming." Some cars, mere vehicles with no purpose above bare locomotion, mechanical drudges such as Lady Metroland's Hispano-Swizo or Mrs. Mouse's Rolls Royce or Lady Circumference's 1912 Daimler or the "general reader's" Austin Seven, these have definite "being" just as much as their occupants. They are bought all screwed up and numbered and painted and there they stay through various declensions of ownership, heightened now and then with a lick of paint or temporarily rejuvenated by the addition of some minor organ, but still maintaining their essential identity to the scrap heap. Not so the real cars, that become masters of men; those vital creations of metal who exist solely for their own propulsion through space, for whom their drivers, clinging precariously at the steering wheel, are as important as his stenographer to a stock-broker. (227)

The "being-becoming" dichotomy of the passage recalls the machine-image of Otto Silenus in *Decline and Fall*. Waugh wishes both actors in the book and of its readers to come to terms with the ultimate question of the nature of man. In both passages, Waugh stresses the sterile furnishings of the machine associated with the modernists. The 'Vile "becoming"' of which Otto speaks in the previous book is of profound relevance to the present one describing as it does the stark and sterile happenings in the lives of the 'vile bodies' of the 1920s. The Speed-Kings especially like Agatha Runcible are at the mercy of cars who "become masters of men." Agatha's career as a race-driver is as haphazard as the rest of her life. Before the race begins, Agatha and her companions (Adam, Miles and Archie) are each given a brassard, which they are asked to tie around the arm. Agatha's brassard says, "SPARE DRIVER": so, quite inebriated, she is obliged to climb into the English plunket-Bouse when its driver has been seriously hurt. She goes in circles, faster and faster and finally clashes. After going through a long period of nightmare and hallucination she dies in a nursing home. Agatha, to quote James Hall, "who had meant to be a clown, becomes a pathetic representative of the group's effort to down self-doubts by frenetic activity."[19]

> I [Agatha] thought we were all driving round in a motor race and none of us could stop, and there was an enormous audience composed entirely of gossip writers and gate crashers and Archie Schwert and people like that, all shouting at us at once to go faster, and car after car kept crashing until I was left all alone driving and driving—and then I used to crash and wake up. (266)

The horrendous end of Agatha Runcible is a dramatic enactment of failure of quests which are not sustained by any kind of faith or conviction or ideology. The other doomed contestants in life's race go through endless circles like Agatha, as though they are motivated by a "strong death wish."[20] Not only the race-track drivers but all other characters—the fallen angels of Mrs. Melrose Ape, the Prime Ministers, the lords of the Press, the drunken Major, the moon-struck Colonel Blount and his daughter and above all, Adam, the book's central figure—they are all like a collection of Catherine Wheels. The brilliant reportage of the auto-race and its disaster is a prelude to the final world-catastrophe which is to be described in the final chapter of the book. With the same artistic control, Waugh pictures a scene of utter desolation in a style characterized by reduction and compression. The symbolic short hand is used to the very end of the book. The disaster of value-free civilization which has already been pre-figured in Agatha's crash, is given a cosmic setting. Adam is seen in the biggest theatre of war in 'human history.' The world of the characters has definitely become worse. Cruelty, hypocrisy and injustice abound more than ever and soldiers like Adam have no noble idealism to fight for or no damsel in distress to save. The letter from Nina gives him and the reader information of the plight of the highly immoral world of the bright young people. Nina herself is pregnant but has given her husband to believe that he is the father of the child. Mr. Beufleet, the notorious publisher who swindles authors, professes patriotism by publishing regular war-news which is pure invention. Betrayal is rife: Ginger, Nina's husband, has managed to send Archie Schwert, member of the set, to prison on charges of spying.

The final chapter of the book is loaded with symbols and is full of telling negative expressions. The general (the erstwhile drunken major) for instance, has broken his spectacles and he "Can't see a thing." His condition signifies the general confusion of the world, in which nobody can hope to make any spiritual progress. Phrases such as "I've lost my platoon," "I have lost my whole bloody division," "have lost the car," "got lost," "I don't know" etc. suggest the world of beknighted knights who are rootless and disoriented. Adam, the hero of modern times cannot face the horrors and he can do nothing but resign: "Then he took out a pipe, filled it and began to smoke. The scene all round him was one of unrelieved desolation; a great expanse of mud in which every visible object was burnt or broken. Sounds of firing thundered from beyond the horizon, and somewhere above the grey clouds there were aeroplanes. He had no sleep for thirty-six hours." (316) Total cruelty is implied in "every visible object was burnt or broken." Adam himself is seen "fighting his fingers about his Huxdane-Halley bomb (for the dissemination of leprosy germs)."

Chastity, the fallen angel of Mrs. Ape, has fallen still further. She has long since lost her identity and is past saving: "I been called a lot of things. I was called Chastity once." (318) The "Woebegone fragment of womanhood" is one of the aptest and most arresting metaphors for ravaged humanity. The plain, unabashed account that she gives of her degraded career is Waugh's criticism on human behaviour in general. The figure of the "lorry I was in got stuck in the ditch" is that of human nature which has lost its moorings and its sense of purpose and direction.

Adam does not want to embarrass the General and Chastity and "obvious to all happy emotion pulsing near him" is reported to "sink into sleep." On one level, his retiring into slumber suggests his fatigue and inability to face race, but on a deeper symbolic level, it suggests the moral stupor of the entire living world. A world which wishes to be cherished by its own illusions is suggested by the General who pulls "down the blinds [of the Dailmer limousine which is sunk to the axles in the mud], shutting out that sad scene" and starts to make love to Chastity.

Adam's inability to make a spiritual warfare is constitutional and has been hinted at earlier in the novel. Adam who has come for the auto-race occupies a bedroom from where he surveys the squalor outside. The room inside is no less squalid. In his aside, the author suggests his hero's regression:

> There was also a rotund female bust covered in shiny red material, and cropped off short, as in primitive martyrdoms, at neck, waist and elbows; a thing known as a dress maker's "dummy" (there had been one of these in Adam's home which they used to call "Jemima"—one day he stabbed "Jemima" with a chisel and scattered stuffing over the nursery floor and was punished. A more enlightened age would have seen a complex in this action and worried accordingly. Anyway he was made to sweep up all the stuffing himself.) (221)

The broken bust in the hotel bedroom and that of "Jemima" in Adam's nursery may serve as objective correlatives for the chaotic multiplicity of the human consciousness. The goal of traditional Christianity has been nothing less than the transformation of man into a being of inner Oneness. Such unity, however in the modern man has been possessed by the Jungian Unconscious, that is by whims, manias and obsessions and as a result been torn up into a multitude of fragments. Young Adam's mutilations of "Jemima" stands for the degenerating or destructive process of the spirit. As for Adam, there has been little moral growth. The picture of Adam in the last chapter, with the lethal bomb clutched in his hand is scarcely different from the little boy in the nursery who tore the doll to pieces. Adam's adolescence—for he rarely attains to complete adulthood—is a hangover from or a regression to his infantile state. The predicament of Adam is indeed that of modern humanity. Even though, like Adam, modern man has an awareness of the fragmentation of existence he is too weak of will to make the consequent search for an all-embracing integrative reality. The contrast between the Fisher King and Adam is of significance. Symbolically, the Fisher King was casting the bait into the depths of his own inmost nature in order to reach the gnosis. Modern man (like Adam), however, is incapable of any such soul-searching.

Waugh never lets the reader forget the spiritual home from where man has exiled himself. His nostalgia for a past golden age is ever implicit in his description of the modern age and of its people. In certain places the nostalgia for a lost Eden is made explicit, as in his quotation from Shakespeare. Ginger the nit-wit to whom Nina is married looks out of the aeroplane and quotes the celebrated description of England from Richard II, although he is not sure of its origin:

> This blessed plot, this realm, this England
> This nurse, this teeming womb of royal kings
> Feared by their breed and famous by their birth . . .

Like T.S. Eliot in his *Waste Land*, Waugh makes an indictment of the post-war world from the perspective of a glorious past which embodied all that was best in human nature. The contrast is quite glaring: the England of *Vile Bodies* is no more a sceptered isle, the earth of majesty, the precious stone set in the silver sea. The land can no longer breed a race of royal men. Nor can it be called "the Other Eden," a citadel of pure ideals. To Waugh, Shakespeare's description of the England of Richard II might equally apply to the Edwardian period in which the laws were the laws of comity and grace. To Waugh the Edwardian era represented a golden and beneficent era of plenty, peace and prosperity. Writers of Waugh's temperament saw the period before 1914 "in the golden haze of lost leisure, of a gracious and unhurried way of living."[21] That period has very definite and valuable qualities of order and stability which were not to be found after 1918. Paul Farr suggests that to Waugh who became increasingly dissatisfied with the aimless rebellion and outrageous insolence the Edwardian period seemed a haven of refinement and sensibility.[22]

Juxtaposed to the Shakespeare quotation is a description of the earth that Nina sees from the aeroplane: "arterial roads dotted with little cars, factories, some of them working, others empty and decaying; a disused canal; some distant hills sown with bungalows: wireless masts and overhead power cables; men and women were indiscernible except as tiny spots; they were marrying and shopping and making money and having children." (284) The narrator's distaste for the meaningless repetition of human activities is discernible.

Waugh's nostalgia for a past age redolent of Yuletide joy and squierarchy in stark contrast to the amoral acquisitiveness and duplicity of the later times is likewise apparent in chapter XIII of the novel in which Nina passes off Adam as her husband at the country house of Colonel Blount in Aylesbury. The novelist's own desire to discover anchorage in stability and tradition amid the whirls of change of his times is made abundantly clear. In the genuine Christmas spirit of the Doubting "All we discern Waugh's longing after 'Ye olde England'."

Ginger Littlejohn, Nina's husband has been called away by his regiment. Adam takes his place and with Nina goes for Christmas to Colonel Blount's country home. The Colonel's old devoted servants – Florin and his wife and the maid Ada – are seen decorating the hall to welcome the newly married couple. There are exchange of gifts, carol-singing visit to the servants' home, and there is universal bonhomie. But this nostalgic idyll is undercut by the adulterousness of Nina and Adam and by more disturbing news of an impending war. The technique of ironic juxtaposition is again at work. We are sharply made aware of our fallen condition, by the contrast. The loyalty of the Florins, the geniality of the Colonel to the carol singers and to his domestics as well as to his daughter and son-in-law are described. The ritual reception of the new bride is most callously violated by Nina who comes not with her wedded husband but with her lover. Their presence poisons the traditional celebration of rustic Christmas.

The central character in *Vile Bodies* as in *Decline and Fall* is not a quester, in the generally accepted sense, that is, one who is in search of his identity or a laudable ideal. What is suggested in these early novels is that the characters lack identity and even if they are to search for identity, their quest is doomed to disaster, benighted as they are in the jungles of modern civilization. Like the characters in the first novel, those in *Vile Bodies* – the young and the old alike – are mere creatures of Fortune. With their wills paralysed they are incapable of the least mental or spiritual exertion and they lack authenticity of existence. Through varied symbols and other stylistic devices such as juxtaposition and contrast, Waugh shows up the hollowness of his characters' aims and the triviality of their quests. One of the dominating thematic-motifs of the first two novels is loss of identity and the moral confusion that results from such loss. *Waste Land* like structure of *Vile Bodies* reflects the fragmentariness of existence of the characters who are trying to run away from the shadow of their own inadequacy.

NOTES

1. *The Critical Heritage*, p. 132.
2. *Ibid*., p. 133.
3. *Ibid*., p. 134.
4. *Ibid*., p. 136.
5. *Ibid*.
6. *Ibid*., p. 138.
7. Evelyn Waugh, *Vile Bodies* (Boston: Little, Brown, 1977), p. 7.
8. Alvin Kernan, p. 214.
9. Stephen J. Greenblatt, *Three Modern Satirists: Waugh, Orwell and Huxley* (London and New Haven: Yale University Press, 1964), pp. 12-13.
10. Frederick J. Stopp, p. 195.
11. James E. Nichols, "Romantic and Realistic: The Tone of Evelyn Waugh's Early Novels," *College English*, 24 (Oct. 1962), p. 46.
12. Alvin Kernan, p. 212.
13. James Hall, "The Other Post-War Rebellion: Evelyn Waugh Twenty-Five Years After," *ELH*, 28 (June 1961), p. 183.
14. David Lodge, "Evelyn Waugh," *Six Modern British Novelists*, ed. George Stade (New York: Columbia University Press, 1974), p. 62.
15. Nirgil Nemoianu, "Evelyn Waugh and the Motley Society," *Clio*, vol. 12, no. 3 (Spring 1983), p. 233.
16. Kurt Bangert, "The Use of Short Story Techniques in *Vile Bodies*," *EWN*, vol. 21, no. 2 (Autumn 1987), p. 4.

17. Alvin B. Kernan, p. 208.
18. *The Critical Heritage*, p. 107.
19. James Hall, p. 193.
20. Jerome Meckier, p. 522.
21. Paul D. Farr, "The Edwardian Golden Age and Nostalgic Truth," *The Dalhousie Review*, p. 379.
22. *Loc. cit.*

An Active But Still Undefined Quest: *Black Mischief*

Black Mischief (1932), although ordinarily grouped among Waugh's early novels, marks a definite progress in the author's novelistic career. The biting satire and the hilarious comedy of *Decline and Fall* and *Vile Bodies* are present in *Black Mischief* and the author's sense of humour has even grown more cruel. But beneath the savagery is noticed an ever-growing seriousness of intent and moral earnestness. Basil Seal, the central character, often described a "cad" is yet in many ways an improvement on the past heroes, Paul Pennyfeather and Adam Fenwick-Symes. Unlike them who are passive and who let things happen to them, Basil is serious and has the ability to retaliate against his society and the value it stands for and launches forth into an unknown future. William Cook's description of Basil "as the roundest character yet" seems accurate and perceptive.[1] A certain moral awareness is noticeable in the hero at the end of the story. Waugh's satire is directed not only at the 'lesser breed without the law' but equally at the Western liberals who think they can impose at all costs their values and standards on an alien people.

As can be expected, contemporary reviews of *Black Mischief* saw it as another of Waugh's brilliant satires. But Eric Linklater notices that the novel showed "an all-round growth of strength" despite its distinguished pessimism.[2] The book equally provoked outrage in some circles. Earnest Oldmeadow's notorious review in the "Tablet"[3] was too strait-laced and bigoted to recognise Waugh's growing ability to control his material and the author's distinction of two entirely different realms of value. More modern and recent criticism which has learnt to guard against the intentional and affective fallacies, sees in the disparate strands of Waugh's novel a centrality of thought and unity of design. The novel is seen as not merely a satire on the absurdities and incongruities produced by collision of two distinct cultures but a serious indictment upon a rapidly degenerating civilization which prides itself on civilizing other people. In travelling from London to Azania, Basil Seal is just going from one kind of barbarism to another. Through Basil, Waugh explores the corrupt and effete upper class society in London and the equally absurd Azanian society whose emperor is making foolish attempts to westernize his primitive people. Basil foreshadows the later Waugh heroes who are all spiritual exiles, of one kind or other. He recognises the emptiness and absurdity of his surroundings and makes a manly attempt to leave home in search not merely of adventure but of a new way of life. While ridiculing the callousness of his hero, Waugh at the same time has some admiration for him because he is an enterprising young man who is endowed with a spirit of adventure. It is often remarked that Waugh's heroes are fictive projections of some part of himself. Basil's search for meaning, however mis-directed, is Waugh's own quest for order and purpose.

The "stylized rebels" of *Black Mischief* like the Bright Young Things of *Vile Bodies* make a bid for attention through exhibitionism, distaste for authority and extraordinarily bizarre behaviour. Their love of sensationalism is symptomatic of a deeply embedded sense of insecurity, a manifestation either of their desire for 'will to power' or of what psychologists term as 'death wish.' A hopeless sense of alienation is at the root of the disaffection between the generations, between the different coteries and indeed between one individual and another. Anarchic impulse is at work. Being unsure of themselves and yet longing for identity and recognition, these "rebels" are in conflict with the society's accepted code of values of orderliness, regularity and responsibility. Father Rothschild's diagnosis of "a fatal hunger for permanence" in *Vile Bodies* applied with equal force to the circularity of life of the characters of *Black Mischief* whose routine consists of prolonged drunkenness and meaningless love affairs. Incapable of new ideas they soon tire of their own brashness and bravado. Their search for identity as a consequence ends in regression to primitiveness and cruelty.

Basil Seal embodies the novel's main theme, namely the plight of the individual who is himself far from perfect, in an increasingly barbaric society. Son of the Late Sir Christopher Seal who had been Chief Conservative Whip for twenty-five years, Basil is a disappointment to his mother. His odd behaviour as the Conservative ball seems to have ruined Basil's own chances as a candidate in the North. All his actions, including his affair with Mrs. Angela Lyne, seem calculated to outrage the members of his society.

It is generally admitted that despite his oddities Basil is a clever, talented and able young man. Gifted with an acute sense of wit, he enjoys embarrassing people and cornering them. But at twenty-eight, he is a froward child, throws away several enviable openings and prefers to waste time in the company of the muddled young people. The room of Sonia and Alastair Trumpington in Montagu Square where Basil goes to dine is a metaphor for the jungle of English civilization. The couple eat in their bed with their dogs messing the floor. Basil joins them on the bed and after dinner all of them play the 'happy family.' Their inane conversation unsuccessfully masks their anxiety and sense of non-entity and despair. But whereas the others content themselves with their parties and social gyrations, Basil Seal knows the meaninglessness of it all and looks restlessly for an anchor of stability. He, however, distrusts the "wisdom, discretion, sympathy, experience and contentment" of an earlier generation whose representative is Sir Joseph Mannering, the confidant of Basil's mother Lady Cynthia Seal. His search for identity, like much else about him, is characterized by an attitude of defiance. Used as he is to being lionized from early youth, Basil gets easily tired of the attention given to him and wishes to explore new avenues of life. His sister Barbara's premarital infatuation of her elder brother borders on incest. Such a psychotic fixation if we are to accept the authority of Girlot's *A Dictionary of Symbols* is itself symbolic of a longing for identity.[4]

Although as Jerome Meckier in his article on *Decline and Fall* has argued, that Waugh set store by Apollonian values in his fiction, he was drawn, even if momentarily, to the Dionysian aspect of human experience. Recent criticism has shown that Waugh's vision of life embraced the polar opposites of the essentialist and the existentialist ways of defining experience.[5] The one has, of necessity, to be defined in terms of the other. Apollonian or the essentialist view with its emphasis on order and objectivity will seem "sterile and inert" without the impulsive chaos of its opposite. Basil Seal is as much a part of Waugh as the other more sober of his fictional creatures. He is Waugh's "man of action" who thinks it is worth one's while to travel afar, not merely to satisfy one's curiosity but to pursue solutions. As he tells his mother Lady Cynthia:"You see I am fed up with London and English politics. I want to get away. Azania is the obvious place. I had the emperor to lunch once at Oxford . . . every year or so, there is one place on the globe worth going to where things are happening. The secret is to find out where and be on the spot in time."[6] The passage provides us with some clues to the character of Basil, the stage of growth to which he has so far attained in life and the nature of his quest. His responses to environmental forces and his disregard of others' feelings seem to have their source in that kind of counter productive cynicism which characterises abnormal adolescence. Waugh makes Basil Seal credible by letting him remain a rogue throughout. David Lodge's reference to Basil Seal as "a true child of 'l'entre-deux-guerres,' so devoid of principle that deception and fraud are reflex responses to him and he is incapable of seeing through his own lies"[7] is an apt characterization of the adult who refuses to grow. Despite his twenty-eight years, Basil appears as one who has had a deferred adolescence. His inability to make permanent life-commitments, his failure to make evaluative responses of perceptual experiences and a general apathy are all what one would expect from one who is in early or middle adolescence, especially of a turbulent type. Most adolescent actions are exploratory and experimental, in character, of an interpretive or evaluative nature. Basil's contempt for conventional values and morals and his apparent nonchalance to the consequences of his actions are symptomatic of a prolonged identity crisis of adolescence in which a few if any commitments are made. This "moratorium" on his moral and spiritual growth issues in inauthenticity and failure to realise his autonomy of self. His theft of his mother's emerald bracelet is in accord with Basil's general attitude to life.

Having said this, it must be admitted however that Basil is genuinely interested in exploring new places and situations. He believes that Azania at least will provide him with opportunities to prove his intelligence. He tells his mother: "History doesn't happen everywhere at once. Azania is going to be terrific. Anyway I'm off there tomorrow. Flying to Marseilles and catching the Messageries ship." (112) One of his problems, as with most adolescents, has been the formulation of a goal. But once the goal has been formulated he will stick at nothing. He undertakes the long and arduous journey with relish and like a true explorer puts up with the inevitable hardships of such an undertaking.

As a symbol, the journey is not merely a passage through space but an expression of the urgent desire for discovery and change that underlies the actual movement and experience of travelling. "Travelling is an image of aspiration, of an unsatisfied longing that never finds its goal, seek where it may."[8] Tennyson's Ulysses typifies such an unfulfilled longing. Waugh's own travels which he has recorded in his *Labels, Remote People, Ninety-Two-Days* among others, afford valuable insights into the author's personality, informative as they are about Waugh's principles and convictions. They have moreover, "sufficient links with his friction." The grotesque and the eccentric that we meet in *Black Mischief, A Handful of Dust* and *Scoop* have their origin in Waugh's travel books. Underlying his accounts in his travel books is a unique kind of paradox: encounters with the unfamiliar enable Waugh to understand the familiar. "In far away places and in the company of strange men and women, Waugh learns about *himself* what he could not have learnt in London, Mayfair, in the midst of the Bright Young People."[9] Waugh's achievement in novels set in remote places lies in his uncanny knack of turning haphazard experiences recorded in his travel books into memorable forms of fiction; in Waugh's own terms in his *Ninety-Two Days*, "like the carpenter who sees a piece of timber and wishes to square and plane it."[10]

The true journey is neither acquiescence nor an escape; it is evolution. Basil's journey to the remote Azania is therefore a symbolic journey representing a quest for identity. In psychological terms, it is a journey from the dark unconscious to the light of understanding of oneself. Waugh's raffish hero, tired of London, is in search not merely of pleasure but of meaning. Whether he ever succeeds in grasping it is a different matter. The fact that he decides to get out of the maze invests his journey with a higher significance. The ordeals with which his journey to Azania is beset may be taken as ordeals of initiation. He will soon discover that the civilized men are not so different from the savages in the African jungle. The resemblances will indeed accumulate, in the course of his journey. Basil Seal will learn, as the readers will do that "man will never be self-sufficient this side of the grave; political and economic conditions can do little to augment either his value or his happiness; inequalities are inevitable."[11] Nevertheless, after his bizarre encounter with an alien culture, he does change, if ever so slightly. The adventure makes him a little more serious than he had been before.

One of the causes of Basil's ennui and disgust with the world of London is the inepitude of the older generation which is "engaged in ritual performances of meaningless manners."[12] The passage which describes Lady Seal retiring to bed is a brief and shining vignette of luxury and indulgence faintly reminiscent of the daily cosmetic ritual of Pope's heroine Belinda in his *Rape of the Lock*:

> So Lady Seal undressed and sank at last luxuriously into bed. Bradshawe softly paddled round the room performing the last offices; she picked up the evening gown, the underclothes and the stockings and carried them outside of her workroom; and straightened the things on the dressing table, shut the drawers, wiped the points of the nail scissors with a wad of cotton; she opened the windows four inches at the top, banked up the fire with a shovelful of small coal, hitched on the wire guard, get a bottle of Vichy water and a glass on the chamber cupboard beside the bed. (113)

A generation which has devoted itself to only creature comforts and other physical supports of life has failed to nurture lasting moral and ethical values in its children. What it has failed to provide Basil Seal and the other members of the younger generation with, is true "experience" which is the harmonization of conformal, evaluative and vectoral feeling. Lady Seal and Sir Joseph Mannering whose own lives seem not to have been touched by "ultimate concern" can hardly be expected to give Basil the right lead in life.

The account of Basil's journey abroad in Chapter Three of the novel bears close resemblance to Waugh's travel books, letters and diaries that he wrote between 1930 and 1939. It is written with the same telegraphic crispness of Waugh's diaries of that period. Like his hero, Waugh "sought adventure and discomfort" in Ethiopia, British Guiana and virtually the North Pole. After the break-down of his first marriage, Waugh had no fixed home and he was travelling constantly both in Britain and abroad. Wastrels like Basil (and his author) who are in search of "novelty" are unmindful of the privation that unconventional voyages entail. Seal is, in the words of Stanley Kaplan, "the embodiment of Waugh's vision of the modern world: he is seal-like, slippery, polytropic, shuttling through a succession of ironic *picaro* who is disenchanted with everything including his own routines. He has ability but no purpose: he tries things and then rejects them with phlegmatic impassivity. He shares the *picaro's* attractiveness in skirting social convention and morality, in the triumphing over adversity, but unlike *picaro* he has nothing to grasp hold at the end of his masquerade."[13]

It is one of the numerous ironies of the novel that its hero who is in search of adventure and identity should go to Azania which is not a land of hope and glory but a land compounded of confusion and alienation. It is "presumbaly an artistic composite of Abyssinia and Tanzania," two of the countries that Waugh visited and wrote about in his travel books and diaries. The similarities between Ethiopia and the fictional land of Azania are striking. In the course of his description of the extraordinary coronation of the Emperor of Ethiopia Waugh writes:

> No catalogue of events can convey any real idea of those astounding days, of an atmosphere, utterly unique, elusive, unforgettable. If in the foregoing pages I have seemed to give undue emphasis to the irregularity of the proceedings, to their unpunctuality, and their occasional failure, it is because this was an essential part of their character and charm. In Addis Ababa everything was haphazard and incongruous; one learned always to expect the unusual and yet was always surprising.[14]

As he remarks elsewhere, Waugh was fascinated "in the remote and barbarous places and particularly in the borderlands of conflicting cultures and states of development where ideas, uprooted from their traditions become oddly changed in their transplantation."[15]

The above quotations exactly describe the conditions in the fictional land of Azania. It is a hodge-podge of races, cultures, and religions but where nothing has taken permanent root. The cry from the minaret mingles uneasily with the Angelus of the Mission Church. Three Bishops, three substantial cathedrals and numerous missions of different denominations are found in the land of the rival Sakuyu and Wanda tribes as well as the Arab descendants. Like the Addis Ababa of Waugh's travel books, Azania resembles the Israel of Saul, and the Scotland of Shakespeare's *Macbeth* but more than anything else it has "the peculiar flavour of galvanized and translated reality" of the world of Lewis Carroll's *Alice* where "animals carry watches in their waistcoat pockets, royalty paces the croquet lawn beside the chief executioner and litigation ends in a flutter of playing cards."[16] In this bizarre and unreal world, surprises are aplenty. Cultures widely different from each other are violently yoked together.

Azania has had a troubled and chequered history. It was first settled by the Portuguese followed later by the Arabs. While it prospered under the Arabs, Amurath, an African negro, who has had a missionary education overthrew its captors and declared himself Emperor Amurath the Great and proclaimed the island a single territory, with its capital at Debra Dowa, the "Dirre-Dowa" of Waugh's travel book *Remote People*. Under Amurath, Azania emerged from barbarism into modern civilization of doubtful authenticity. The irony is in Amurath's declaration of Christianity as the official religion of the empire. When the novel opens, the empire is under Amurath's grandson Seth. " Chief of the chiefs of Sakuyu, Lord of Wanda and Tyrant of the Seas, Bachelor of Arts of Oxford University." (21) Seth carries the modernization to ludicrous lengths and yet Azania remains barbarous underneath the veneer of modernity.

The futility of transplantation of an alien culture in the Azanian soil is suggested in many ways. Debra-Dowa the capital is a "haphazard jungle" of foreign legations and primitive huts.His success over his rival Seyid has made Seth a bit over-confident of himself but despite his repeated claims that he is the "New Age and the Future" and a symbol of progress, Azania remains a land of darkness. Azania is so "full of mixed items with no context"[17] that it has no identity of its own or has lost what little it had before the importation of foreign culture and notions. In a land of strange contiguities and an odd assemblage of disparate elements of life, where vernacular hymns and drum beats collide with ancient liturgy, one may expect to see only fragmentation and dissipation. Spiritual alienation is a logical consequence of such jumble. He remains cut off from his friends and countrymen. Frequent references to "darkness" suggesting darkness of soul and spirit abound in the author's account of Azania:

> Night and the fear of darkness. . . . Night was alien with beasts and devils and the spirit of dead enemies; . . . warm, naked bodies

> breathing in the darkness an arm's reach apart, indivisibly unified so that they ceased to be six or seven scared blacks and became one person of more than human stature, less vulnerable to the peril that walked near them. Seth could not expand to meet the onset of fear. He was alone, dwarfed by the magnitude of the darkness, insulated from his fellows, strapped down to mean dimensions. (35)

The one constant emotion that is strikingly apparent in the young Emperor's face is blank terror and he is utterly lonely: He keeps saying: "I am alone, there is no one." (41) Everything around him is "Expressive of nothing; followed by nothing; no foot steps, no voices; silence and the distant beat of the tomtoms." (42) Sandwiched between the two seeming irreconcilabes, Seth seems to have lost his identity altogether and suffers from a loss of communication. He is one of T.S. Eliot's Hollowmen, bereft of beliefs and convictions, an uncertain composite of primitivism and sophistication. In his quest for modernity Seth loses his own identity because modernity produces only depravity and loss of spirituality. His "brave new world" is a world which is lacking in warmth of humanity and communitarian feeling. The res nova (new thing) that he is pitting against the res publica[18] (public) is fraught with predictable consequences. Tradition is violently uprooted but in its place there is nothing tangible for him and his people to pin their faith on. Waugh discovers that civilized men are not so different as the natives of the dark continent. He fires, as Voorhees remarks, "with a double-barreled hilarity at both the savage and the civilized."[19] If the attempts of Emperor Seth to modernize are ludicrous, the modernism to which he aspires and those who have come from modern West are even more so. Waugh has remarked in his *Remote People* that "the resident aliens were as extraordinary as the natives," by which he meant that the Europeans were litttle better, if not worse, than the natives of the land, both in terms of culture and social behaviour. The representatives of western civilization are as far removed from Christian manners and morals as the natives are from their traditional ways of living. The modern West, according to Waugh, is sterile and degenerate since it is more and more divorced from conservative Christian values. The cretinuous behaviour of the Western residents in Azania makes them, to use one of Waugh's oft-quoted phrases, "potential recruits for anarchy."[20] The irony of the novel which is multiple, is directed not only at the primitive parasitic mind but at the "intransigent irrationality of man" in general.

Azania is a wasteland, spiritually arid, beneath which, to borrow the image from Bertrand Russell,[21] the fiery depths of a volcano into which an unwary walker might sink at anytime. The scales of values of the alien residents – Sir Samson Courtney, the British envoy Extraordinary and his like – is trivial. It can hardly provide them with any moral sustenance and their veneer of respectability is as vulnerable as the thin crust of barely cooled lava which covers the seething volcano. In his appraisal of the minor characters, – chief of whom is Sir Courtney – Waugh seems quite objective and seems willing to ridicule as well as sympathise. Sir Samson Courtney is the very emblem of imbecility and is the embodiment of modern futility and failure. A man of singular personal charm and wide culture, Sir Courtney is however, a signal diplomatic failure because of his inattentiveness to the things of the world. His reckless inability to learn to make himself competent has earned him a certain notoriety in his career and has had to be shifted from post to post. Once in Washington, he caused scandal by devoting himself exclusively to bicycling and entering his name for an international long distance championship. In Sweden he made himself ridiculous by his total inability to make even rudimentary conversation in a foreign language. However thanks to his family connections in the Foreign Office in London, despite his innumerable faux-pas, he has made a knight of St. Michael and St. George and relegated to Azania where he is outwitted by the diplomats of other foreign missions. The fifty-year-old diplomat is an adolescent like Basil Seal. His day-dreaming in the bath-room is illustrative of his stunted mental and moral growth:

> Prudence and William had left an inflated Indian rubber sea-serpent behind them in the bath-room. Sir Samson sat in the warm water engrossed with it. He switched it down the water and caught it in his toes: he made waves for it: he blew it along; he sat on it and let it shoot up suddenly to the surface between his thoughts: he squeezed some of the air out of it and made bubbles. Chance treats of this kind made or marred the happiness of dream. (81)

The envoy's total indifference to the momentous events outside shows, as Ian Littlewood has observed, that the claims of office rate low in his inverted scale of values.[22] In his peculiarly personal hierarchy of values, what is trivial is treated with utter seriousness where serious matters of life and death are treated with frivolity. The inconvenience of lending a tennis racket seem more serious than the news of the war that is raging around him. His casual tone "Which side won?" is like a school boy's interest in the latest cricket-match. His "disillusionment" in the bath and his disgust with "the stale, crowded world" of the twentieth century are symbolic of the modern man's refusal to grow out of his childhood ways and his consequent inability to rise to the challenges of manhood. Sir

Samson Courtney represents the modern man who cannot make decisions to assume personal responsibility for his speculative growth and development and to assume responsibility for the formation and consequences of his own decisions. Modern man would rather go back to the "womb" and feel absolutely secure rather than go back to the process of the experimental evolution of life.

Lady Courtney, his wife, is similarly divorced from the realities around her; practically all her time is taken up by gardening in the legation lawn. Their daughter Prudence who is a victim of ennui, like most others, relieves the tedium by sexual assignation first with the young man William and later with the novel's hero and by writing a book ironically entitled "Panorama of Life" which is a day-dreaming account completely out of touch with the outside world of teeming chaos.

Azania is what General Connolly, the stocky Irish commander-in-chief of Emperor Seth calls an "abandoned country" where wars are won by two very ancient weapons – lies and the long spear. What Waugh has to say about General Connolly on his victorious return after crushing a mutiny, that he looks "like a lost explorer than a conquering commander-in-chief" may be applied with equal truth to most other inhabitants of Azania. Youkoumian, the wily Armenian hotel-owner and trader embodies the law of the jungle. With what Ian Littlewood calls his "immaculate callousness," he tries to bridge the cultural gap in Azanian life. His complete lack of humanity which is especially evidenced in his shameful treatment of his meek and loving wife, his abject servility to the white man for consideration and his lack of all trading scruples make him a veritable symbol of what Carens calls "an amoral and indestructible force,"[23] a kind of manic energy of anarchy which sets at nought all civilized norms of order and propriety.

To Waugh who is pessimistic about the possibilities of human nature, such anarchistic impulse is the general human condition. Cut off from all tradition and incapable of absorbing the best modernism, Azania is a parched land desperately in need of the waters of spiritual life. The heap of stones at the roadside which was a continual reproach to Sir Samson's diplomatic failure also serves as a metaphor for the failure of human spirit unaided by moral and religious values in general. All of the Envoy's attempts to improve the outrageous road which connected the legation to the capital has ended in disaster and all that now stood by the roadside was "the heap of stony rubbish" (to use T.S. Eliot's phrase) which was a monument to his single ineffective excursion into statesmanship. Misdirected human effort, Waugh seems to say, is bound to end the same way.

Within the novel's ironic perspective, it is easy to understand why Basil has to go to Azania, a place with a uniquely elusive atmosphere. Besides providing the novelist with an opportunity to further explore the comic possibilities inherent in a situation in which a character faces something totally new, Basil's journey is a novelistic necessity from the point of view of the quest-motif. Azania provides the searcher with objects of knowing, for it is part of the process of self-knowledge that one knows people and objects among whom one is cast. However, the hero's attempt at self-identity in the novel is undercut by the pervasive irony in the book. It is all one buzzing booming confusion and the hero's own constitutional inability to communicate coupled with the lack of sympathetic understanding of a hostile culture makes it hard for him to achieve any degree of self-discovery. It is one of the novel's basic assumptions that self-discovery comes from meaningful relationships with those around us. Basil's personal dilemma takes on serious overtones once he is in Azania. As the story proceeds, the reader begins to sympathise more and more with the hero's predicament for it becomes apparent quite early on that the latter's quest is doomed to failure.

Critics who regard Evelyn Waugh primarily as a satirist have described *Black Mischief* as a savage satire of manners which follow a collision of two widely different cultures. Carens described it as a bitter and pessimistic book full of "savage irony." To Greenblatt it was a book of "comic cruelty."[24] Christopher Hollis saw the book as "the study of the politics of an Abyssinia-like African island whose Emperor Seth attempts to impose on his barbarous subjects what he conceives to be the customs of "modern progress."[25] Some have detected "snobbery" in the white man's racial superiority to the people of the African principality. However, most critics have agreed that the author's attack is not always one-sided. The book is a blistering attack on the Western liberals who believe that their manners and values alone can refine the savage race 'without the law.' Kernan calls it a "grotesque image of Western civilization in the twentieth century."[26]

An over-emphasis of the book's satire ignores its serious concern. In their preoccupation with Waugh's style, these critics have called into question his moral concern. It cannot be denied that Waugh's whole fictional oeuvre was concerned in one way or other with the moral predicament of human beings. Lawrence Ruff's assessment of the moral aspect of Waugh's work seems sound and just. He points out for instance that to call Waugh's novel "decadent" is based on the false assumption that language in Waugh is an end in itself, and that the one and only distinguishing characteristic is its conscious artistic form. "Vocabulary, syntax, and imagery develop in elaborate patterns which become the real foci of attention."[27] But as Ruff has demonstrated it is not quite right to say that

Waugh was obsessed with form and consequently lacked a moral purpose. Waugh's achievement lay in combining an entrancing style with serious matter. He has a consistent moral purpose throughout all his work. His early novels, from *Decline and Fall*, to *Put Out More Flags* and "in fact all his pre-*Brideshead Revisited* novels express a definite ethical/didactic purpose in Waugh's highly stylized, craftsman like prose."[28] For example, a lighter purpose is evident in the two apparently chaotic novels: *Vile Bodies* and *Black Mischief*.

Two things follow from this. First amoral cultures of the West, England in particular as Waugh knew it, and the barbarism in the heart of Azanian darkness are indistinguishable. Azania is a darkly ludicrous caricature of the "civilized" West: "The apostles of jungle progress, the crude profiteers, the ludicrous aristocracy, and the cannibals of Azania are but extensions of attitudes and people who appear in more normal clothes and speak in more normal familiar accents in the novels set in England."[29] In Azania, as in England, life goes in meaningless circles, like the maddened dance of the cannibals described in the novel. Attempts of the Protectorate which takes over the Government of Azania after the death of Emperor Seth to bring back order and progress symbolised by the paved roads and neat bungalows, are only "another form of the old power game." Back in the jungle one hears the drum-beat of the cannibals while the tribesmen tear up the rail road irons for spear heads and rip down telegraph lines to make copper bracelets for their wives. Kernan's use of the well-known French adage, "Plus ca change, plus c'est la meme chose" is most apt – the more it changes the more it is the same thing. No amount of superficial or apparent change can alter the essential human nature. Much of human activity is misdirected and fails in its purpose essentially because it lacks a spiritual or moral dimension. In the absence of a teleology in human thinking, all activity is bound to prove inane or absurd. The characters in the Waugh novel spend their time with the mundane round of activities, unmarked by the Coleridgean joy when emotional and intellectual faculties are in equipoise. The characters in *Black Mischief*, the Whites and the Africans alike, are empty-headed inhabitants of the twentieth century jungle, without the least sense of moral or aesthetic discrimination. What Waugh presents in refined prose is a vision of man reduced to his most primitive and brutish level. He tells the story not of corrigible folly but of all-out degradation and baseness which sours the flesh and scents the air, a tale of human retrogression, of isolation and barrenness. Behind the apparent chaos of sentimentality and jumbled human relationship, is the standard of medieval love of order and a horror of hell.

The second corollary that derives from the propagation that Waugh's novel is not to be solely judged as a satire, is that it is not quite correct to deny the author's sympathy for his characters. Critics who see Waugh as a satirist regard his 'criticism of life' untempered by sympathy or understanding. Waugh's novels, especially the early ones, have earned the notoriety of masterpieces of inconsequence in which the satirist–the author/narrator – remains completely anonymous, merely a speaking voice who tells nothing directly and distances himself from his heroes and their fortune. The narrator-persona of these "menippean" satires is to be regarded as but a poetic device of the author to express his satiric vision. Even if there is such a thing as plot in Waugh's stories, they do not eventuate in any significant change; there is only an intensification of the original condition. Like the heroes in other satires, those in Waugh's are pathic creatures and their stories are ever in a state of stasis. Savagery, despair and sadism are innate in Waugh's satires and he gives no one any quarter. A "contriver of farragoes, rather than articulated wholes," Waugh is not interested in the growth of his characters or of any interaction between them and their environment.

Such criticism, however, overlooks the basic distinction between the detached stance of a critic and his own personal disinterestedness. The objectivity of the satirist is clearly confused with the author's own attraction or repulsion for his characters. Such objectivity is only a technique, "a method of contrasting unpleasant or shocking material with calm, restrained, dispassionate expression."[31] It does not prove, as Feinberg goes on, that the satirist, in the case Waugh – does not care about the events he is describing. All that the writer has done is to choose a particular form to describe such events. Such accusations by critics of Waugh's hardness of mind or harshness of tone result from the confusion of the author's detachment with his own attitude to or involvement in his characters. A.E. Dyson's remark belongs to that category: "This [deep human] concern is exactly what Waugh lacks. His novels do not extend our awareness of why people are as they are, and they inhibit rather than create compassion."[32] But as William Cook rightly protests, Waugh's detachment and "seeming" of lack of concern is the result of his masterful control of his mateiral, not of misanthropy, as Dyson's criticism implies. An "increasing identification with the plight of his fictional creatures" is apparent in Waugh's development as a novelist. Waugh ably conceals his own involvement with his characters behind his brilliant satiric artistry and entrancing style. He is not such a cold-blooded and unsympathetic observer of human foibles, as critics make him out to be. On the contrary, there is what Rolo calls "a core of tragic awareness"[33] behind the satires. Carens, Ruff, G.S. Fraser and O'Faolain among others hold a similar view. The last-mentioned critic, especially notes the delicate balance which Waugh strikes between his detachment from characters "which allows him to satirise them and his affection for them which allows him to pity them."[34]

The foregoing 'digression' on Waugh's art as a satiric writer is germane to our discussion of the quest-motif in *Black Mischief*. Waugh shows sympathy not only for the hero but for most of the secondary characters of the novel and not as William Cook seems to imply that it is limited only to the main character. The sympathy that he showed to Agatha Runcible in *Vile Bodies* is seen in his treatment of Emperor Seth in the present novel. As Ruff has argued, the collapse of Seth's confused ideals in the face of primitive ignorance and civilized ineffectualness and greed is poignant. Lady Seal and Joseph Mannering, Sir Samson Courtney, his daughter Prudence, and Madame Youkoumian, the long-suffering wife of the grasping Armenian trader – all these characters claim some of the author's sympathy by turns. Individually and collectively these characters, most of whom are fictional transmutations of real-life people, are either haunted by a nostalgia for a long-forgotten past or, to use Waugh's own phrase in *Robbery Under Law* "in search of an oppressor who will take responsibility"[35] for their ills. They are dreamers of one kind or another, who indulge in their emotion without analysing the object that is supposed to be responsible for it. They are now and then touched by a sense of pathos, if not genuine tragedy, in their hopeless attempts of living by hope.

Basil Seal, and to a lesser extent, Emperor Seth carry the thematic burden of the novel. Representatives of widely differing cultural values or disvalues, they are united in their bizarre zeal to realise themselves. Each after his grotesque fashion is a comment on the nature of man in contemporary society. They are both a couple of groping, puzzled and isolated men, who are never quite able to see life steadily and see it whole. In existential terms, these melancholy and isolated men are thrown into a grotesque and uncontrollable world whose challenges they are pitifully ill-equipped to face.

Basil of London and Emperor Seth of Azania are visionaries – the one is in search of something different from the wasteland of London and the other has grandiose dreams of modernization of his barbaric country. Imprisoned in their own subjectivity, they are both unable to transcend themselves or realise all the ontological potentialities, energies and desires within them. Their egocentricity disables them to contemplate absolute truths and deprives them of meaningful communication with others. An ego thus divided and alienated from itself is subjected to a kind of spiritual schizophrenia, or, to borrow the terminology of the existentialist, "the actual *defacto* self (what I actually mean) is separated from the real or *dejure* self (what I ought to be)."[36] The careers of these two men illustrate the dangers of solipsistic self-sufficiency and point to the fact that man, in the words of Newman, is implicated "in some great aboriginal calamity." Divided within himself modern man is in a state of deprivation and is unable to come to terms with himself. Waugh's irony thus becomes cosmic, for what is involved in the plight of Basil and Seth, is human fate.

In his conviction that he has been set apart from his countrymen for a higher destiny, Seth alienates himself from his native culture. The naivete with which he adopts the half-understood Western culture makes him an easy butt of ridicule. His reign is a catalogue of misconceptions and disasters. The Emperor's proclamation with which the novel gives a clue to the nature of the man and of his intellectual understanding:

> "We, Seth, Emperor of Azania, Chief of the Chiefs of Sakuyu, Lord of Wanda and Tyrant of the Seas, Bachelor of the Arts of the Oxford University, being in this the twenty-fourth year of our life, summoned by the wisdom of Almighty God and the unanimous voice of our people to the throne of our ancestors do hereby proclaim. . . . Seth paused in his dictation and gazed out across the harbour where on the fresh breeze of early morning the last dhow was setting sail for the open sea. "Rats" he said, "stinking curs. They are running." (9)

This opening passage with its combination of "royal rhetoric and back-alley slang"[37] while giving the reader a clue to the character of the speaker, sets the tone of the novel. The absurdities that flow from the cultural confusion implicit in the situation are obvious. The insertion of the definite article "the" in his academic title shows that he has not even understood what the initials "BA" stand for. His proclamation suggests that he has learnt the arts of Oxford University as one might learn the law of the jungle.

A setback to the Emperor's idea of progress on the ruins of native tradition is sounded even on the day of his first triumphal journey from Matodi to Debra-Dowa, the modern capital on the renovated railway, the Grand Chemin de Fer'd Azania. Despite the elaborate official arrangements and the Emperor's own clear directions, all is disorder and chaos. The Emperor arrives an hour later than the appointed time and when the time to start arrives, the engine gives a great wrench, shakes itself free from the rest of the train and shoots "by itself" into the country. The station master laments: "It is a thing I did not foresee. . . . Our early engine has gone away alone. I think I shall be disgraced for this affair." (132)

Seth's grand gestures are of no avail. His attempts to modernize a land where people still believe that an engine can "go away alone" as if moved by an ancestral spirit are bound to end in dismal failure.

The coincidence in Basil Seal arriving in Matodi on the day of the Emperor's ceremonious train journey and his travelling on the same train is aesthetically significant. Basil and Seth are soon to meet on the idea of the dishonest businessman Youkoumian who is on hand when Basil wants a ticket on the crowded train to Debra-Dowa. At the victory celebrations later the Emperor recognises Basil as the young man whom he had met at a luncheon as an undergraduate at Oxford. Basil had then enjoyed a reputation of peculiar brilliance among his contemporaries. He was the man the emperor needed, "a man of culture, a modern man . . . a representative of Progress and the New Age." To Seth, Basil was the personification of all "that glittering, intangile Western culture to which he aspired." Seth's dream of a modern state is a mere ignis fatuus and by falling an easy victim to the cool opportunism of Basil he hastens towards his doom. The world of Azania with a young hopeful as its head has a false bottom. The Victory Ball that Seth gives in the capital at which every side of Azanian life is liberally represented shows up the hollowness of Seth's world. It has exceeded the highest expectations of the organisers in splendour and gaiety: "A gross of assorted novelties – false noses, papers, trumpets and dolls – had arrived by the mail from Europe, but demands exceeded the supply. Turbans and tarbooshes bobbed round the dancing floor: there were men in Azanian state robes, white jackets, uniforms, and reach-me-down tail coats; women of all complexions in recently fashionable gowns, immense imitation jewels and lumpy ornaments of solid gold." (138)

Basil Seal finds an outlet for his energies in the demanding work as Seth's Minister of Modernization with extraordinary powers. He is to carry out endless schemes under the emperor's new-fangled One-Year-Plan, by which the latter hopes to bring order to the primitive life of Azania. Basil falls to his new and prestigious assignment with amazing gusto. One suspects, however, in his unbounded enthusiasm not merely a love of work for work's sake but his innate desire to do anything that is out of the way and even perverse. He is a "civilized" white savage in complementary contrast to the black Emperor. He shows, in Hall's words, "genius for uproar" and for the first time feels his talents truly engaged.[38] Basil's duties are breath-takingly multifarious and they range over practically every aspect of living. Undismayed, he and his assistant Mr Youkoumian who is the state's finance secretary, cope with the enormous correspondence and the crowded daily routine with a certain roguish relish. The other ministers and officials of the Empire are content and relieved that "here was an Englishman who was willing to leave them their titles and emoluments and take all their work off their hands." Papers from all other departments are referred to the bureau of modernisation and even Lord Chamberlain, the Justicia, the City Governor and Seth himself have readily relegated all decisions to Basil "with one firm stab of indelible ink." Only the Nestorian Patriarch and General Connolly in their conservative dislike of Seth's progressive thinking fail to avail themselves of the new institution. Basil is even involved in the codification of the criminal law. He buys the leading journal of Azania, Courier but lets the old proprietor M. Bertrand retain his position of editor and nominal proprietor. He falls in easily with the Emperor's large plan of the capital.

Basil's conflict with General Connolly over the issuance of boots for the army is a point of high comedy in the story. When the boots are delivered, however, the men make a feast and eat them.

In all this, Basil shows remarkable resilience and endurance, qualities which he shares with his assistant Youkoumian and which the men are endowed by nature. His disillusionment over Seth's One Year Plan is, however, soon evident. He fails to find any real spiritual value in his escapades in the jungle of Azania in the same way he has failed to find any meaning in London and English politics. Tired of the enterprise, he begins to "miss Connolly." Living all the time between Seth and Youkoumian has become "rather a business" and he is so tired that "he could die." The Emperor's adumbrations of the New Age have left him edgy and have begun to sour his outlook. Seth's currency notes which he has printed himself and stacked in the shelves and his latest passion for "Nacktkultur" that destroy Basil's confidence in the permanence of the One Year Plan. His reaction to Seth's gilt-edged menu-card laced with silk-ribbons in the Azanian colours and embossed with a gold crown which the Emperor has got ready for the dinner in honour of the two English ladies is one of overt boredom with a trace of disdain in it: "Basil looked at the card. A month ago he might have suggested emendations. To-day he was tired." (218) We are soon to enter the heart of Azanian jungle and witness, along with Basil Seal, the *dance macabre.* The Emperor's Birth Control pageant ends in a most violent fiasco when the revolutionists under the aegis of the three conservatives – General Connolly, the Earl of Ngumo and the Nestorian Patriarch – stage a coup d'etat.

Seth is hounded out and his old uncle Achon who has been for long years a prisoner in away the far monastery of St. Mark's is made the new monarch. Achon, however dies even before the coronation is over and all is chaos again. The forces of barbarism are knocking at the wall. The

British Legation is crowded with all its nationals much to Sir Samson's impotent annoyance. In abject fear, they cower in shelter in the drawing room and in Lady Courtney's garden. Word comes that bombers are to arrive anytime now and evacuate the entire British population. Basil Seal in his native dress who has joined the party lately is seen to have taken command the last few days. He is his usual defiant self and regales them with tales, mostly imaginary, of Sakuyu savagery. Prudence asks him to give up his absurd Emperor and go along with them but Seal is determined to watch the "racket" with the air of roguish defiance of the London days. The people in the legation are ready to leave in the five aeroplanes and Basil "suddenly reduced to unimportance" stands "a solitary figure in his white Sakuyu robes."

He then undertakes a long and arduous journey towards the lowlands with rain pouring incessantly, and seems inured to undue hardship of the enterprise of finding his lost Emperor. Seth meanwhile has met with an ambiguous death; one is not sure whether he died of his own hands or through poisoning.

Seth's body is carried to Moshy, the capital of the Wanda country, the tribe to which the Emperor belonged with Basil at the head of the procession. A pyre has been lit and there is a large crowd ready for the cannibal feast in honour of their departed hero. As the highest man present Basil delivers the funeral oration, speaking in Wanda-tongue of which he has a reasonable command. The peroration is semi-Biblical in tone and has a tinge of Basil's native irony.

> Peace be among you. I bring the body of the Great Chief, who has gone to rejoin Amurath and the spirits of his glorious ancestors .... He was a great Emperor. . . . Seth's name was a name of terror. Seyid rose against him and is no more. Achon also. They are gone before him to prepare suitable lodging among the fields of his ancestors. Thousands fell by his right hand. The words of his mouth were like thunder in the hills. Weep women of Azania, for your royal lover is torn from your arms. His virility was inexhaustible, his progeny numerous beyond human computation. . . . Weep, warriors of Azania. . . . In council the most guileful, in justice the most terrible. Seth the magnificent is dead. (299)

The feast accompanied by fast and furious dancing follows the cremation.

All this prepares the reader for the ultimate savagery—the feasting of Prudence who has died of the plane accident, by Basil and the cannibals. The irony of the conversation of Basil and his mistress earlier in the story stands revealed in all its starkness.

> "Darling, what's the good of talking. . . . We'll see each other again, whatever happens. You do promise that do you?"
> "You're grand girl, Prudence, and I'd like to eat you."
> "So you shall, my sweet . . . anything you want." (237)

Waugh's comic cynicism and narrative control alleviate the grimness of the conclusion of Prudence's life. Basil's quest is very different from the tragically grim conclusion of the life of Celia Coplestone in T.S. Eliot's *Family Reunion*. There is no hint of potential sainthood in the lives of the characters in *Black Mischief* as in that of Celia. What is emphasised in *Black Mischief* is the absurdity and the meaninglessness of the lives of the so-called "civilized" men and women, little different from those less "civilized" than themselves.

Although Basil remains essentially the same person at the end of the story, his experiences in Azania have to some extent, awakened at least, a few compunctions in him. On his return to London after his "expediton" Sonia remarks on Basil that he is somewhat changed: "Later Basil went round to see Angela Lyne and Sonia as she undressed said to Alastair, 'D'you know deep down in my heart I've got a tiny fear that Basil is going to turn serious on us too.'" (305-6) Basil's search for identity has, thus, not been wholly in vain or is negative. The self-transcendence that one links with a character's moral growth may not be there, but the fact that Basil has achieved some degree of moral awareness"[39] is evidence that *Black Mischief* is not wholly a farce on collision of cultures.

Seth is a visionary of a different stamp. Entranced by his own dreams of Progress and the New Age and fired by an irrational zeal to impose order on an unwilling race, the Emperor of Azania eagerly absorbs all ideas coming from the West which to him symbolise all that is best and positive. He is ashamed to claim kinship with his people who are "insupportable barbarians," "ruffans" and "buffoons." His own early brief contact with Western education and the books from the West have provided him with the cues to modernize Azania. Seth becomes one of Waugh's chief figures in fun insofar as he is incapable of fully comprehending the ways of Western thought and culture. So fanatic is his reformist zeal to promote the adoption of modern organisation and habits of life throughout the Empire that he sets out hourly fiats to his Ministry of Modernization which has launched the One Year Programme. As days pass, Seth becomes increasingly impatient, capricious and volatile and his imagination is a seething volcanic lake. The "black lunatic" as Basil Seal designates him dreams of a Utopia in which there are Swedish drills for the entire population, a first rate astronomical institute, an up-dated

Museum – all at a moment's notice. His interests are wide and demonic. Every aspect of life comes within his intellectual orbit: architecture, speculative biology, surrealism, birth control, humanistic treatment of animals, latest uniform for his men and *Nacktkultur*. He will tear down anything even if it is the magnificent Anglican Cathedral, that stands in the way of progress.

The New Guest House of German architecture is to be constructed of steel and Vita Glass, unsuitable to the tropical climate. In the idea of communal physical exercises and communal signing he out-Platos the idealism of the *Republic.* Renaming avenues or places and rechanging them are his crowded daily agenda of reforms. Several if not all of his hare-brained schemes have predictably hilarious effects. The Museum which he accommodates easily after throwing the Earl of Ngumo from his premises, is designed to house historical, zoological and other specimens. In the end however it becomes an exotic junk shop.

The Birth Control Campaign in preparation for the great pageant, is typical Waugh. The message of the posters is misread by the natives who take the birth control aid – "the Emperor's juju" – as a fertility god and grow wild with joy. A good modern dinner, in Seth's thinking, is one that consists of several courses of greasy flesh and fish all of them rich in all the vitamins known to the nutritionists. Further edge is given to the irony when such imperial banquet is given to two distinguished women who have come from England to promote humanitarianism to animals. So obsessive and monomanic does Seth grow in his idea of Progress that he becomes incoherent in speech and his directives to his men irrelevant. His ideas come from the desultory reading of the book he is reading at the moment: "'Heaven knows what will happen if he ever discovers psychoanalysis,' remarked Basil, gloomily foreseeing a Boulevard Kraft-Ebbing, an Avenue Oedipus and a pageant of Coprophagists." (187) It is when the Emperor has begun to print and stack worthless currency notes for about three million pounds under the name of the Imperial Bank of Azania that Basil, who has been humouring him so far, thinks of distancing himself from Seth.

Seth is a personification of "misplaced faith in western ideas of Progress," which is one of the causes of his hopeless alienation and subsequent downfall. His indiscriminate and ludicrous adoption of the manners of the West which are themselves degenerate because they woefully lack an ethical perspective, makes him not merely a figure of fun but a representative contemporary man who is uncertain in his beliefs. The task that he has set for himself is out of all proportion to his inner resources. The lonely figure of Seth tearing down the Anglican Church is that of a twentieth century Sisyphus performing an evidently hopeless labour:

"That evening Dame Mildred and Miss Tin saw a very curious sight. . . . As they passed the Anglican Cathedral they noticed a young man working alone. He wore light grey and parti-coloured shoes and he was engaged in battering at the granite archway at the West End with an energy very rare among Azanian navvies." (242)

Waugh's style, as has been noted in the previous chapters, is emotive and richly allusive. With him the style is the subject. Waugh achieves a high degree of aesthetic fulfilment largely because he has what Schorer calls, adequate technique.[40] Engaged in a constant struggle against chaos, Waugh's technique enables him to discover, explore and develop his subject, convey its meaning and finally evaluate it.

Waugh knew that the resources of language were an inalienable part of his theme. His sensitivity to the English language was extraordinary and he used it to create a certain texture and tone which in themselves, stated and defined his themes and meanings. Through conscious manipulation, he forced his medium into "those larger meanings which our ordinary speech never intends."[41] The structure and rhythm that he imposed upon the lump of his experience resulted in an enrichment of his own and the reader's apprehension of the world of action. By the limits imposed upon it, fiction can never be a completely lucid mimesis. However, what a stylish like Waugh succeeds in doing is to create convincing illusions of a reality which is beyond our grasp, through masterful handling of his medium. Form and content, technique and subject-matter thus become one. The value of Waugh's style lies mainly in the subtle means by which sensuous details become symbols. His symbols provide a network which awakens in us a new and startling awareness of our existence. They perform a further function, namely, of objectifying the writer's experience. In a way, Waugh's technique is a means of his own discovery as a man and writer, for his style and fictional method continuously help him in evaluating his own experience as a writer. In evaluating the quest of his characters by means of symbols and other stylistic devices, Waugh is trying at the same time to discover himself.

The Waste Land manner of evoking endless association through ambiguous and multivalent imagery and symbolism is noticeable in Waugh's fiction beginning with *Decline and Fall.* In *Black Mischief,* contemporary civilization is presented as a chaos of disparate elements, devoid of discipline, purpose and direction. Viewed with an ironic detachment, these disparities appear to Waugh as aberrations from a norm which might be called moral or religious. In fact critics have argued that Waugh was a Christian writer from first to last and that we cannot divide the Waugh of the thirties from the forties quite as sharply as it is generally done.

Waugh's symbols are often meant to point a contrast between the past and the present, usually to the detriment of the latter. The notion of the fallen man in exile from a world of primordial perfection is often the staple of his fiction. He challenges the idea that we live in a unique age and that "the achievements and dangers and changes of today are such as our ancestors never had to consider."[42] The true situation, it seems to Waugh, is that the individual is an exile on earth, an echo from St. Augustine. No amount of superficial modernism can change the hopeless condition of man as an exile from Eden.

The relevance of this discussion on Waugh's use of symbols in general will become apparent when we turn to *Black Mischief.* Through his use of ironic leitmotifs, Waugh traces the alienation, sterility and the inertness of the characters in the novel. The sterility campaign of Emperor Seth establishes forcefully the thematic argument of spiritual impotence and isolation of contemporary man. The futility of Seth's mission to Westernize his Empire is at the same time the futility of modern man's search for identity. The conservative forces, whose chief representative is the Nestorian Patriarch, are scandalised by the Emperor's enthusiasm for birth control. But the influence of the established church is not weighty enough to mount an assault on the campaign which has got vast support from the tribesmen and the villagers. Copies of the large, highly coloured poster calculated to convey to the illiterate the benefits of birth control attract the attention of the whole population. The pictures show two contrasted scenes:

> On one side a native hut of hideous squalor, overrun with children of every age, suffering from every physical incapacity—crippled, deformed, blind, spotted and insane; the father prematurely aged with paternity squatted by an empty cook-pot; through the door could be seen his wife, withered and bowed with child bearing, desperately hoeing at their inadequate crop. On the other side a bright parlour furnished with chairs and table; the mother, young and beautiful, sat at her ease eating a huge slice of raw meat; her husband smoked a long Arab hubble-bubble (still a caste mark of leisure throughout the land). While a single healthy child sat between them reading a newspaper. Inset between the two pictures was a detailed drawing of some up-to-date contraceptive apparatus and the words in Sakuyu: WHICH HOME DO YOU CHOOSE? (192)

Ironically, however, the message goes completely awry. The natives take the advertisement to mean the very opposite of what it intends to convey. The campaign is a great success but for the wrong reason. The interpretation of the ambiguous poster by the islanders is Waugh's own comment on the lack of understanding between two alien cultures.

The birth control apparatus has an entirely different connotation for them: the "fine new magic of virility and fecundity," not at all what Seth expected to mean. Waugh's irony is double-edged. While it is a satire on the Western notion that their idea of progress can be easily transplanted on a soil which utterly resists them, the passage at the same time indicates, as Kaplan notes, the "instinctive life-affirming attitude that appreciates hard work, multitudes, and a tolerance of disorder – the 'insane' child is 'very mad, very holy.'"

Black Mischief is Waugh's scathing indictment of the West, which, divorced as it is from traditional Christian values, is trying to impose its sterile culture on a society which is struggling out of barbarism. Basil Seal, the Courtneys, the two S.P.C.A. women and the other men of the British and other foreign missions who represent modern civilization are spiritually paralysed. Sterility is indeed the presiding metaphor in the novel in which the characters are alienated from each other and from life-sustaining values. Sterile as Seal and Seth are, their quests lack meaning and fulfilment. They live in a void of nothingness, an abyss upon which they construct the vain structures of their meaningfulness. Theirs is a broken world made desolate by the absence of God. Negating traditional absolutes, modern men wander through fields of nothingness in search of a being to give their life meaning. They muddle "through sterility to Culture," as Seth's Birth Control banner proclaims in orange and green.

The broken car in the land of Azania is a recurring image of abandonment and inertness of not merely of the setting of the novel but of contemporary society at large. The rusty motor car abandoned by its Arab driver blocks the main road connecting between Matodi and the terminus of the railway to Debra-Dowa. Its parts rusty and its tyres eaten away by white ants the car is an image of modern degeneracy.

Another of the novel's motifs is cannibalism which is almost universally present in London as much as in Azania. The disorderly scenes of the young people gorging their food in London are structural equivalents of the feasts in Azania which culminate in the cannibalistic feast of Seth's funeral when Prudence is eaten.

The return of Basil Seal to his old familiar chaos of London in the last chapter of the book is a parody of the triumphant return of the romantic hero after his long quest. Seal's adventures have not been an unqualified success, since he has not yet found the spiritual values that can sustain his existence. He has been in Azania long enough to recognise that the land of exotic people and customs can offer him no underlying support. His failure is intensified by the further economic impoverishment and spiritual degradation of London society and politics. The flippancy of Sonia's tone is indicative of the growing decline of values of the upper classes: "Just the same. She's the only one who doesn't seem to have lost money. Margot's shut up her house and is spending the winter in America. There was a general election and a crisis – something about gold standard." (304) Basil notes a slight estrangement between his old friends and himself, as his frequent references to his Azanian adventures imply. His adventures abroad have made him somewhat serious in outlook as Sonia tells Alastair: "D'you know, deep down in my heart, I've got a tiny fear that Basil is going to turn on us too." (305-6) Basil's career is, to adapt Bradbury's phrase, a "bleak reminder of the folly of seeking fulfilment inside time or history."[43] Living in an unteleological universe where coherent motives or aims are impossible, Basil fails to achieve complete spiritual fulfilment or moral evolution. Unlike his friends, however, he realises that self-centred happiness soon wears itself out and ends in boredom and emptiness.

NOTES

1. William J. Cook, Jr., p. 113.
2. *The Critical Heritage*, p. 129.
3. *Ibid.*, pp. 132-39.
4. Jack Sage, trans., *A Dictionary of Symbols*, p. 157.
5. Robert Murray Davis's review of George McCartney's *Confused Roaring: Evelyn Waugh and the Modern Tradition*, *Evelyn Waugh Newsletter*, Spring 1988, pp. 7-8.
6. Evelyn Waugh, *Black Mischief* (Boston: Little, Brown, 1960; rpt. 1971), p. 112.
7. David Lodge, *Evelyn Waugh*, p. 64.
8. *A Dictionary of Symbols*, pp. 164-65.
9. Richard Voorhees, "Evelyn Waugh's Travel Books," *Dalhousie Review* (Summer 1978), p. 248.
10. *Ibid.*
11. *Ibid.*, p. 245.
12. Stanley R. Kaplan, "Circularity and Futility in *Black Mischief*," *Evelyn Waugh Newsletter*, vol. 15, no. 3, Winter 1981, p. 2.
13. *Ibid.*, p. 3.
14. Evelyn Waugh, *Remote People* (UK: Penguin, 1985), p. 48.
15. Evelyn Waugh, *When the Going Was Good* (Penguin, 1951; rpt. 1984), p. 187.

16. *Remote People*, p. 23.
17. Stanley R. Kaplan, p. 3.
18. *Ibid.*, p. 1.
19. Richard Voorhees, p. 243.
20. *Robbery Under Law*, p. 279.
21. Bertrand Russell, *Portraits from Memory and Other Essays* (London, 1956), quoted in Ian Littlewood, p. 214.
22. Ian Littlewood, p. 39.
23. James F. Carens, p. 141.
24. Stephen J. Greenblatt, p. 20.
25. Christopher Hollis, *Evelyn Waugh* (London: Published for the British Council), quoted in William J. Cook, Jr., p. 115.
26. Alvin B. Kernan, *The Plot of Satire*, p. 161.
27. Richard A. Long and Iva G. Jones, p. 216.
28. Lawrence A. Ruff, "Comments on the 'Decadent Novel'," *College English*, 23 (October 1961), p. 64.
29. Alvin B. Kernan, "The Wall and the Jungle," p. 215.
30. Much of what has been said here on the nature of Waugh's satire is an adaptation of Alvin B. Kernan's views in his "A Theory of Satire" in *Satire: Modern Essays in Criticism*, ed. Ronald Paulson, pp. 249-74.
31. Leonard Feinberg, *The Satirist: His Temperament, Motivation and Influence* (Iowa, 1963), quoted in William J. Cook, Jr., p. 35.
32. A.E. Dyson, "Evleyn Waugh and the Mysteriously Disappearing Hero" in *The Crazy Fabric: Essays in Irony* (New York: St. Martin's Press, 1965), p. 195.
33. Charles J. Rolo. *The World of Evelyn Waugh* (Boston: Little, Brown, 1958), p. x.
34. Sean O'Faolain, *The Vanishing Hero: Studies in Novelists of the Twenties* (London: Eyre and Spottiswoode, 1956), p. 53.
35. *Robbery Under Law*, quoted in Ian Littlewood, p. 109.
36. Max Charlesworth, "The Meaning of Existentialism," *The Thomist*, no. XVI (October 1953), pp. 173-95.
37. William J. Cook, Jr., p. 118.
38. James Hall, "The Other Post-War Rebellion: Evelyn Waugh Twenty-Five Years After," p. 194.
39. William J. Cook, Jr., p. 122.
40. Mark Schorer, "Technique as Discovery," *20th Century Literary Criticism*, ed. David Lodge (London: Longman, 1922), pp. 387-400.
41. *Ibid.*
42. Francis O. Mattson, "Man in Exile," *Evelyn Waugh Newletter* (Winter 1972).
43. Bradbury, "Possibilities," p. 154.

The Quest of the Defeated Romantic: *A Handful of Dust*

A Handful of Dust (1934) has been considered by critics as Waugh's best novel. Hailed frequently as a minor classic and written, as William Plomer remarked at the time of its publication, "with a neatness that is perhaps French rather than English"[1] the novel shows Waugh's ever-growing maturity as a writer. The world of *A Handful of Dust* is the familiar Waugh world of barrenness and disorientation where no human salvation seems possible, but whereas the heroes of *Decline and Fall, Vile Bodies* and *Black Mischief* fit easily into the stereotypes common to the writer and his readers, the hero of *A Handful of Dust* is a three-dimensional figure, "credited with purposes and values."[2] Waugh relaxes his iron-grip over the central character and allows him a degree of existential right to assert himself. In his sympathy for the hero's helplessness in a cruel and contingent universe, Waugh makes him a potentially tragic character while preserving at the same time the comic mode which is his forte. Such a 'chilling' blend of the tragic and the farcical makes *A Handful of Dust* an outstanding fictional achievement. The parody and "low-norm satire" of the earlier comedies have given way to a more uniquely intellectual brand of indictment. *A Handful of Dust* marks what Northrop Frye calls "the second phase satire" in which literature assumes a "special function of analysis, of breaking up the lumber of stereotypes."[3]

Like the heroes in the earlier novels, Tony Last in *A Handful of Dust* is the sole connecting link of the different segments of the society, as William Cook has ably argued.[4] Waugh directs his satirical thrust at the corrupt world of the Beavers, Tony's wife Brenda and of Polly Cockpurse and others from all of whom Tony stands apart. In the same way, Waugh ridicules the dream world of Tony's Gothic splendour and of the hollow aristocratic values (unsupported by religion) which Tony tries to uphold. Equally, Waugh's indignation is directed at the farcical legal systems in which Tony is hopelessly involved. In satirising Tony's romantic love of exploration, Waugh ridicules also the explorations of shams like Dr. Messinger and Reggia.

The strange coexistence of pathos and force, of artistic withdrawal of emotional attachment contributes to the ambiguity of the novel's rhetoric and to its superb tonal effects. Two entirely opposed and paradoxical levels of thematic meaning are made apparent. On one level, *A Handful of Dust* is a critique of the secularity of Victorian values while on the other, the novel upholds certain of the cherished ideals of order and beauty of the Victorian ethos, sadly absent in contemporary life. A similar ambivalence is apparent in Waugh's attitude to his hero Tony and his wife Brenda. While embodying the classical virtues of elegance and propriety, Tony yet remains the object of the author's satirical ridicule. Brenda is at once a shallow adultress of the modern age and a charming fairy princess immured in an ugly castle. "The irony and poetry," to recall Brigid Brophy, "echo in the interstices of the narrative."[5] It is because of this remarkable narrative equipoise the book escapes being a vulgar tragedy for all the vulgarity of its many characters. This poetic tension lies at the root of the 'two-world' view— the romantic and the eschatological—of the whole of Waugh's fictional oeuvre and his travelogue. *A Handful of Dust* is the tale of a decent country gentleman, a Gothic hero, who is stripped eventually of his romantic illusions. The sad and improbable end is inevitable in the scheme of a Gothic man who escapes from one set of savages to a more real and horrible one. The quest of Tony Last for the city is his muddled and romantic search for self.

Like Eliot, Waugh deplored the passing away of tradition and like him, was deeply pessimistic about the condition of the modern man who lived in a world without morals and inherited culture. Both men were fiercely hostile to the cult of vulgarity and decadence. Waugh was drawn to Eliot's view that the present civilization was doomed because it repudiated all versions of the doctrine of original sin and refused to acknowledge the insane and irrational springs of wickedness in human nature. From Eliot's High-Church perspective the idea that a lasting Utopia could be built sustained merely by human intuitions of the good and the virtuous, untroubled by outward restraints of convention and inflexible rules of conduct seemed arrogantly irreligious. Such a view of the imperfectability of human nature accorded with Waugh's own Roman Catholicism—which emphasised institutional sanction and authority.

Exploring as it did the theme of 'death's other kingdom' and the need for religion, Eliot's *Waste Land* was the vade-mecum of writers of the post-War generation, who were led by their overwhelming sense of crisis to a sort of religious attitude which took the form of an intensely personal concern with some form of salvation. We have already seen how skilfully Waugh has employed in his *Decline and Fall* the 'waste-land' technique of imitation, of contrast, of juxtaposition of the corrupt and the innocent and of the past and the present. The fragmentariness of thematic presentation of *Vile Bodies* has also its origin in the Eliot poem. But Waugh's indebtedness to Eliot, both in terms of theme and of the general design is more obvious in his *A Handful of Dust* than in the earlier works.

The 'Waste Land' echoes are heard in the varied thematic modulations and at different structural levels of the novel. The title itself is a line from Eliot and Waugh obligingly hints at the connections in the epigraph which is a quotation from the first part ('The Burial of the Dead') of *The Waste Land:*

> I will show you some thing different from either
> Your shadow at morning striding behind you
> Or your shadow at evening rising to meet you;
> I will show you fear in a handful of dust.[6]

In a stridently ironic tone of challenge similar to that of the speaker of the desert landscape of the poem, Waugh sets out to confront his central character with what he knows but will not admit to himself, namely, that he is only a handful of dust and that it is what he is destined to return. The world of Tony Last, the novel's hero is a vast "stony rubbish" where people know nothing but a heap of broken images. They worship discredited idols while the images that their mind conjures up are mere illusions with which they can never make a coherently meaningful relation to reality. Sandwiched between two shadows – the delusion of the youthful morning shadow and the shadow of death of the evening and living in a fragmented and arid world bereft of traditions and a sense of order, the characters of *A Handful of Dust* cling to the illusion of the permanence of life's history. Void of the least eschatological significance of life, they are gripped with the morbid fear of death and nothingness and they show no evidence of a life beyond the grave. All their life experiences are coloured by the dominant emotion of death-in-life with no possibility of the rest of quiet sleep. The corrupt world of *A Handful of Dust* with its evident devaluation corresponds in most particulars to the dead dusty and relentless world of Eliot's poem. The speakers of *The Waste Land* and the characters of *A Handful of Dust* share a similar fate. With their perception dimmed and troubled by vague memories of another order of life they are left unfit to face the glare of reality. The casual and sordid sexual encounters, and the muddled waterways are common to both. The climax of both shows the disintegration of experience into grotesque, phantasmagoric nightmare. Tony Last's journey into the baleful Brazilian jungles is Waugh's fictional equivalent of the frightful scenes in the poem's climax. The characters of both writers are afraid of death and its consequences precisely because they are conscious not of what Eliot called, in his *Hollow Men* "death's other kingdom" the land of infinite promise but only of "death's dream kingdom" which is a world of the living dead, full of hallucinatory terrors and heart-breaking disappointments. Alienation from a world where they seem to be only "partly living" an uneasy existence is a direct, predictable consequence of such consciousness.

It is however in the treatment of the central motif of the quest that Waugh shows a remarkable affinity to Eliot's poem. As in *The Waste Land*, oblique connections are established between the figures of the Arthurian legends and the characters in the Waugh novel. Like the questing knights – Sir Gawain, Sir Percival and Sir Galahad – Tony Last undertakes a long journey in quest of a vision. The landscape of *A Handful of Dust* is not specifically that of the Arthurian romance but Waugh's intentions are perfectly plain. He parodies and contrasts the two. Waugh found Eliot's "mythical method" quite handy, for such a method (in the words of T.S. Eliot) gave the modern writer a "way of controlling, of ordering, of giving a shape and a significance to the immense panorama of futility and anarchy which is contemporary history."[7] The "mythical method" manipulates a continuous parallel between contemporaneity and antiquity. In the myths of the Arthurian Grail legends, Waugh found a mode of continuity with the past. Such a manipulation of a continuous parallel between the present and the past or "two-plane" writing, Waugh has most likely learnt from Eliot. Peter Firchow[8] goes as far as to suggest that Waugh may have read Jessie Weston's *From Ritual to Romance* recommended by Eliot in his notes to *The Waste Land.*

The novelist's attitude to the quester of the modern idyll is complex and ambivalent. Tony Last as his name suggests, is the "last" and lone survivor of the old order. He alone among the characters has a "strong sense of the past and of his place in tradition."[9] His respect for the vanished past is reflected in the names of the Arthurian characters of the different parts of his great and decaying house, Hetton Abbey. The general aspect and atmosphere of the place with which he has grown up are a "source of constant delight and exultation to Tony": The bed rooms with their brass bedsteads, were each named from Malory: "Yseult, Elaine, Mordred and Merlin, Gawaine and Bedievere, Lancelot, Perceval, Tristram, Galahad, his own dressing room Morgan le Fay and Brenda's Guinivere where the bed stood on a dais, . . ."[10]

Tony's love of classical values is symbolised by his attachment to Hetton Abbey. Formerly one of the notable houses of the country, the Abbey was entirely rebuilt in 1864 in the Gothic style but is now devoid of interest and is not altogether amenable to modern ideas of comfort. An Englishman raised in the great tradition, Tony is deeply attached to his home, cares for the huge Victorian house long after its upkeep has ceased to be economical, loves his wife and son John Andrew, has pleasant manners and goes to church every week, although he has no religious beliefs.

In his description of the book years later that it was a "study of other sorts of savage at home and the civilized man's helpless plight among them"[11] Waugh implied once again the permanent polarities – Apollonian and Dionysian – of life's values of his characters. Tony Last is the civilized man who makes continuing albeit futile warfare against the forces of corruption and barbarity. In his deportment, in his enormous capacity for love and in his centrifugal concern for others in the moment of sorrow caused by the death of his son John Andrew, Tony is the ideal gentleman of Cardinal Newman. His sheer selflessness and dedication to a principle in a ruthless world makes Tony eventually a victim of overwhelming isolation. Tony's story is the Innocent's progress through a world of chaos, not dissimilar to that of Paul Pennyfeather but the difference lies in the degree of moral awareness of two heroes. The seriousness of Tony's plight in his search with its tragic implication is not found in the earlier and even in some of the later Waugh heroes. The novelist infuses our sympathy through his own positive emotional identification with Tony Last. In all the hero's crises Waugh is on the side of his hero. His descriptions of the many moments of Tony's agony and frenzy are penetratingly moving.

Waugh's attitude towards Tony Last may easily be inferred from the many directions provided by the author's stylistic devices. Steering a middle way between "under-" and "over-" aesthetic distancing, and aided by his controlled use of irony, the author gains our sympathy for his hero. Waugh's maturity as an artist is in direct proportion to the degree in which he submits himself to the discipline of aesthetic distance. While artistic distancing permits him to incorporate in Tony Last certain qualities which have Waugh's approval, it enables the reader at the same time to recognise Tony as an object of Waugh's irony. By virtue of his self-contained and inviolable innocence, Tony becomes nearly a boob but Waugh's narrative tone in the moments of crises of his hero shows the implicit sympathy of the author.

The death of young John Andrew, Tony's son, all but crushes Tony and the facade of respectability and calm which he studiously maintains in front of his household is rudely torn apart, revealing his utter inability to cope with life's problems. The card game that Tony plays with Mrs. Rattery Jock's 'blonde' to pass the painful hours before the arrival of Tony's wife Brenda from London is symbolic of the respective mental make-up of the two characters. Tony is fretting and incoherent and totally distraught while Mrs. Rattery is doing her best to be in command of what seems a hopeless situation: "Mrs Rattery sat intent over her game, moving little groups of cards adroitly backwards and forwards about the table like shuttles across a loom; under her fingers order grew out of chaos; she established sequence and precedence; the symbols before her became coherent, interrelated." (110)

But the strain in playing with Tony is too much for her and she gives up what she calls the "heart-breaking card game" and suggests a game of animal snap instead. The irony of the situation is revealed in its starkness when the two players "bow-vow" and "coop-coop" at each other with a child in the house lying dead after an accident. The description is an implicit critique of the "absurd" modern man, insecure of identity, and unaided by the consolations of religion, and miserably inadequate to face up to life's problems.

The drunken antics of Tony Last in London in Jock Grant-Menzie's company earlier on in the novel dramatise the radical instability of being of the individual in contemporary world of chaos. Brenda's frequent absences from Hetton Abbey in London have left Tony and his son Andrew desolate. He spends a day at Bratt's club in London and drinks more than he is even used to with Jock. Together they visit the Old Hundredth, a low joint of bad repute, from where the tipsy Tony speaks to Brenda in her flat at Mrs. Beaver's. Brenda, however, puts him off with her native finesse and charm. Back in Hetton Abbey the next morning, Tony is tired and heavy with guilt. He is torn by pangs of remorse and shame when alone: "'Two men of thirty,' he said to himself, 'behaving as if they were up for the night from Sandhurst – getting drunk and ringing people up and dancing with tarts at the Old Hundredth. . . . And it makes it all the worse that Brenda was so nice about it." (76) Tony's plight illustrates the collapse of will endemic on the modern scene. His mind is easily preyed upon by undue sense of errors and anxieties and foreshadows the later scenes in the South American jungles where Tony is tortured by nightmares brought on by malarial fever. Early in the book Waugh hints at the kind of future that is in store for Tony and at the need for the consolations that only an authentically institutionalized religion (the Catholic Church in Waugh's case) can offer to an individual. Neither has Anglicanicism which has a purely social function nor his romantic love of the past can sustain Tony. Having no inner resources, he is knocked all of a heap by the least of life's bludgeons. Having shut himself in a world of romantic and Gothic values, he cannot comprehend the values the real outer world of bestiality and anomie.

Tony's love of Brenda like his attachment for Hetton Abbey is tinged with romanticism. This unreasoned attachment for an attractive wife of whose disloyalty he does not have an inkling makes Tony an absurd figure of fun. One of the tasks of the novelist is to make an unbiased appraisal of romanticism, stripping his hero of his sentimental illusions. Brenda, shrewd and practical, knows her husband well, as she tells her friends: "The trouble is that I've become such a habit with him." (88) Brenda's assessment is that of the novelist. So used is Tony to the habit of loving his wife that he cannot suspect her of cuckolding him even when she herself acknowledges it. His reaction to the letter that Brenda writes telling him of her love for Beaver and her decision to ask for divorce, is one of disbelief:

> 'I'm sorry it should have happened like this.'
> 'But it's not true, is it?'
> 'Yes, I'm afraid it is. Everyone has known for some time.'
> But it was several days before Tony fully realized what it meant. He had got into a habit of loving and trusting Brenda. (125)

The habit of loving and trusting Brenda that he has contracted since his marriage has such a stronghold on him that he easily acquiesces in Brenda's plan for divorce in which she would appear as the plaintiff. It doesn't cross his mind to question the terms of settlement even when his lawyer advises caution. His Victorian upbringing prevents him from questioning the impropriety of the proceedings. Just as he is arranging to take Milly, the girl of the Old Hundredth to Brighton on the lawyer's instructions, his thoughts run to Brenda and of his love:

> Tony had not slept much lately. He could not prevent himself, when alone, from rehearsing over and over in his mind all that had happened since Beaver's visit to Hetton; searching for clues he had missed at the time; wondering where something he had said or done might have changed the course of events; going back further to his earliest acquaintance with Brenda to find indications that should have made him more ready to understand the change that had come over her; reliving scene after scene in the last eight years of his life. All this kept him awake. (132)

The shabby and dubious ways of obtaining a divorce is symbolic at once of the decay of all civilized norms and of the fall of standards in the modern legal system. Waugh plunges his hero relentlessly deeper into worlds of disillusion and horror hitherto unknown to him, in order to enforce his thesis that ours is a socially and spiritually depraved world. In such world Tony Last, "the last spark of human decency in a vile world," strikes a ridiculous figure, with his finicky sense of propriety and good sense. Waugh's descriptions of the moments of Tony's mental agony are meant to win the reader's sympathy for the hero. The condition of Tony who has lived a life of decency and according to a strict code of honour is not untouched by tragedy. In the Brighton hotel where he has been obliged to take a tart and her obnoxious little daughter, he is sick with unexpressed disgust at the passing of the old order:

> A change of clothes brought to both Tony and Milly a change of temper . . . for a month now he had lived in world suddenly bereft of order; it was as though the whole reasonable and decent constitution of things, the sum of all he had experienced or learned to expect, where on the dressing table; no outrageous circumstance in which he found himself, no new, mad thing brought to his notice, could add a jot to the all-encompassing chaos that shrieked about his ears. (137)

The passage is a moving description of the deep distress of a man who has taken seriously the institution of marriage which has however become shallow and farcical in the world of the Beavers, of Brenda and of Polly Cockpurse. The Brighton scenes provide a poignantly grotesque dimension to Tony's situation. He is pushed around by a mere child of eight, the ill-bred daughter of Milly. On the beach, he is the object of scorn of the on-lookers. The corrupt legal system which is adept at framing convenient adultery cases for effecting divorces comes in for implicit criticism. Naive and well-bred gentlemen like Tony Last fall easy victims to the ploys of shyster lawyers and private detectives who are shameless sponges.

The "all-encompassing chaos" harks back to the Waste Land theme of collapse of values and general degeneracy. Tony is hedged in by corruption on all sides. Living in a world which is bent on destroying everything he cherishes, Tony is an alien spirit and a misfit. The values or disvalues that his attractive wife Brenda stands for are in direct opposition to Tony's. Shallow and deceitful, she succumbs to the amorality of the world of the Beavers. The structural implications in introducing the animalistic Mrs. Beaver and her son John, a vulgar social-climber at the very beginning of the novel cannot be missed. Theirs is the jungle that Alvin Kernan talks about, which has made inroads into civilized life.[12] Mrs. Beaver's opening words in the first chapter of the novel set the tone, providing as they do clues to her grasping nature and total depravity:

> 'Was any one hurt?'

> 'No one, I am thankful to say' said Mrs. Beaver 'except two housemaids who lost their heads and jumped through a glass roof into the paved court. They were in no danger. The fire never reached the bedrooms, I am afraid. Still, they are bound to need doing up, everything black with smoke and drenched in water and luckily they had that old-fashioned sort of extinguisher that ruins everything. . . . (7)

Mrs. Beaver whose portrait is said to be based on the uppish Mrs. Maugham, the decorator-wife of the novelist Somerset Maugham[13] owns a shop where she constantly badgers her shop assistants. Through her business, she claims acquaintance with most people who matter and this enables her son, the unemployed twenty-one-year-old John get frequent invitations to luncheon parties. John Beaver himself from leaving Oxford has worked briefly as an advertising agent gets up late and sits near the telephone most of the day, hoping to be rung up. His present weekly income varies around six pounds a week which he wishes to save by going to parties given by women known to his mother. He wheedles an invitation to Hetton Abbey from Tony Last whom he hardly knows. In symbolic terms, his arrival at Hetton Abbey at the week-end, is the invasion of the forces of barbarism on order and propriety. Not that the Abbey is idyllic in its purity before Beaver appears on the scene. That there is corruption already is seen in the influence that Ben Hacket, the stable groom exercises over John Andrew, Tony's son. Young John has caught all Ben's rude expressions improper for the son of a country gentleman. Brenda's instant attraction for Beaver speaks of an inherent vulgarity in the fairy princess. There is irony in the names of the bedrooms: Brenda's is named after Guinivere, the disloyal queen of King Arthur; Beaver is given "Galahad" the purest of King Arthur's knights who alone was privileged to catch sight of Excalibur.

In spite of its present state of disrepair, Hetton Abbey stands for certain solid virtues – medieval grandeur and nobility. The descriptions of the Abbey in the Guide Book that it "was one of the notable houses of the country, entirely re-built in 1864 in the Gothic style and is now devoid of interest" speaks not only of the fall of a great country house but along with it of the standards of civilized taste. To most people some of Tony's close relatives included, the abbey smacked of Pecksniff, the unctuous curmudgeon in Dickens's *Martin Chuzzlewit.* Hetton Abbey is not altogether amenable to modern ideas of comfort, but despite its ecclesiastical gloom and the enormous expense for its upkeep, it is a source of constant delight and exultation to Tony, its present owner. His romantic temperament has been nurtured by tender memories of the place from childhood. Brenda's confession to Beaver that she detests the place shows what gulf has separated her from her husband in their eight years of "happy marriage." The subtle sexual connotation in Brenda's use of "coping" gives a clue to her nature:

> 'Darling, you're being heroic with Beaver.
> 'Oh, I quite enjoy coping . . .'

There is no evidence to show that Brenda has been unfaithful to her husband before Beaver arrives but her readiness to "bitch him" as she says is an indication of the nature of things yet to come.

The readiness with which Brenda strikes up acquaintance with Beaver and the eagerness with which she laps up the latest gossip in London shows the difference between her and Tony. Brenda and Beaver, temperamentally so alike that they do not share Tony's enthusiasm for the abbey; they have indeed a plebeian contempt for the values that Tony would have people cherish. The London society that Brenda is soon to embark upon stands in direct opposition to Tony's ideas of noble living. Waugh sums up the low moral ebb that the 'high' London living has touched in his sketch of Polly Cockpurse, one of the doyennes:

> Although Polly's fortune was derived from men, her popularity was chiefly among women, who admired her clothes and bought them from her second-hand at bargain prices . . . some time ago she had married a good natured earl, whom nobody else happened to want at the time; since then she had scaled all but the highest peaks of every social mountain. (41)

Brenda finds enough initial encouragement to her affair with Beaver from her sister Marjorie who after her marriage with Allan, has had similar escapades. Instead of the weekly Wednesday visits to London in which she did her shopping and saw the bone-setter, Brenda now hires one of Mrs. Beaver's flats in London on the pretext of doing courses in economics in order to carry on her intrigue with John Beaver.

Mrs. Beaver, the crassest of the London set, typifies modern vulgarity which erodes into the civilized life of order and refinement. The chromeplating of the rooms in the Hetton Abbey on Brenda's recommendation is the most gross attack of barbarism on the rusty yet noble precincts of the Gothic structure which, with its dilapidated battlements, is at least in Tony's eyes, a monument of a by-gone age. In the deft hands of Mrs. Beaver which can easily convert a lavatory into slap-up apartment for base love, the old order will yield place to new and fashionable disorder. The subsequent invasion by the dreadful females with Mrs. Beaver at the head of the castle is heavily symbolic of the defeat of values hallowed by tradition.

The references to the pack of cards in the novel link the novel's theme with that of *The Waste Land.* As in Eliot' poem, the function of the pack of cards in Waugh's novel, to adapt F.R. Leavis, is 'to evoke . . . cosmopolitan "high life" and the charlatanism that battens upon it.'[14] The cards evoke a resonance of fate which threatens to destroy the characters who have neither pasts nor futures. An element of chance which is an indispensable part of the game of cards characterises the lives of the men and women who muddle through their allotted space of time. Bereft of faith of any kind, they become willing victims of blind fortune. The fortune-telling of Beaver with the help of cards is an apparently minor, yet subtly significant detail, relevant to the novel's theme and tone. Beaver's card-game on his very first visit to Hetton Abbey is one of the things which hold the empty-headed Brenda in his thrall and seal her fate:

> Beaver was telling Brenda's fortune with cards, ". . . Now cut to me again," he was saying, "and I'll see if it's any clearer. . . . Oh yes . . . there is going to be a sudden death which will cause you great pleasure and profit. In fact you are going to kill someone. I can't tell if it's a man or a woman . . . yes, a woman . . . then you are going to go on a long journey across the sea, marry six dark men and have eleven children, grow a bear and die." (35)

The vagueness in Beaver's predictions is a satire on much the fortune-telling in a sick society which is ready to catch at a straw. Brenda's little son John Andrew is to die in an accident when Brenda is away in London and the news of which does indeed cause her some relief. When Jock Grant-Menzies, the friend of the Lasts bears the painful news Brenda mistakes 'John' for her lover John Beaver and bursts into shameful tears when she realises her mistake. The child's death provides her with an excuse to make a complete break from the hated Hetton Abbey and her husband Tony Last. In her letter to Tony in which she informs her husband of her love for Beaver, she makes it appear as if things might not have happened the way they did, if their son John Andrew had not died. Beaver's predictions apply not only to Brenda but also to Tony who will go on a long and hazardous journey in quest of a lost South American city. Brenda's own quest for happiness through extra-marital love is to come to grief as predicted by Beaver.

The long games of solitaire that Mrs. Rattery plays with Tony in the hours following young Andrew's death is a symbol which carry meanings different from Beaver's card-game. Serene and distant, as Tony describes her, Mrs. Rattery has cool self-command and seems for a while the only point of rest and sanity amidst a world of chaos. However, we suspect that Mrs. Rattery's detachment is not what one would associate with Christian stoicism but is rather a kind of resignation of someone who is strong-willed and stubbornly self-controlled. Peter Firchow connects her to Eliot's sybil. Like her, Mrs. Rattery has had a good share of life's experiences and is now "killing time waiting to die."[15] Most modern questers who find the odds too much against them soon give up their attempt to self-discovery and are willing to die like the latter-day sybil.

Mrs. Northcote, the exotic new fortune-teller is a descendant of Madame Sosostris, the clairvoyante in *The Waste Land*, the lady with the Tarot cards. Mrs. Beaver has introduced her to the women of London at some profit for herself. Mrs. Northcote tells fortunes in a new way, by reading the soles of the feet. The house of Lady Cockpurse where the fortune-telling is done thus becomes a pagan temple and a modern secular substitute for a traditional church. When Jock arrives in London with the news of the tragedy at Hetton Abbey, Brenda is having her fortune told by Mrs. Northcote. She tells Brenda that four men dominate her fate, one of whom, she warns is rapacious and bodes no good for her. The prediction is taken by Brenda to refer to Beaver who has just gone to France.

The introduction of Princess Jenny Abdul Akbar, the alleged widow of the Prince of Morocco, gives a further grotesque dimension to the waste land of fashionable London. Brenda, in collusion with her London friends, chooses the Princess as the woman to divert the bored and lonely Tony in Hetton Abbey. The response that this 'joke woman,' as Tony calls her, evokes is one of immediate disgust. Her behaviour, which is a bit comic, is entirely devoid of good sense. The scene which describes her first encounter with Tony and the readiness with which she eats muffins illustrates her animal nature: "'Muffins stand for so much' said Jenny. She ate heartily; often she ran her tongue over her lips, collecting crumbs that had become embedded there and melted butter from the muffin." The description of the Princess's flat in London later further emphasises the litter and confusion of the London scene—a description faintly reminiscent of the lady's chamber in *The Waste Land:*

> The princess's single room was furnished promiscuously and with truly Eastern disregard of the right properties of things; swords meant to adorn the state robes of a Moorish caid were swung from the picture rail; mats made for prayer were strewn on the divan; the carpet on the floor had been made in Bokhara as a wall covering;

> while over the dressing table was draped a shawl made in Yokohama for sale to cruise-passengers; an octogonal table from Port Said held a Tibetan Buddha of pale soapstone; six ivory elephants from Bombay stood along the top of the radiator. Other cultures, too, were represented. (114)

Critics have remarked that in presenting these characters who are embodiments of vulgarity and bad taste, Waugh comes close to modern life. The infidelity of Brenda thus becomes an indictment on the "colossal failure of taste" of the twentieth century. Seen in this light, Tony's predicament in the "all-encompassing chaos" is the condition of the human soul which pines for the lost state of innocence before the Fall – a recurring theme in Waugh.

The Brighton experience has left Tony emotionally exhausted but for the first time opens his eyes to the gross reality around him. His disillusion is complete when Brenda's brother Reggie, one of Waugh's most boorish characters, comes to demand two thousand pounds as monthly allowance for his sister to enable to marry Beaver. To Tony's protest that he not only agreed to five hundred pounds but also went through the farcical adultery to make Brenda's divorce easy, the vulgar Reggie insinuates that Tony has been less than fair to Brenda and even calls him vindictive. When Tony is convinced that Brenda is in on Reggie's proposal, his attitude to her and to the entire situation begins to harden. The whole moral world has collapsed: "A whole Gothic world had come to grief . . . there was now no armour glittering through the forest glades, no embroidered feet on the green sward; the cream and dappled unicorns had fled." (151) So hardened has Tony become that he now refuses the five hundred that he originally offered. Brenda is not going to get her divorce, since his Brighton evidence is worth nothing. Should the case come up at all, he will defend and win. He finally tells Reggie that he is going away for six months and on his return, he may divorce Brenda if she still insists, without settlements of any kind.

Biographical criticism maintains that even the most trifling detail of the author's life can provide an important key to the interpretation of his work. This is especially the case of Waugh who turned life-events to art-events. His wide travels provided him, as we have already noted, with material for his fiction. But even more significant than the actual life events are some of the psychological hurts that find subtle and unconscious artistic expression. Martin Stannard's biography of Evelyn Waugh, for instance points out that Waugh smarted throughout under the rebuffs of his early life.[16] Waugh's own diaries and letters seen to confirm this view. Waugh's novels, it has been argued, reveal an unremitting persecution mania to which he was subject most of his life. One of the lasting sources of injury was the desertion of "She-Evelyn" and the break-down of his first marriage. Allowing for flamboyant self-pity characteristic of Waugh, there is still a sediment of truth in the claim of the bio-critics that Waugh was touchy on the subject of the behaviour of his first wife. Written a few years after the dissolution of his first marriage, *A Handful of Dust* is seen by Waugh's critics as a personal story of a man who took his wife's desertion very much to heart. The behaviour of Tony Last when he realises his wife's disloyalty is that of Waugh the injured husband. Tony's subsequent quest for the lost city is a fictional transformation of Waugh's own travels that he made in the years following his wife's desertion.

Be that as it may, artistic integrity is sedulously preserved in the transformational process of personal feelings into credible fictional content through Waugh's control over his material. Tony's anger against the world and his decision to go on a long expedition are an artistic necessity for Waugh will not rest content until he has stripped his hero of all his Gothic illusions. The appalling knowledge of the moral rottenness of the world to which his wife belongs is only the first stage of the discovery of himself. He has yet to be cured of his romantic dreams, such as his attachment to the old decrepit Hetton Abbey and his search of a lost city. He refuses to make any more payment to Brenda for the real reason is that he needs all the money he has to maintain the abbey.

From the start Tony's search for the lost city of the Incas in the remote Brazilian hinterlands is made to appear futile. Neither in his school days nor in his early manhood has Tony had any experience of travelling abroad: "He was going away because it seemed to be the conduct expected of a husband in his circumstances, because the associations of Hetton were for the time poisoned for him, because it seemed to be the conduct expected of a husband in his circumstances . . . because he wanted to live for a few months away from people who would know him or Brenda, in places where there was no expectation of meeting her or Beaver or Reggie St. Cloud at every corner he frequented." (156) Waugh classes Tony, the honest but incohate and bleary-eyed explorer with the other two less reputable men—Reggie St. Cloud and Dr. Messinger. Waugh's attitude of derision to Reggie is easily guessed:

> He was prematurely, unnaturally stout and he carried his burden of flesh as though he were not yet used to it; as though it had been buckled on to him that morning for the first time and he were still experimenting for its better adjustment; there was an instability in his gait and in his eyes a furtive look as though he were at any moment liable to ambush and realized that he was unfairly hand-

> icapped for flight. (145)

Tony makes his acquaintance with Dr. Messinger at Greville Club. The bearded and prematurely bald young man has the air of a seasoned explorer and is about to go on an expedition to Brazil for the lost city. Tony is impressed with Dr. Messinger's knowledge of the City's obscure traditions and history. His description of the City has all the Gothic splendour of Hetton Abbey and Tony's fate is sealed. He agrees at once to go with Dr. Messinger. That Waugh intended Dr. Messinger to be Tony's unreliable guide and means of undoing is suggested, as Peter Firchow remarks in the footnote to his article, in Waugh's choice of the name.[17] He is the messenger, the angel (from the Greek root angelos) of death. His disastrous mishap on the river and his untimely death may have some significance. His death is described with Waugh's characteristic deftness. Leaving behind Tony who is ill with malaria Dr. Messinger goes in a frail canoe but is caught in a swift current of water:

> he rolled over twice, found himself in deep water and attempted to swim, found himself among boulders again and attempted to grapple with them. Then he reached the falls.
>
> They were unspectacular as falls go in that country—a drop of ten feet or less but they were enough for Dr. Messinger. . . . Dr. Messinger's hat floated very slowly towards the Amazon and the water closed over his bald head. (197)

The sudden death of Dr. Messinger, who is death's own harbinger, symbolically foreshadows Tony's incarceration in the jungle and his irretrievable spiritual alienation. Firchow notes an interesting parallel between Dr. Messinger's demise and that of the disappearance of the hero and his companions in Rider Haggard's *Alain Quatermain*, thus linking Waugh's novel to that of the famous Victorian.

Unmistakable echoes from Eliot's *Waste Land* and Tennyson's *Idylls* have been noticed by Giovanni Gerchin, Peter Green and Richard Wassen[18] in the foolhardy journey of Messinger and Tony into the perilously infested jungles of the Pie-wie Indians. Firchow's arguments that Eliotean echoes especially from Part V of his *Waste Land* are strong seem convincing, even if a bit ingenious, despite La France's assertion to the contrary.[19] From the point of view of the quest-motif in the novel, these discoveries have immense value. Eliot's influence on Waugh, in general, as Jeffrey Heath has remarked, has been pervasive.[20] The quester in Waugh's novel, like the quester to Chapel Perilous in *The Waste Land* is beset by countless nightmarish trials and privations. The nights seem interminable to Tony; twelve hours of darkness, noisier than a city square with the squealing, and croaking and trumpeting of the bush denizens. Tony lies awake scratching. Waugh constantly juxtaposes the scene in the darkest Indian jungles with those of London in order to inform the reader that his hero has merely left behind one set of savages to live and "die" among a slightly different kind of savages. The only difference between England and the Pie-wie jungle is the difference in time. England is east of America and so Tony and Dr. Messinger get the sun later. At the same time as all the Macushi men go after the bush-pig, leaving behind their women, Jock Grant-Menzies, raises the question of pigs in Parliament at question-time. He wishes to know whether in view of the dumping in England of Japanese pork pies, a modification of the eight-and-a-half-score basic pig from two and a half inches of thickness round the belly to two inches may be considered. The under secretary's reply to this preposterously trivial question is couched in equally ponderous language: "With regard to the specifications of the basic pig, I must remind the honourable member that, as he is doubtless aware, the eight-and-a-half-score pig is modelled on the requirements of the bacon curers and has no direct relation to pig meat for sale in pies. This is being dealt with by a separate committee who have not yet made their report." (175)

The world inhabited by Brenda, the Beavers and Jock is a spiritually arid wasteland comparable to the impenetrable jungles in far away South America, with its dark terrors and fear of death. Dr. Messinger's remark to Tony that they have no need of a map in their expedition is applicable to the entire generation of the Depression years; the savage both "civilized" and primitive are bereft of a sense of direction.

The general secular aimlessness and the spiritual fragmentariness of the wastelanders in the novel are artistically embodied in the phantasmagoric dreams of Tony Last when he is deliriously ill in the Indian jungles. The figures in the jungle are conflated with those in England even as the events of the past are indistinguishable from those of the present. Waugh's narrative brilliantly captures the 'Alice in Wonderland' logic of which he has always been fond. In his feverish dream, Tony sees himself tried in a mad-hatterish council where all the odious figures of Tony's past—Mrs. Beaver, Winnie, the hateful child of Millie among others—unanimously accuse him of misdeed. Brenda is seen declaring her hot adulterous love for John Beaver. Just as Mrs. Rattery scoops in the cards and says 'Bow-Wow,' Tony Last catches glimpse of the City for which he has been searching all along:

> From the turret of the gatehouse a heraldic banner floated in the tropic breeze. . . . He picked his way through the surrounding

> thornscrub; the sound of music rose from the glittering walls; some procession or pageant was passing all along . . .
>
> At last he came into the open. The gates were before him and trumpets were sounding along the walls, saluting his arrival; from bastion to bastion the message ran to the four points of the compass; petals of almond and apple blossom were in the air; they carpeted the way, as, after a summerstorm, they lay in orchards at Hetton. Guilded cupolas and spires of alabaster shone in the sunlight. Ambrose announced, 'The City is served.' (203)

In Tony's fevered romantic fantasy, the City has all the lineaments of Hetton Abbey, only slightly transfigured. What Waugh has been attacking so strenuously is Tony Last's incurable romanticism. At the end of his quest, there is no sign of Tony's maturation or evidence of self-discovery, but rather he shows signs of growing regression. He is seen crying more and more like a child. His quest has been a failure insofar as the object of the quest has been wrong one, on which he has expended all his energy and time. It is in large measure, a matter of taste, as Heath had argued. The uncritical love or Gothic idealization of the past unsupported by faith or religion is indicative of bad taste.[21] Like Eliot's quester, Tony struggles through the wasteland and when he reaches the destination he fails because he does not put the right questions. In the Parsifal legends the pure knight undertook a long and arduous journey to the castle where was immured the impotent Fisher King. On the right type of questions put by the knight depended the salvation of the land which was under a curse owing to the king's impotence. The fact that the questions concerned the sacraments implied that only a knight who possessed profound faith could undertake such a mission. Tony does not seek the right kind of goal nor does he put the right questions at the end of the quest. His quest should end therefore the way it does—instead of being a liberator he finds himself a hapless citizen of a wasteland. The City that he glimpses in his dream is Eliot's Unreal city, the "urbo aeterna" declined into "l'immonde cite." It is the Babylon of *Apocalypse,* "the Blick ins chaos," the imperial city which is the whore and the mother of harlots, with Mystery written on her forehead. It is not the fabulous Eldorado of the classical explorer's dream but a city laid waste by sin of the modern secularity. It has the run-down look of Boa Vista, the city of which Waugh himself went in search. The experience is recounted graphically in his travel book *Ninety-Two Days.* But Waugh expects his readers not to be content with this identification. He does expect his readers to see more than that in the City of Tony's dreams.

Like Eliot Waugh reminds us that in times of the break-down of civilization the individual has to remember that he lives not just in this disreputed City of Man but also in eternity and in the City of God. Critics have justly pointed to the Augustinian dialectic between the City of Man and the City of God in Waugh's novels. Augustine's classification of the cities into polar opposites dramatises the struggle between the flesh and the spirit. Tony's city is thus the City of Man devoted as it is to carnal desires and lust of the flesh, a secular city without the least hint of a spiritual dimension. It is the city where good is perverted into evil and where the means become ends themselves. Caught "in this sensual delight," to recall Yeats, the dwellers in this city neglect the universal design of Providence, namely union with the Higher Thing. There has never been any place for true religion in Tony's life. Consequently his quest has been doomed to failure and frustration. The idea of the fleshly appetite is contained in the announcement of Tony's butler Ambrose "the city is served." At the same time, the reversal of roles may have been meant by Waugh, as Peter Firchow remarks. It a tale which parodies the Grail legends, it seems possible that Ambrose the butler may stand for monk Ambrosius in Tennyson's idyll "The Holy Grail" whom Percival tells of his quest for Grail and his vision of the City of God. The heroes of the two quests see their journey end in "dust and nothing." To Percival at least is given the gift to see Galahad's ascension into "the spiritual city and all her spires/And gateways in a glory like a pearl."[22] Tony Last, however, literally catches sight of a "man of exceeding age" and a "ruinous city." Heath sees a further allusion to the Reformation in England in Dr. Messinger's description of the city to Tony Last earlier on: "It was the result of a migration from Peru at the beginning of the fifteenth century when the Incas were at the height of their power. It is mentioned in all the early Spanish documents as a popular legend." (139)

Waugh maintained that one of the causes of spiritual malaise in England was the heresy of Protestantism. While Catholicism stood for wholeness and health, Protestantism, like romanticism, came to represent sickness and fragmentariness of existence. Dr. Messinger's (and Tony's) city, cut off by "five hundred years of isolation" might be Anglican England itself, a heretical land, spiritually immature and refusing to fulfil God's design.[23] Tony's brief romantic encounter on board the ship with the young Catholic Therese de Vitre may have its symbolic function too. In refusing to be guided by Therese, Tony refuses the chance of being guided by true faith, and he prefers instead to be guided by unaided human reason symbolised by the bald-headed Dr. Messinger.[24]

That alienation is universal in the landscape of *A Handful of Dust* is indicated by the frequent juxtapositions of the scenes of London life with those of the South American jungles. While in his torturing phantoms

Tony confuses Brenda with the Indian Rosa, Brenda's position in London has been steadily deteriorating. Her abandonment is stressed again and again. After a hopeless interview with Tony's counsel, ironically named Mr. Graceful, to know her financial standing, Brenda is seen walking "alone into the sunshine." A little later the narrator gives a description of her loss of stature in London society:

> Brenda awoke in the lowest possible spirits. The evening before she had spent alone at a cinema. Afterwards she felt hungry—she had no proper meal that day—but she had not the strength to go alone into any of the supper restaurants. She bought a meat pie at a coffee stall and took it home. It looked delicious but when she came to eat it she found she had lost her appetite. The remains of the pie lay on the dressing table when she awoke. (200)

Brenda is abandoned by practically everybody and at the same time Tony Last is crying like a child in his illness. Brenda is seen crying herself to sleep in any agony of resentment and self-pity. She touches the nadir of respectability when she ponders how people can't invite her at least occasionally: "'Me? Oh, I'm all right,' said Brenda, and she thought, 'It might occur to her to sock a girl a meal once in a way.'" (180)

Waugh does not let us forget that his novel is a satire on the untenable attitudes towards life and that the quest of Tony Last is an absurd quest of a decent modern gentlemen who is devoid of genuine religious convictions. Despite therefore his sympathy for the hero's values, Waugh has yet to maintain his detached artistic stance. The starkly grotesque and frightful end of the hero is made to conform to the laws of the novel's "poetic justice." Tony's incarceration in a hut in the Brazilian jungle by the half-breed madman to whom he has to go on reading the novels of Dickens endlessly, would therefore appear wholly deserved. In meting out such treatment to his hero, Waugh explodes the Victorian myth that innocence always pays. *A Handful of Dust* thus becomes a blistering attack on the romantic idea of searching for a Gothic Utopia, a non-existent city in remote places. A genuine search for the City of God, the "New Jerusalem" would have been the proper thing to do. Tony's quest for an illusional Camelot has been an ill-advised effort to redeem his romantic ideals symbolised by Hetton Abbey which has been despoiled by his wife's vulgar friends. Tony goes on his excursion without adequate preparations. His quest of the Peruvian lost city is a parody of the search for the Holy Grail which presupposed strenuous spiritual training and a unique sense of vocation.

Chapter VI—"Du Cote de chez Todd"—in which the hero meets with the madman was originally a short story called "The man who liked Dickens," which Waugh wrote based on his own Brazilian expedition. The chapter is pivotal to the story for it gave Waugh the idea of writing a full-length study of the two types of savages – those inhabiting the civilized city and the primitive ones living in jungles. Mr. Christie, the religious maniac whom Waugh met in the wilds of British Guiana and who claimed to have seen Waugh's arrival in a vision, becomes Mr. Todd of the novel. Waugh records his meeting with Mr. Christie in his *Ninety-Two Days.* Tony's incarceration by Mr. Todd is the fictional rendering of Waugh's fear that he might be held for life by Mr. Christie whose conversations made Boa Vista, "a finger's breadth above reality."[25]

Waugh's treatment of Todd is complex, characteristic of the ambiguous and symbolic nature of his style. The name rhymes with "God" but remembering the law of inversion that rules the Waugh-wasteland, it may stand for death, or as Jeffrey Heath suggests, death-in-life.[26] ("Tod" in German does signify death.) From the perspective of the quest myth of Eliot to whom Waugh owes his title, Todd may represent the Fisher King who is waiting for the quester to arrive and redeem his land and himself by asking the right questions and slaying the dragon who keeps guard of the Chapel Perilous. But in the Waugh story there is once again an inversion. It is Todd, not Tony the latest arrival from civilization who poses the questions. He asks Tony first whether he can read and then whether he believes in God. The wound of the latter-day Fisher King is not sexual, but spiritual. Todd represents the spiritual lethargy of the modern world which is in sore need of God. Jeffrey Heath in his notes,[27] draws attention to Waugh's biography of the English Jesuit martyr Edmund Campion. In his listlessness and apathy, Todd represents the spiritually exhausted post-Reformation England. Todd's insular existence resembles the spiritually alienated England under Tudor Queen Elizabeth: "Although Mr. Todd had lived in Amazonas for nearly six years, no one except a few families of Pie-wie Indians was aware of his existence." (204)

If Dr. Messinger was an angel of death, Mr. Todd is Death – that is spiritual death – itself. Most of the descriptive epithets about him are of a negatively connotative value. He is the offspring of an apostate father, a Barbadian missionary who after deserting his wife began to prospect for gold and married Todd's Pie-wie mother. In his apostacy and illegitimacy, Mr. Todd bears a curious resemblance to Waugh's portrait of the Tudor monarch of Campion's day. For all the vast exuberance of Renaissance England of Elizabeth's day seems to Waugh a land of cruelty, degradation and savage intolerance. Waugh maintains that cut off from the true source of religion – Roman Catholicism – the inhabitants of the country were living a sham existence and were in dire need of the healing waters of true faith.

The unteleological nature of Tony's quest which is secular in origin, is in sharp contrast to the absolute clear-sightedness of goal of Edmund Campion who guided by the light of the true faith willingly died as a martyr. It is the purity of motives that distinguishes Edmund Campion, who died a hero's death, a "spectacle unto God, unto angels and unto men"[28] from the pathetically absurd figure of Tony Last, a prisoner in a mud hut in Brazil. Misperceptions disable Tony from achieving the actuality which Campion brilliantly achieves. *A Handful of Dust* tells us that man's passions, affections and his intellect require to be chastened and held in subjection. The highest life consists in the conscientious discharge of plain manifest duty, not in search of something extraordinary. King Arthur in Tennyson's idyll seeks not only to "wander from the allotted field until his work be done." Like Tennyson Waugh is warning against the vision which is merely due to the excited imagination of crazy enthusiasts. Such a quest is mere delusion. No one should leave his allotted sphere of duty to run after some self-chosen object. Such a transcendental pursuit is suited only to exceptional beings like Sir Galahad. Others would only waste their time and energies which might be better bestowed elsewhere. Tennyson's idyll contains the warning that "no man could sit on the Siege Perilous but he should lose himself." Galahad loses his old self, his share in the world and all that it has to offer in order that he may be crowned king in the spiritual city.

With the imprisonment of Tony in Todd's hut the wheel has come full circle once again. The familiar Waugh motif of circularity illuminates the structure of the present novel. Parallel characters and situations complete the thematic structure. The satirical symmetry of events in the novel is further indictment on the sterility of action in the modern age. Tony and Todd have a curious affinity to each other while Todd's hut is only a transformed Hetton Abbey. The insane repetitiveness of Todd's life is a distortion of Tony's own meaningless routine of earlier days when he lived the life of a country gentleman in Hetton. Tony's role as Todd's lector is the one he has played before:

> They took down the first volume of *Bleak House* and that afternoon Tony had his first reading. He had always rather enjoyed reading aloud and in the first year of marriage had shared several books in this way with Brenda, until one day, in a moment of frankness, she remarked that it was torture to her. He had read to John Andrew, late in the afternoon, in winter, while the child sat before the nursery fender eating his supper. (210)

What was torture to Brenda years ago is soon going to be even worse to Tony who will have to read on and on, to Todd. Tony's voice is like that of the Cumaen sybil in Ovid who longed for death.[29] Like the sybil, with all powers of discernment gone, Tony must remain Todd's voice, pleading in vain for liberation from his living death.

The choice of Dickens may not be as arbitrary as it may seem. Casual and pejorative references to the Victorian novelist have already been made in the early part of the novel. One of the less likeable of Dickens's characters, Mr. Pecksniff, is mentioned in connection with Tony's Hetton with its decrepit Victorian facades. An early hint such as this gives us a clue to Waugh's attitude to Dickens and the use to which he is going to put an author who has held the imagination of several generations of readers but who, in Waugh's opinion, has been the insidious cause for the pernicious secularization of religion. Men like Todd with no proper religious upbringing fall an easy prey to the hollow sentimentalism and spurious religious values of Dickens. Jerome Meckier thinks that Tony's quest of the Eldorado is a parody of Dickens's notion that a "Principle of good in quest of its rightful inheritance invariably succeeds."[30] Tony goes to Todd who is his *alter ego* and reads Dickens. In an earlier essay on the Cycle and Parody in Waugh's novel *Decline and Fall* Meckier has referred to the allusions to Dickens in the novel and has hinted that Dickensian ethics has contributed to the ongoing decline of the Western civilization.

The religion of Dickens to which Todd is devoted is as bloodless as Tony's Anglicanism. In bringing the men together Waugh emphasises the mutual complementarity of two natures: Tony's gothic attachment to Hetton and love of Arthurian romance is counterpointed by Todd's maudlin response to the melting sentimentalism of Dickens's morality. Tony and Todd are both shown as victims of humanism, a philosophy which in Waugh's view was spurious and inadequate. Waugh said in 1946 that *A Handful of Dust* contained all that he had to say about humanism.[31] The humanism propagated by Dickens, in Waugh's view, was particularly nefarious in so far as it sought to uphold the kind of Anglicanism to which Tony and Mr. Tendril the eccentric clergyman owed allegiance. Like the Anglicanism that was preached by Mr. Tendril the humanism of Dickens which nearly replaced the New Testament in the Victorian age, failed because it sought to do without the forms and dogmas of the Christian faith, especially of the Catholic variety. In their search for lasting consolation, Tony and Todd are baulked of their goal like the search party which comes from England looking for the lost Tony but which has to go back with a mere bagatelle, Tony's watch. The routine of daily Dickens reading has had as little spiritual effect on Todd as the repetitious religious routine on Tony's had been. The gruesome living-death of Tony in a madman's hut in a jungle is a metaphor for the anguished failure of the modern man to escape from the spiritual dungeon which is a product of the self-defeating humanism of his time. Dickens's pseudo-religion does not provide Todd or Tony with a panacea precisely because theirs is spiritual malaise which only an unquestioning obedience to the dogmas of the Church will cure. The Dickensian divorce of forms from truths has been the cause of much muddled modern thinking.

That Dickensian humanism is impotent against man's inherent savagery and the savagery without is illustrated by Todd's growing cruelty towards Tony. Waugh ridicules the idea of the educational worth of good secular literature. Dickens's novels cannot change an illiterate savage like Todd. The metamorphosis has been palpably negative. Todd is devoid of the least human sympathy. A year after Tony has been a prisoner reading Dickens day-in, day-out, his gloomy foreboding of permanent exile becomes acute when between the pages of *Martin Chuzzlewit* he finds a document written in pencil in irregular handwriting:

> Year 1919.
> I James Todd of Brazil do swear to Barnabas Washington of Georgetown that if he finish this book in fact *Martin Chuzzlewit* I will let him go away back as soon as finished. There followed a heavy pencil X and after it: Mr. Todd made this mark signed Barnabas Washington. (213)

Barnabas Washington whose grave Todd has already shown Tony was Todd's predecessor. Dickens's ethics has failed to instil in Todd any sense of honour. Giving one's word has no significance to him any more than the cross he has put on the black man's grave. A cross on the grave is another "pretty idea" to him. When Tony realises the growing menace of Todd, he stops reading but is consequently starved into submission by the jailer. Tony has been led to believe that a boat will be ready when the rains come, but none of the villagers most of whom are Todd's natural children will make him a boat. Todd has known all along the villagers' superstition about making a boat in the rains. Todd put Tony to long sleep which lasts for two days by means of one of the Pie-wie concoctions. He relieves Tony of his watch while the latter is sound asleep and gives it to the search party from England, as "a little souvenir" as Todd later says heartlessly. The search party has wanted something to take back to England where a reward is being offered for news of Tony. Todd has let them take photographs of the little cross he has put up in commemoration of the black man's death and Tony's arrival. The kind of fate that awaits Tony is hinted at in the horribly sinister tone of Todd: "But I do not suppose they will visit us again, our life here is so retired . . . no pleasures except reading. . . . We will not have any Dickens to-day . . . but tomorrow, and the day after that, and the day after that." (217)

The Brazilian jungle is reminiscent of the setting of Conrad's *Heart of Darkness*. The similarity in the initial letters in the titles of the novels of Waugh and Conrad may not be purely coincidental. Waugh's novel, like that of Conrad is an exploration of evil of the fallen man but the religious dimensions of *A Handful of Dust* is absent in Conrad's great work. This, as Meckier has said, hints at Waugh's distrust of Conrad's idea of nihilism and his contention that man has somehow come to terms with it. Neither Dickens's moralism nor Conrad's secular humanism can aid modern man in his struggle to combat barbarism.

Victims of the temporal order, Tony Last, Mr. Todd and the new heirs of Hetton Abbey cannot discover their true natures. In the concluding chapter of the book "English Gothic III" Waugh presents the hopeless spectacle of England in steady decline. The clock "high overhead among the gargoyles and crockets" striking fourteen when it is half-past eight (like Tony's stolen watch) is another of Waugh's symbols of the tyranny of time. No intersection of the timeless with the time is noticed in the lives of Richard Last and his family, the successors of Tony Last, believed dead. Molly Last on her two-stroke motor cycle, "with bran mash on her breeches and in her hair" and Teddy Last aged twenty two living at home and busy with silver foxes and Agnes always late for breakfast are the representatives of their generation. Nothing is sacred to them as their parents complain. Brenda without showing the least wifely grief has married Jock Grant-Menzies. Tendril the mad clergyman who believes Tony has died in Afghanistan conducts the brief service of dedication of the memorial put up in Tony's memory. The idea of the memorial is that of the notorious Mrs. Beaver. Hetton is completely overrun by Dionysian forces which characterise modern life. Teddy and their generation, the modern savages indistinguishable from the silver foxes they hunt, hope one day to restore Hetton to "the glory that it had enjoyed in the days of his cousin Tony." The inference is easy to draw. Waugh sees no hope for the modern wastelanders who nourished by the secular, time-bound humanism of their times hide themselves from the Celestial City.

Tony's quest is self-defeating and purposeless – like that of Martin Chuzzlewit who goes in search of non-existent city. Waugh also expects his readers to make another connection – to Proust. Two of the chapter headings in *A Handful of Dust* are meant to recall Proust's novel *A la Recherche du temps perdu*. Whereas Proust's novel is a story of spiritual quest, "a journey from the magically ordered world of childhood into an adult view of life as an inhuman mechanism of senseless laws and thence to a completely satisfying ordering of his [the narrator's] experience," *A Handful of Dust* is a tale of a smug romantic whose quest fails because he lacks the moral strength which springs from faith and an allegiance to the authority of the Catholic Church. In their unvarying routine of daily Dickens-reading, Tony and Todd are like the inhabitants in Dante's *Inferno* who are condemned to move in endless circles.

A Handful of Dust may be described as a religio-philosophical satire of modern values. In Tony's nostalgia for the past and his quest for the lost city, Waugh satirises the doomed quest for value in the post-war world, doomed because of the lack of religious faith. In the theological implications of the novel we can recognise, as Otto Beer has said,[32] a precursor of *Brideshead Revisited.* In the insistence on the need for self-knowledge the novel looks far ahead to the war-trilogy.

NOTES

1. "Spectator," 14 September 1934, in *The Critical Heritage,* p. 154.
2. Malcolm Bradbury, "Possibilities," p. 161.
3. K.M. Burke, "Dialogue and Satire in Three Novels of Evelyn Waugh," *Evelyn Waugh Newsletter* (Autum 1984), p. 4.
4. William J. Cook, Jr., p. 121.
5. "New Spokesman," 25 September 1964, *The Critical Heritage*, p. 161.
6. *Collected Poems and Plays of T.S. Eliot*, p. 61.
7. *The Modern Tradition*, ed. Richard Ellmann and Charles Feidelson, Jr. (N.Y., 1965). Quoted in Monroe K. Spears, *Dionysus and the City Modernism in Twentieth-Century Poetry* (New York, 1970), p. 67.
8. Peter E. Firchow, 'In Search of *A Handful of Dust:* The Literary Background of Evelyn Waugh's Novel,' *Journal of Modern Literature*, 2 (1972), p. 415n.
9. *Ibid*., p. 410.
10. Evelyn Waugh, *A Handful of Dust* (Penguin Books, 1951; rpt. 1987), p. 15.
11. *A Little Order*, p. 33.
12. Alvin Kernan, pp. 200-20.
13. *Evelyn Waugh Newsletter*, vol. 21, no. 1 (Spring 1987), pp. 1-2.
14. F.R Leavis, "The Waste Land" in *T.S. Eliot*, ed. Hugh Kenner (Englewood Cliffs: Prentice Hall, 1962), p. 92.

15. Peter Firchow, p. 409.
16. Martin Stannard, *Evelyn Waugh: 1903-39. The Early Years*.
17. Peter Firchow, p. 412
18. Giovanni Cecchin, "Echide T.S. Eliot nei romanzi di," Evelyn Waugh, *English Miscellany, XV*, 1963; Peter Green, "Du Cote de Chez Waugh," *Review of English Studies,* 11 (1961); Richard Wasson, "*A Handful of Dust*: Critique of Victorianism," *Modern Fiction Studies*, VI (1961).
19. Marston La France, "The Year's Work in Waugh Studies," *Evelyn Waugh Newsletter* (Spring 1973), pp. 5-7.
20. Jeffrey M. Heath, "The Lush Places," *Evelyn Waugh Newsletter* (Autumn 1979), pp. 5-7.
21. *The Picturesque Prison*, pp. 30-36.
22. Tennyson, "The Holy Grail," *Poems of Tennyson*, ed. Christopher Ricks (London: Longman, 1969), quoted in Peter Firchow.
23. *The Picturesque Prison*, p. 117.
24. Teresa Jungman, daughter of Mrs. Richard Guiness, was the original of Therese de Vitre in the novel. Waugh mentions in his *Diaries* that he once proposed to Teresa ("Baby") and was rejected.
25. Evelyn Waugh, *When the Going was Good* (UK: Penguin, 1951), p. 219.
26. *The Picturesque Prison*, p. 117.
27. *Ibid*., p. 300n.
28. Evelyn Waugh, *Edmund Campion* (London: Cassell, 1945), p. 164.
29. Robert Murray Davis, "Title and Theme in *A Handful of Dust,"* *Evelyn Waugh Newsletter* (Autumn 1972), p. 1.
30. Jerome Meckier, "Why the man who liked Dickens reads Dickens instead of Conrad: Waugh's *A Handful of Dust—Novel—A Forum or Fiction*," vol. 13, no. 2 (Providence: Brown University, 1980), p. 172.
31. Evelyn Waugh, "Fan-Fare," p. 58.
32. *Evelyn Waugh; A Reference Guide*, p. 42.

The Spiritual Odyssey: *Brideshead Revisited*

No other novel of Waugh has provoked so much controversy as his *Brideshead Revisited* significantly sub-titled *The sacred and profane memories of Captain Charles Ryder*. The book took the critical world by storm and set the critics by the ears. On its publication it won Waugh more detractors than admirers, and even those who were his one-time enthusiasts walked over to the enemy camp. Readers long used to thinking of Waugh as the greatest of the century's satirist were disappointed by Waugh's latest performance. To many Waugh seemed to have sacrificed artistic integrity to a private loyalty. Waugh's Catholicism which unabashedly broke into the novel's surface seemed barely palatable. Waugh became the critic's despair. Curiously, even those critics who professed the same religious faith as Waugh were divided in their appraisal of the book. O'Faolain thought that a religious theme given institutional treatment was liable "to get lost in the embroidered folds of ecclesiasticism."[1] Waugh's *Brideshead* in O'Faolain's opinion was an artistic failure. But there were other critics of Catholic persuasion who praised the book and predictably, not always for the right reason. *Brideshead* therefore seemed an embarrassing conundrum to many.

What great impact the novel had on the critical sensibility of the time of its publication may be guessed from the opinions of some of the critics of note. Edmund Wilson ordinarily an admirer of Waugh found his *Brideshead* a piece of banal romantic fantasy. He confessed to being unsympathetic by conviction with the point of view of the Catholic converts such as Waugh but that he found it impossible to feel that Waugh's novel conveyed "any genuine religious experience."[2] In a similar vein Rose Macaulay writing to the *Horizon* in December of the same year, praised Waugh's ability to create the lunatic logic of the Alice-in-Wonderland type but found that once he abandoned his "circus tent," he became sentimental and distastefully self-indulgent.[3] However it is the *Bell* controversy begun by Donat O'Donnell in the December number of 1946 that reflects the cross-section of critical estimate of this most remarkable Waugh novel. Writing under the pseudonym of O'Donnell, Conor Cruise O'Brien, pointed to the pervasive Catholicism by most readers especially those in America. He however found Waugh's Catholicism an amalgam of romanticism which was at the roots of cloying sort of nostalgia. Furthermore Waugh's snobbery and class loyalty made him partial to the aristocratic Marchmains who alone in his opinion were fit candidates for religious salvation. Hooper and his ilk were made ineligible by their middle class origin.[4]

T.J. Barrington replied to O'Donnell's charges that the latter was "brilliantly wrong." Dismissing O'Donnell's interpretation of the novel as materialist, Barrington argued that it was nonsense to hold that in Waugh's theology the love of money was the preliminary form of the love of God. To support his argument he drew attention to Lady Marchmain's awareness of the enormous evil latent in riches and of God's grace which could change that evil into good. If Sebastian, the drunken son of Lord Marchmain was saved it was not because he was a lord but that he was one who loved God, despite his infirmities Donat O'Donnell replied to Barrington, reiterating his former arguments. Waugh himself ended the controversy by writing a brief reply to O'Donnell's arguments. With an irony characteristic of him, Waugh wrote that his attack was not zeroed-in on the middle class Hooper but also on Lady Celia Ryder, a lady of high birth and Rex Mottram, the vulgar millionaire.[5]

What put some of Waugh's well-meaning critics off *Brideshead* is (what D.J. Dooley[6] termed) an overstatement of faith, coupled with lush prose. Waugh himself in the Preface to the 1960 revised edition of the novel wrote that he found his own writing in the novel distasteful. However he made plain the purpose of his book:

> Its theme—the operation of divine grace on a group of diverse but closely connected characters—was perhaps presumptuously large but I make no apology for it. I am less happy about its form, whose glaring defects may be blamed on the circumstances in which it was written. . . . It was a bleak period of present privation and threatening disaster—the period of soya beans and Basic English—and in consequence the book is infused with a kind of gluttony, for food and wine, for the splendours of the recent past and for rhetorical and ornamental language, which now with a full stomach I find distasteful. I have modified the grosser passages but have not obliterated them because they are an essential part of the book.[7]

The "high seriousness" of the novel to which Waugh has pointed the reader's attention had been noticed by many critics even at the time it first appeared. Amidst all the cacophony of dissenting opinion, we frequently hear of the significance of the invisible order in the novel's thematic structure. As Hutchins remarked in his review of the book, in *Brideshead* Waugh has moved into "more spacious spheres."[8] One of the insistent themes of Waugh's fiction – the futility of security and the need for a spiritual order of things – finds loud utterance in *Brideshead*.

Post-*Brideshead* criticism of Waugh has tried consistently to come to terms with Waugh's philosophy of life. Much of recent Waughiana has emphasised Waugh's artistry in bodying forth his moral message. Betjeman's assessment of Waugh in 1947 that he is a whole person with a complete philosophy[9] has found reverberating echoes in the writings of serious and imperial critics of more recent times. That *Brideshead* marks a revolution in theme and technique is the opinion of most present-day critics. The influence of T.S. Eliot to which attention has been called continues to be felt in Waugh's work. His world, as Cecchin remarks, like Eliot's represents a gradual process of clarification and reflects extraordinary discipline.[10] What is even more noticeable is Waugh's growing mastery of characterization. Charles Ryder, the narrator/hero of *Brideshead* is a "round" character, even if he is, at times, the mouthpiece of the author. The view that Julia Flyte, with whom Charles falls in love, is "dead as mutton" has been rejected lately. She, even more than Charles is seen to grow in complexity as the story proceeds.

The thematic continuity with the earlier novels, especially in antithetical opposition of civilization pitted against the forces of barbarism has also been noticed. To defend civilization from the "cultural terrorism"[11] of the modern times as Jeffrey Hart remarks, has been one of Waugh's obsessive preoccupations as a novelist. Waugh makes no apology for his conviction that the Catholic Church, the repository of culture and order, is a bulwark against the ravages of modern secularity which is really barbarism. The Catholic framework in *Brideshead* helps Waugh to enforce his moral that the phenomenal world is in desperate need of a supernatural, "noumenal" world-order. This intersection of the timeless on the temporal is brilliantly illustrated in the death-bed scene of Lord Marchmain in the final pages of *Brideshead*. The novel provides resolution to the Waste Land theme. Whereas Tony Last in *A Handful of Dust* has no means of redemption, the characters in *Brideshead* save themselves from damnation, each in his unique way. Waugh's Catholicism does not merely give the novel its great dramatic power but it provides the world of the novel's characters with coherence and a sense of meaning.

In the opinion of many perceptive writers on Waugh in the present-day, far from being an artistic failure *Brideshead* is Waugh's great aesthetic achievement. The stylistic precision and conscious artistry in the novel continue to stimulate Waugh study, as evidenced by many learned articles which appear in *Evelyn Waugh Newsletter* and other literary periodicals. Sensitive use of symbols and of contrapuntal imagery are employed to bring home to the reader the author's purpose. Critics have begun to heed to the tip given by Waugh that a word for word reading of the novel is bound to pay off.[12] The novel's structure is dexterously welded to its texture and layers of meaning relevant to the theme can be detected beneath the surface of the language.

The quest-motif, which is the subject of our study, is most artistically conceived and integrally related to the novel's theme. Here again the Catholic framework has proved functionally successful. In a sense, *Brideshead* is a "conversion novel" dealing as it does with the hero's conversion to the Catholic faith. As in the earlier novels, Charles Ryder in *Brideshead* is an alien – only he is aggressively agnostic, unlike the previous ones – in a hostile society, which in this case, is the world of Catholics. Critics who complained before of Waugh's nihilism and of the negative epiphanies of the former heroes can have no complaint with the positive affirmations of the novel. The quest of Tony Last in *A Handful of Dust* ends in the hero's gruesome incarcerations in the Brazilian jungles with no hope of redemption. The chief quester in *Brideshead*, on the other hand, is seen leaving the dilapidated chapel with renewed vigour to face the ravages of cultural values brought about by the war. In exploring the hero's spiritual dilemma and his ultimate acceptance of Catholicism, Waugh is in fact making a moral commentary on the modern agnostic world which knows no way out of its impasse. Charles Ryder's assent to the church dogmas is his discovery of self and identity. The name "Ryder" is symbolic of pilgrimage which involves a long ride into hitherto unexplored realms. The hero travels from the ephemeral joys of his profane world to the sacred love of God, as the sub-title of the novel symbolically proclaims. Waugh had this in mind when he later described *Brideshead* as "romantic and eschatological."[13] The Bright Young Things of *Vile Bodies* were irredeemably romantic and had no sense of eschatology. Consequently the temporal world of *Vile Bodies* was pointless whereas (as Jerome Meckier has observed) in *Brideshead* Waugh wants to posit that this world of men can "providentially conduct one to realities that prove timeless."[14]

Oblique allusions to and at least one direct quotation from the writings of St. Augustine unmistakably underpin the parallelism between Ryder's search for truth and the spiritual Odyssey of the saint of Carthage. Augustinian allusions are often made through images with theological connotations. Ryder's vain pursuit of florid and vulgar aestheticism and his stubborn agnosticism are reminiscent of Augustine's early attraction to the philosophy of the Manichees and his love of carnal pleasure. The two straying sinners are brought back to faith with a "twitch upon the thread" (to anticipate Waugh's quotation later in the novel). The recurring image of the "shadows" (with a glance at Wordsworth) in the novel recalls the "angelic darkness" of evil that Augustine repeatedly mentions in his writings. He could emerge from such darkness only after he attains internal illumination following a long period of spiritual struggle and privation. Augustine's fundamentally true search for a spiritual sanctuary has been a classic prototype of the quest for the meaning of existence. In different ways, Augustine's *Confessions* and Waugh's *Brideshead* tell the story of the inevitability of Providential grace. The hound of heaven pursues the lapsed sinner with relentless mercy and follows him through the tortuous metaphysical and intellectual maze he has entwined himself and brings him back to the fountain head whence proceeds the wisdom and knowledge that truly nourish the human soul. Ryder, like Augustine learns at great cost to himself, that a vision of a higher order of reality awaits only those who are prepared to abandon the natural appetites. It involves, to recall T.S. Eliot, a continual self-sacrifice and self-surrender.[15] When natural morality is taken up by christian life, it must totally reorient itself. The search of Ryder, like that of Augustine, ends in the discovery of the primacy of the supernatural over the natural life, defined with clarity by the dogmas of the Catholic Church.

The man-in-exile doctrine dear to St. Augustine is worked out in fully artistic terms in Waugh's *Brideshead*, a theme, incidentally, which runs through the entire gamut of Waugh's fiction. Instead of finding scapegoats for the regression of oneself or of the civilization in which the modern man lives, it were better if he came to terms with his own fallen nature. Ryder finds his identity, like Augustine long before him, only when he realises that each soul, has individually, to make peace with his Creator. Alone in the presence of the Eucharist, Ryder understands the meaning of the vulgarity of the world without. The moral and material chaos of the age is a consequence of the primordial sin and modern man's refusal to face that fact.

In *Brideshead Revisited* Waugh employs a complex narrative technique in which the main body of the novel is sandwiched between a "Prologue" and an "epilogue." Besides giving the narrator/author a degree of externality to the events of the story such a framing device enables the narrator to present the reader the needed contrast between the past and his present maturer vision. Through the first-person retrospective narrative the narrator/hero attempts to regain unity of self of reconstructing the past through memory. The knowledge of the self is one of the essential aspects of the spiritual quest which is given dramatic expression in the novel. Not only is time fragmented but also the self of the hero and both regain unitive reconstruction in the novel.

The multiplicity of consciousness in the narrative structure traces the different stages in the hero's spiritual development. Such a novelistic structure, to quote David Brailow, makes it easy to "accept both end and process, however dubiously we may view the beliefs in Ryder's conversion."[16] There are at least three "I"s–the "now I," the "intermediate I" and the "then I"—as William Cook has observed.[17] An evolutionary spiritual process is made articulate by these three "voices" of the same narrator at different structural points of the novel.

The world of the Prologue is that of people who thrown upon the filthy tide of modernism are wrecked by its formless spawning fury. From the privileged perspective of a convert Charles Ryder views such a world with disgust and boredom. The traditional loveliness and sanctity which Catholicism once provided are absent from England of the post-war times. In the face of banal preoccupations and pressures of secularization, the men are blind to the mystery of the universe in which they live and have their being. The opening pages of the book epitomise for us the "dull, plodding unheroic self of twentieth century man"[18] and the stark irrevocability of his condition. Ryder is one of the few who have heeded the promptings of Grace and who as a consequence has achieved his quest, while those around him are pale spectres moving in unknown worlds. The feverish mobility and restlessness of the officers and men bespeak their loss of spiritual direction in contrast to the stability and permanence that Catholic Christianity has provided Ryder and the Flytes.

The dominant thematic motifs are announced in the Prologue—the degeneracy of the times and the narrator's ultimate search for significance. In highly-charged symbolic language, characteristic of the author, the Prologue encapsulates the horror and boredom of the modern wasteland. The camp outside Glasgow under snow is an outward symbol of the hero's disillusion with the war. Half-hidden in the embosoming trees lies the municipal lunatic asylum which is the correlative for modern man's perverted state of emotions. Charles Ryder, infantry commander, is aged thirty nine but feels prematurely old. The death of his love for the army is spoken in terms of "the whole drab compass of marital disillusion." Ryder is entirely "indifferent to the destination" of the camp. It is a "planless maze." Ryder wryly muses on what future archaeologists would have to say on the tribal anarchy of his times. Most characters in the novel are benighted in a world of shadows. The wrong pursuit and love of false sanctuary that is the lot of the men and women in the novel are hinted at early on: "I had played every scene in the domestic tragedy, had found the early tiffs become more frequent, the tears less affecting, the reconciliations less sweet, till they engendered a mood of aloofness and cool criticism, and the growing conviction that it was not myself but the loved one who was at fault. I caught the false notes in her voice." (14-15)

The notion of union with God contained in the novel's title will be touched upon later. It will be, however, useful to mark the author's use of the metaphor of matrimony to define human relations in general. Ryder's descriptions of his disenchantment with army-life for which he had once a passion is close to the break-down of his own marriage described in passing later in the story. The error of the military men in believing to be destined for the defence of Calais when they were actually going the wrong way, the frequent change in the army's locations, the image of the broken window on which the C.O's accusing eyes fall are some of the metaphors by means of which the author/narrator picture a world of aimless men. References to a sense of loss occurs with iterative forcefulness: "'I say, any idea where we're off to?' 'None.'" (20) The sense of loss is accompanied by a sense of intolerable boredom captured brilliantly by the description of the men travelling in a train of antiquated coaches: "They ate sandwiches and chocolate, smoked and slept. None of them had a book. For the first three or four hours they noted the names of towns and leaned out of the windows when, as often happened, we stopped between stations. Later, they lost interest." (21)

The figure of Hooper, one of Ryder's officers, "A sallow youth with hair combed back . . . and a flat Midland accent" is a symbol of young England which has no code of values. No other character in Waugh's fictional oeuvre has provoked the critic's wrath more than that of young Hooper. Waugh's undisguised contempt for Hooperism has been traced to his snobbism and dislike of the lower sectors of society. But Hooper is at once a figure of fun and an object of pity. Ryder himself shows a bit of love and sympathy for Hooper. He apologises later to the young man when the colonel has had Hooper's hair cut in front of everybody. To Waugh as to Charles Ryder Hooper is only a representative of the erosion of values of the times.

> Hooper had no illusions about the army. . . . He had come to it reluctantly, under compulsion, after he had made every feeble effort in his power to obtain preferment. He accepted it, he said 'like the measles.' Hooper was no romantic. He had not as a child ridden with Rupert's horse or sat among the camp fires at Xanthus-side; . . . Hooper had wept often, but never for Henry's speech on St. Crispin's day, not for the epitaph at Thermopylae. The history they taught him had few battles in it . . . and the Battle in the West where Arthur fell . . . sounded in vain to Hooper. (17-18)

Much as he deplores the England which is saturated with Hooperism, Ryder shares Waugh's contempt for mean men like the commanding officers.

Captain Charles Ryder finds himself accidentally stationed on the site of Brideshead mansion, now fallen in woeful disrepair. The sight of the mansion early the following day calls up memories, both Arcadian and Purgatorial. Brideshead, which Charles is now revisiting, is a symbol of the achieved quest. At the sound of its name from his servant the "phantoms of those haunted late years began to take flight." That Brideshead is the central and unifying structural symbol of which the other symbols in the book are vital parts is indicated in the description with its Keatsian overtones.

> Our camp lay along one gentle slope; opposite us the ground led, still unravished, to the neighbourly horizon, and between us flowed a stream—it was named the Bride and rose not two miles away at a farm called Bridesprings . . . it became a considerable river lower down before it joined the Avon—which had been dammed here to form three lakes, one no more than a wet slate among the reeds, but the others more spacious, reflecting the clouds and the mighty beeches at their margin. The woods were all of oak and beech, the oak grey and bare, the beech faintly dusted with green by the breaking buds . . . Did the fallow deer graze here still?—and, lest the eye wander aimlessly, a Doric temple stood by the water's edge. . . . All this had been planned and planted a century and a half ago so that, at about this date, it might be seen in its maturity. (25)

The symbolism of Brideshead house, the seat of the Marchmains, is fully and brilliantly worked out in the course of the novel. Suffice it to say, at this point of our discussion, that Waugh makes it quite explicit at the beginning that the symbolism of the title is vital to the quest-motif in the novel. Hooper's reference to the chapel, "a sort of R.C. Church" gives the reader a further clue, if he needed one, of the symbolic identification of the estate of the Marchmains with the Church itself. The Church has often been referred to as the Bride of Christ and Christ himself as her bridegroom. Waugh is obviously thinking of the description of St. Paul in his *Epistle to the Ephesians* and of the passage in *Apocalypse*.[19]

In the quotation from Keats's *Ode on the Grecian Urn* ("still unravished") is implicit in Waugh's contrast between Art as a refuge from the flux of time and the Church. It is the latter, in Waugh's opinion, which is the true sanctuary, although Waugh agreed with Keats on the value of Beauty. The chapel, even in its present ruined state, is the "still unravished bride" in a chaotic world of loss and rejection, the "still centre" of T.S. Eliot. In it resides all that Ryder has been searching for all his youth and manhood. Rodney Delasanta has drawn several parallels between the bride in Keats's urn and the Bride of Christ which is the Church.[20] But unlike in Keats, the beauty of art is not an end in itself. To Charles Ryder aesthetic beauty is going to lead him to the imperishable values that the Catholic Church alone can and does offer. Whereas, in Keats, Beauty is equated with Truth, in Ryder's story, Beauty is only the forerunner. Brideshead, the "unam, sanctam ecclesiam" is a perfect synthesis of Keats's aesthetic joy at the wonder of man's salvation.

The thematic significance of Brideshead is stated at the outset of the story. How seriously Waugh himself took the book's theme can be seen in his own apologia for the book:

> I believe you can only leave God out [of a novel] by making your characters pure abstractions. Countless admirable writers, perhaps some of the best in the world, succeed in this. Henry James was the last of them. The failure of the modern novelists since and including James Joyce is one of Presumption and exorbitance. They are not content with artificial figures which hitherto passed gracefully as men and women. They try to represent the whole human mind and soul and yet omit its determining characters – that of being God's creature with a defined purpose. So in my future books there will be two things to make them unpopular: a preoccupation with style and an attempt to represent more fully, which to me, means only one thing, man in his relation to god.[21]

If Waugh's *A Handful of Dust* treats of a failed quest his *Brideshead Revisited* exemplifies an achieved quest. Where the former sounds pessimistic about the possibility of man's redemption, the latter offers a positive response to the destructiveness of the modern world. *Brideshead Revisited* is an achieved art insofar as it deals with an achieved quest. All the elements in the book have an artistic and semiotic meaning. Ryder's memory stirred by an old familiar name has to be perpetuated in a tale which is an artistic whole.

The main events of the story of Ryder's early days, his introduction to Brideshead family and his final conversion fall into three distinct parts structurally mirrored in the book. As William Cook[22] has noted there is a Hegelian triad at work here: the first stage tells us of the carefree days of Arcadian joy; the second "negative" stage marking the hero's agnosticism and rebellion; and the final stage in which the hero's search ends in transcendent vision of the finite perfection embodied in the One true faith. As in Proust's *Recherche*, *Brideshead Revisited* traces the hero's growth from childhood and innocence through adolescent agnosticism to his maturation as an adult who has realised himself. Francis Heck notes a further analogy between Ryder's conversion and the conversion theme of Andre Gide's *La Porte etroite*.[23]

The events described in Book One of the novel take place twenty years before those of the Prologue. Entitled ironically as "Et in Arcadia Ego" it recounts the days of careless youth of the hero and his friend Sebastian Flyte, who plays the part of the imitator in the quest story. They are a pair of young men who are greatly attracted to each other but do not yet know life's purpose. The heady days at Oxford are described with Arnoldian wistfulness: "In her spacious and quiet streets men walked and spoke as they had done in Newman's day; her autumnal mists, her grey springtime, and the rare glory of her summer days—such as that day—when the chestnut was in flower and the bells rang out high and clear over her gables and cupolas, exhaled the soft airs of centuries of youth." (29-30)

Much as the Oxford scenes in the book reflect Waugh's own sense of nostalgia, there is a touch of irony in the descriptions. Writing long after the days of youth, the narrator persona looks upon the period with a detached view of a man who has no more illusions of his past. The epigraph gives a clue to the ironic detachment of the narrator. Evoking as it does the golden Arcady of a forgotten age, it suggests a sense of inevitable doom. Amidst a chaotic assortment of articles in Ryder's rooms in Oxford is seen a human skull ("that noisome object" as his cousin Jasper names it) which bears the motto "Et in Arcadia Ego" inscribed on its forehead. Along with the Biblical quotations used later in the book, this Latin tag might serve as an epigraph to the whole of not only *Brideshead Revisited* but to the entire oeuvre of Waugh. There is death even in Arcady. Ryder did not *then* realise that the Oxford days were numbered and that he would encounter before long the teasing questions of existence. Waugh makes the same cynical use of the phrase from Virgil which the inscription on the tomb in Poussin's picture 'The Arcadian Shepherds' sought to evoke. In the post-lapsarian world, rife with evil and pain as a consequence of its abandonment of God, it would be futile to look for rural innocence and simplicity. The shadows of the Godless world close upon Charles Ryder and Sebastian Flyte of the Marchmain family. The Flytes—Sebastian and his sister Julia—as their name suggests, are apostates who separate themselves from the traditional values which their religion has helped nourish in their childhood. Young Sebastian himself with his exquisite charm and beauty is ever trying to escape from a painful, self-conscious present by retreating more and more into infantilism. *Brideshead Revisited* is a highly structured work in which not only the characters but the language of the book itself is charged with a high degree of metaphor. Sebastian's ever-present companion the teddy bear plays more than one symbolic role. Apart from the hagiographical symbolism of his name, the teddy bear is as critics have remarked, a Freudian throw-back to Sebastian's childhood, the type of regression that we have noticed in the earlier heroes. His isolation is emphasised very early on. Ryder himself, another figure of alienation, who in his own words was "in search of love" strikes an immediate acquaintance with Sebastian. While pointing to his house to Ryder, Sebastian refers to it not as his house; but that of his family: "'It's where my family live'; and even then, rapt in the vision, I felt, momentarily, an ominous chill at the words he used – not, 'that's my house' but 'it's where my family live.'" (44) This is the lot of Ryder himself. There is little sympathy between Charles and his callous and eccentric father. Right from the start, the idea of modern man's alienation from God and the true home symbolically manifests itself in the all-pervasive alienation of children from their parents and from other fellow-beings. It is structurally appropriate that Anthony Blanche, the aesthete par excellence, one of the novel's memorable grotesques should be reciting passages from T.S. Eliot's *Waste Land*, a poem which describes the condition similar to that of the Oxford scenes. The bric-a-brac in the young men's rooms externalises the internal confusions of the children of the lost generation The sense of spiritual exile is conveyed by the image of the enchanted garden in Ryder's description of his first visit to Sebastian's room: "I went full of curiosity and the faint, unrecognised apprehension that here, at last, I should find that low door in the wall, which others, I knew had found before me, which opened on an enclosed and enchanted garden, which was somewhere, not overlooked by any window, in the heart of that great city." (40)

Fallen in a comically limited and fragmented world, the characters are yet unaware that they are helpless victims of time, mutability and death. The Keatsian echo of youth dying is heard in Ryder's prognostication of Sebastian's future: "He was entrancing, with that epicene beauty which in extreme youth sings for love and withers at the first cold wind." (40) As Ryder confesses, it is retrospectively easy to endow one's youth with a false precocity or a false innocence. Nanny Hawkins the childhood nurse of the Flytes is another of the symbols of a bygone stage for which Sebastian yearns with psychopathic longing. His extreme possessiveness of Charles Ryder betrays his total lack of stability which is at once the cause and consequence of his inability to form meaningful relations with the others. Sebastian's condition is metaphorical of the state of acute self-consciousness of the modern soul which has separated itself from the Universe.

Not only bustling Oxford with its innumerable attractions but the home of the Flytes, Brideshead, constitutes the seductive illusions which blind Ryder and others to life's true meaning. Brideshead is one of Waugh's poetic paradoxes. Housing as it does the ancient English Catholic family, the recusants for whom Waugh has always had sympathy, Brideshead stands symbolically for the beacon light of truth in a world of shadows. Yet the house itself with some of its apostate inhabitants, in one sense, is a false refuge. For all its splendour, in earthly terms, it is a mere shell, like Ryder's "human skull" with its ominous inscription containing the warning of the brevity of life's joy. The "dome" which housed Nanny Hawkins is described as "false." But one has to beware of the poetic ambiguity of the description for it is made by a youth who has yet to attain true knowledge. Nanny Hawkins seated among a confused heap of objects and with a rosary in her hands is a figure of serenity and repose.

What attracts Charles to the Flytes – Sebastian first and then his twin-like-sister Julia – is not the beauty of Catholicism of which Lady Marchmain is a solid and a living symbol but their incredible physical charm. His love for Julia Mottram later in the story proves one of the biggest obstacles to his faith, although at the same time his love for Julia is a forerunner of the greater love of God. The other "Circean bride"[24] as Jeffrey Heath calls it, who keeps Ryder from the true path is the secular art. A devotee to pagan beauty, Ryder becomes a celebrated architectural painter but in his own later maturer estimate, he is not a true genius. Anthony Blanche again is the true judge of the matter. He calls Ryder's work as "terrible tripe." But in the early Oxford days Ryder is charmed by the aesthetic beauty of Brideshead: "It was an aesthetic education to live within those walls, to wander from room to room, from the Soanesque library to the Chinese drawing-room, adazzle with gilt pagodas and nodding mandarins, painted paper and Chippendale fretwork, from the Pompeian parlour to the great tapestry-hung hall which stood unchanged, as it had been designed two hundred and fifty years before; to sit, hour after hour, in the shade looking out on the terrace." (96) The irony in the passage can hardly be missed. What he calls "aesthetic education" is to turn out in the end to be a more genuine and vitalising kind of education namely self-integration through the discovery of God. Ryder himself wonders whether "in the mansions of Limbo the heroes enjoy some such compensation for the loss of the Beatific Vision; Perhaps the Beatific Vision itself has some remote kinship with this lowly experience; I, at any rate believed myself very near heaven, during those languid days at Brideshead." (94) Somewhere in the ("Jungian") unconscious lay intimations of immortality which troubled Ryder's waking moments. The fountain in the Brideshead estate which Sebastian sets Ryder to draw is a dominating symbol, carrying the theological message of the novel. Ryder, struck by its uniqueness, is yet unaware of the wealth of meaning that lies hidden in the springs: "in the centre dominating the whole splendid space rose the fountain; such a fountain as one might expect to find in a piazza of southern Italy." And Ryder goes on: "This was my conversion to the Baroque. I sat, hour by hour, before the fountain probing its shadows, tracing its lingering echoes, rejoicing in all its clustered feats of daring and invention, I felt a whole new system of nerves alive within me, as though the water that spurted and bubbled among its stones, was indeed a life-giving spring." (96-97) As Mario L. D'Avanzo has shown, the "life-giving spring" is at once Ryder's Hippocrene and the baptismal font of the Catholic Church.[25] Ryder is gradually led through the beauty of profane art to catch a glimpse of the eternal truth. The contemplation of this "life giving spring" fills him with an ineffable artistic inspiration. An unknown hand takes hold of his brush and "the intricate multiplicity of light and colour became a whole," without difficulty. Through the pursuit of art, unconscious to himself, Ryder is led along the path of redemption. Already as an artist, he is able to see the underlying pattern of meaningful unity behind all the fragments of material existence. The *art nouveau* chapel of the Brideshead Castle, which Ryder finds somewhat vulgar in taste has a similar symbolic function. The sanctuary lamp has the same mysterious attraction for Ryder. It is bound to twitch him along to the heart of God and as Bridey, the eldest of the Flyte boys, predict, with Ryder art will be means to a theological end.

One of the chief intrumental causes in Ryder's maturation is Lady Marchmain, the saintly materfamilias, who is not yet a saint. As in the mythical quests, Lady Marchmain performs the function of a sage counsel. With her lofty religious scruples, she stands for the formidable exaction of the Church herself. She wields an almost preternatural influence on all the characters including Charles Ryder. In her death might be seen a fictional analogue of the Christ-figure – a sacrifical death for the sins of her erring children, Sebastian and Julia. Anthony Blanche describes her as a monster who sucks people's blood. But there is enough evidence in the text to show that of all the characters Lady Marchmain is the most misunderstood and by irresponsible men like Blanche the most vilified. Cordelia, who has often been described as the "heart" of the book and in some ways the author's spokeswoman rights the balance. She tells Ryder that when people wanted to hate God "they hated mummy." Her argument that people who wanted to hate God and couldn't dare do so, chose instead to focus their hatred on God's saints such as her mother is central to an understanding of Lady Marchmain and of the novel. Lady Marchmain's fate as prophet and the voice of truth in an unsympathetic world is that of the true disciple of Jesus who will forfeit the sympathy of his family. She is compared, in the novel not only to the Lady of Sorrows but also to God the Father and God the Son. Like the *Hound of Heaven* in Francis Thomson's poem Lady Marchmain loves her children (with Ryder included among them) and her husband with a consuming love and twitches them back to that abode of blessedness from where they have gone astray.

Blanche himself is another representative of Ryder's agnostic generation. He is barely Ryder's senior but seems even then to be "burdened with the experience of the Wandering Jew." He is indeed a nomad of no nationality. His dislike of Lady Marchmain is typical of men who are afraid of the Grace of God. Blanche combines humanistic reason totally unaided by God's grace and perversion of natural appetite.

Bridey, Sebastian's elder brother, is the exact opposite of Sebastian. Hard of countenance and Jesuitical in deportment and with his passion for matchboxes he is another of Waugh's grotesques. Yet, it is he who awakens in Julia, a sense of sin by his remark on her adulterous relation with Ryder.

It is, however Cordelia, the plain younger daughter who, by her fervent Catholicism, makes a lasting impression on Ryder. Like Lear's daughter, she cares for her renegade father the Byronic Lord Marchmain, when the latter returns to Brideshead from Italy where he has been living with his mistress Cara.

To one who thought he "had no religion," (101) the atmosphere of Brideshead must have seemed forbidding: "Religion predominated in the house; not only in its practices – the daily mass and Rosary, morning and evening in the chapel – but in all its intercourse." (146) With Waugh, as with some of his post-war contemporaries, chiefly Graham Greene, the quest of the hero is a spiritual quest which deals not so much with some abstract humanist ideal but principally with God and what he means to man. An agnostic like Ryder and reprobates like Sebastian and Julia, are unaware that Providence has designs on them. In spite of themselves they are being pulled constantly God-ward. Their attempts to escape the Grace of God turn eventually into spiritual pilgrimages.

If Ryder's attitude is one of disbelief characteristic of youth, the career of Sebastian is becoming even more threatening. Isolated spiritually and emotionally from the rest of the family, he is on the way to becoming a dipsomaniac. Whereas Ryder gets drunk often but only through an excess of high spirits, Sebastian drinks "to escape." He sits up late and alone in the college rooms and is found soaking. A succession of drinking disasters come on him. His days of Arcadia are relentlessly coming to an end. His despairing prayer is to be let alone. Cara, Lord Marchmain's Italian mistress, warns Ryder about the danger to Sebastian. What makes things intolerable for Sebastian is his religion, which like his teddy bear seems a mere "foible" to Ryder. But to Sebastian himself, being a Catholic is a far more serious matter. He confesses to Charles that he is "very, very much wickeder" than his friend and yet he would remain a Catholic. Like St. Augustine, Sebastian finds the call of God irresistible and like him he prays, "O God, make me good but not yet." Catholicism which seems an awful lot of nonsense to Ryder, sounds "terrible lot of sense" to Sebastian. What his mother Lady Marchmain calls the Alice-in-Wonderland side of the Catholic faith, the crib, the three kings and so on attract Sebastian. Like his sweet sister Cordelia who makes novena for the pigs, Sebastian himself has once prayed to St. Antony when his Aloysius was found lost. Nowhere is the spiritual tension dramatised as movingly as in the case of Sebastian. It is God who wins in the end when, like St. Augustine whose prayer he used once, he finds his vocation in North Africa but till the very end drink will be his cross. His quest nonetheless is an achieved one, but it is not "just yet," as Sebastian has said. He has to chase many an unsubstantial shadow before he sees the light. In the meantime, Sebastian betrays the deviousness of a dipsomaniac. Drinking heavily on the sly, he is frequently seen missing. The imminent physical and moral collapse of Sebastian is told in movingly economic language: "His year of anarchy had filled a deep, interior need of his, the escape from reality, and as he found himself increasingly hemmed in, where he once felt himself free, he became at times listless and morose, even with me." (125)

Lady Marchmain's friendship with Charles through whom she hopes to wean Sebastian away from his weakness arouses the latter's angry suspicion of his once close friend and ally. The brief imprisonment that Sebastian along with Ryder and Mulcaster undergoes for drunken driving in the company of a couple of prostitutes, instead of sobering him up, only makes him more introverted and uncongenial. Lady Marchmain's treatment of the incident with humorous resignation only exacerbates Sebastian's hatred of himself and others. The Easter day party at Brideshead at which Charles is a guest culminates in a painful incident. Sebastian gets disgustingly drunk and marks another stride in his flight from the family which brings him to ruin. He is especially resentful of Ryder whom he unfairly suspects of taking sides against him. The thought that he is being spied upon by his mother's friends, chief of whom is Mr. Samgrass, the history don drives him to worse bouts of drinking until in the end he gets sent down from the University.

If Sebastian's apostasy consists in his alcoholism, that of his sister Julia's takes the form of defying the Catholic code of the family by choosing a Canadian Vulgarian, also a divorcee, for her husband. This debutante with her "quatro cento beauty" is a self-willed, spoilt child. She hates the very values that her pious mother represents and even delights in hurting the religious sensibilities of her parents with impunity, fully confident that her father Lord Marchmain who is living in sin outside the family is on her side. The sterility of her mad pursuits is symbolised by the birth of a dead child to Rex Mottram. Her adultery with Charles Ryder later in the book, while being an instrumental cause for bringing Ryder to Catholicism also awakes in her a strong sense of sin long since dormant within her. Their struggle to escape from the truth embodied in the Church ends in failure and frustration. Julia's nun-like life of chastity and service is an allegory of the triumph of the soul over the temptations of the flesh and the senses.

Like the heroes in the earlier novels, Charles Ryder is the one character who moves in all the worlds presented in the book. His experiences are part of his growing up. He himself is unaware of the impact his introduction into the Brideshead household was going to have on his life. It is as if Ryder is predestined in the economy of God's grace to be one of his elect. So vital seems his presence in Brideshead family that Lady Marchmain not only looks upon him as part of the family but comes to depend on him in restoring her son Sebastian back into the health of the community. Lord Marchmain approves of the idea of Julia divorcing Mottram and having Charles as her second husband. The possible inheritance of the property is a hint of the wealth of spiritual inheritance that is in store for Ryder.

The leitmotifs of the "shadows" in the first book are a constant reminder of presence of death in the spring time of youth of the main characters. That the pleasures of Arcady are touched by death is reinforced by the image of the skull in the book. Not only is there a skull in Ryder's collection of objects but one of the girls in the disreputable Old Hundredth is described as a skull: "One had the face of a skull, the other of a sickly child. The Death's Head seemed destined for me." (135) Ryder's confession to Collins that he is the loneliest man in Oxford since Sebastian Flyte's expulsion is the despairing cry of a helpless victim of temporality and death. That his life lacks a centre is suggested by his decision to become a painter, abandoning his academic career at Oxford.

The Arcadian phase of innocence of the Oxford days is rapidly giving way to a severer phase of spiritual weariness and cynicism. Lady Marchmain's abortive attempts to cure Sebastian from his "illness," in spite of his recuperative trips in the company of Mr. Samgrass one of Lady

Marchmain's chief retainers make matters worse. With money stolen with Ryder's aid and connivance, Sebastian slips out of England and disappears for a long while from the novel. Ryder himself fares no better; he is, as has been remarked by critics, exiled from Brideshead rather unfairly, by Lady Marchmain, because he is suspected of collusion. Like Lady Marchmain's husband years ago, these two young men are compulsively driven out of Brideshead by the apparently unimaginative and fanatical religious zeal of the matriarch of the Flyte household. Sebastian's flight takes him to remote Africa while Charles goes to Paris to pursue art. Paradoxically, however, the "quest" of Ryder and Sebastian are in the long run journeys backwards to the seat of "grace" embodied in the religion of Lady Marchmain, which the two men heartily reject. Their paths (that of Sebastian especially) are attended upon by hardships and frustrations of some kind. But as Cordelia remarks later, "no one is ever holy without suffering." Sebastian's apparent moral collapse and Ryder's hardened agnosticism are mere preludes to their final redemption. One of the theses of *Brideshead Revisited* is what Hinchliffe remarks, "Human failures are divine victories."[26] Correlatively, the bleak and threatening landscape these pilgrims traverse are the "dryness and the interior desolation" which is the experience of great mystics and saints of the Church who are beset by a sense of spiritual aridity and an utter sense of loss. Beginning in an illusion of romance the path of these men leads to the disillusionment of irony.

Ryder's reaction to Lady Marchmain's veiled accusation of ingratitude is one of hatred and revulsion. As he drives away from Brideshead he thinks he has seen the last of the castle and of the inhabitants: "I felt that I was leaving part of myself behind, and that wherever I went afterwards I should feel the lack of it. . . .'Henceforth I live in a world of three dimensions with the aid of my five senses.'" (195)

Ryder's 'hopeless search' takes him to the far corners of the earth. But he has since learnt, as he writes in the page following, that apart from Brideshead with its "indwelling grace" (to echo M.L. D'Avanzo) and from Sebastian and Julia, he can never ever hope to find spiritual fulfillment. The rash assertion that he can live in a three-dimensional world with the aid of his five senses is characteristic of a man who suffers from metaphysical alienation which is far more crippling than other kinds of alienation. For ten long years, he drifts along producing second-rate paintings and writing equally sterile art criticism. Through repeated ironic references to modern art and architecture, Waugh emphasises the futility of existence in the "modern waste lands" (a phrase used by Ryder himself). The great houses represent only the unsubstantiality of modern man's "three dimensional" life: "there were countless substantial houses in the squares of Mayfair and Belgravia, alight and thronged, one or other of them, night after night. Foreigners returning on post from their own *waste lands* wrote home that here they seemed to catch a glimpse of the world they had believed lost for ever among the mud and wire." (207)

The three-dimensional world to which Ryder is glad to come back to, fails to provide him with what Wordsworth called in his great *Ode* the "gleam," the creative impulse which is a most essential pre-requisite for true art. In the terms of the novel such life-giving inspiration sprang from the tenets of the Church which were symbolised by Lady Marchmain and her art-nouveau chapel at Brideshead. A world which is lacking in metaphysical dimension can boast of sumptuous but tasteless buildings. The fate of such buildings would be that of the great London house of the Marchmain house which is in imminent danger of being sold and later transformed into vulgar, chromium-plated modern flats, such flats that vandals like Mrs. Beaver in *A Handful of Dust* delighted in putting up. A further link to the earlier novel is provided in Ryder's journey into the jungles of South America. Finding that the three-dimensional human civilization cannot give him the needed artistic impetus, Ryder like Tony Last travels a long way from England, only to become even more disillusioned. In the meantime, his uninspired study of secular architecture results in several books which an uncritical public acclaims as great works of erudition and research.

Ryder's lovely but inane wife Celia cannot give him "the authentic impulse to action," which comes only from genuine spiritual commitment. Long before, plain Cordelia spoke with characteristic perceptiveness when she described the kind of art that Ryder espoused as "bosh." His quest for theme and inspiration for his art in the remote Mexican and Central American jungles is the long journey of the human soul into the impenetrable darkness of obdurate doubt and ignorance. The Wordsworthian echoes mingled with those of Eliot's *Waste Land* become insistently resonant: "In quest of this fading light I went abroad, in the Augustan manner, laden with the apparatus of my trade, for two years' refreshment among alien styles. I did not go to Europe . . . by slow but not easy stages, I travelled through Mexico and Central America in a world which had all I needed." (261) This is the fate of the quester who deserting the Church goes into a mapless terrain full of physical and spiritual perils. His career as an architectural painter is told by Ryder in moving terms. His work, he confesses has nothing to recommend it except "my growing technical skill, enthusiasm for my subject and independence of popular notions." The financial slump of the period, serves to enhance his success which is itself a "symptom of the decline."

A growing awareness of his inadequacy both as a painter and as human being is a mark of the hero's growth. He senses a "presage of doom." What he has been after is only a "mirage" where people seek to drink when the "water holes are dry." Yet despite his lack of a "settled routine," his isolation and his long sojourn in a strange world, he remains still unchanged, "still a small part of myself pretending to be whole." Real discovery of himself is still to come. The irony contained in the review of Ryder's art by the most respected of all critics is deadly: "By focusing the frankly traditional battery of his elegance and erudition on the maelstrom of barbarism, Mr. Ryder has at last found himself." (263)

Through ritual repetitiousness, the quest-motif gains in value and complexity as a dominant symbol in the novel. Like countless other images and symbols in the language and action of the story, that of quest hints at a latent meaning of greater consequence than some of the other experienced events in the narrative. The different varieties of quest in the novel through the subtle variations create deep emotion in the reader's mind, even as the subtle use of light and shade give depth and urgency to Ryder's paintings executed in moments of "authentic impulse" of creativity. Within the narrative structure of the novel, one sort of quest is set off against another, of slightly less or more aesthetic intensity. Such juxtapositions, while providing the reader with a degree of aesthetic distancing from the experiences of the characters involved in the novel's action, also enrich its texture. Contrapuntalism which is one of Waugh's favourite narrative strategies deepens the complexity of the metaphor of quest. The quest that Ryder undertakes a few years before he goes in search of inspiration in the South American jungles, is contrastive in nature and contains within it one of the several thematic ambiguities.

Charles who has returned from Paris to London in 1926 for the General Strike learns from Julia that Lady Marchmain is very ill and does not have long to live. The latter has been sorry to have treated Charles rather nastily and secondly she has been anxious about Sebastian who is running to seed somewhere far away. Julia wonders whether Ryder will try and get him.

The motive behind Ryder's ready acquiescence in Julia's request is obscure. Does such willingness to serve foreshadow a future romance? Or is it that Ryder is unable to break the charm that the family has exercised over him? Could it be that he wanted to pursue Sebastian who has his own shadow? Ryder's "quest" for Sebastian, in fact, serves the function of a symbol from which several meanings radiate, some of them mutually contradictory. Jeffrey Heath, for instance, argues that Ryder has seen the last of Sebastian in Morocco. It is just as well for Ryder for in one sense Sebastian with his creamy charm has done Ryder enough moral and aesthetic harm. But in quite another sense, Sebastian with his message of sacrificial love, draws his old companion to the end of the world. As Ryder wistfully ruminates in the first book of the novel, "to know and love one other human being is the root of all wisdom." This is the lesson that Sebastian has learnt as well. His friendship for the parasitic young German Kurt seems a sort of purgatorial penance that Sebastian has to perform. Sebastian knows that Kurt is a shady character and yet he himself has come to depend on Kurt for emotional and spiritual fulfilment. Waugh makes Sebastian indeed a saint, with his self-effacement and his struggle against drinking. Like his mother who now represents the Lady of Seven Dolours, Sebastian himself is on his way to his beatification. The barefooted brother of the monastery where Sebastian eventually becomes a door porter, is convinced of his holiness, as Cordelia is assured that her brother has a unique sort of vocation. The symbolic function of Sebastian's teddy bear named Aloysius now strikes us with forceful clarity. Like St. Aloysius Gonzaga of the twelfth century who is the patron saint of young male students, Sebastian the aristocrat has given up his former wealth and attachments and has gone to North Africa (the home of St. Augustine) there to live a life of austerity until his last days. Waugh who, like Graham Greene, does not trouble about maintaining orthodoxy, makes Sebastian a complex hagiographical figure at the end. Ryder's journey to North Africa in search of Sebastian foreshadows his own glimpse of the transcendental love of God, after ten long wasteful years as a secular artist. To attain salvation Ryder has to follow Sebastian's example. Ryder has still to learn that self-sacrifice precedes self-enlightenment.

It is one of the aesthetic requirements of the novel that Ryder's quest in the dreamy wasteland for long years should be paralleled by those of Julia. There are several surface similarities between Ryder and Julia: both of them rebel against the values that Lady Marchmain stands for; their marriages have been failures and upto a certain point they share the same existential situation. Their interdependence and their later parting underscore the deep theological implications of the novel. Symbolically, Ryder's sexual, albeit adulterous union with Julia (who is unhappily married to Rex Mottram) is his first essential step towards his redemption, for it is through her repentance and conversion to the old faith that Charles himself knows the meaning of the greater love of God. She is the last crucial step in Ryder's spiritual awareness. By giving up the one thing that she loves most, namely Charles, Julia redeems herself and her sacrifice has tremendous consequences for Ryder.

The futility of Julia's quest for marital and material fulfilment is brilliantly summarised in the grotesque image of the tortoise shell, Rex's gift to Julia during their courtship: "a small tortoise with Julia's initials set in diamonds in the living shell, and his slightly obscene object, now slipping impotently on the polished boards, now striding across the cardtable, now lumbering over a rug, now withdrawn at a touch, now stretching its neck and swaying its withered, antediluvian head." (190) With its suggestion of triviality ("catch the attention when larger matters are at stake") and obscene slitheriness, the object serves as a metaphor for the spiritual and moral impotence of men like Rex Mottram. Years later, Julia in fact equates Rex with an undeveloped organism low in the scale of human evolution: "He simply wasn't all there. He wasn't a complete human being at all. He was a tiny bit of one, unnaturally developed; something in a bottle, an organ kept alive in a laboratory. . . . A tiny bit of a man pretending he was the whole." (222-23)

In her 'search' for a husband and light-flung life, Julia Flyte recalls the Bright Young Things of the earlier novels. Devoid of her mother's religious scruples and her sense of the 'fourth dimension' Julia likes to be drawn into the vortex of secularity. "Not for her the cruel, delicate luxury of choice, the indolent, cat-and-mouse pastimes of the hearth-rug. No Penelope she; she must hunt in the forest." (210) To the protestations of Lady Marchmain and her brother Bridey about the unsuitability of the marriage on the grounds that Rex has been divorced once before and that he is not really keen on becoming a Catholic, Julia replies that it is too late; she has been his mistress for some time. So the wedding takes place in an obscure Protestant Church, with very few attending—another of Lady Marchmain's cross! But unlike the earlier "heroines," Julia has an enviable capacity for growth. The obscure image of the kingfisher associated with Julia may hint at the heroine's nostalgia for her lost spiritual home: one of the traditions has it that the kingfisher, also called the blue bird may be seen flying along the river bank looking for Noah's ark or for some of its remains. When Noah sent the blue bird to take wing and see if the earth was invisible, the bird flew high into the ether until her plumage became a brilliant azure. Later when she was scorched by the sun, she came down to bathe in the water. In the process however she forgot her mission but when she remembered the Ark was gone.[27] Waugh makes a consistent use of the image of the Ark signifying the true spiritual home in contrast to the vulgar luxury liner later in the novel.

With all their weaknesses, Ryder and Julia, like Sebastian earlier, are potential recruits for redemption. At the end of Book Two Ryder thinks of Cordelia's argument that "if you have a vocation, you can't get away from it" as mere "convent chatter." He has just finished painting the front of the Marchmain House in London and in a glow of satisfaction calls himself a "Man of the Renaissance" of the Browningesque type. But the passage is of course ironic. In his contempt for religion, Ryder resembles the Godless man of Browning's Renaissance, who had "spurned the friars, with their dusty tomes and their sunken eyes and their crabbed hairsplitting man." A return to Brideshead as Julia's lover in the not too distant future is going to change all this. In the place of the sneering, the cynical man is going to be a more mellow and philosophical individual transformed by faith.

Brideshead Revisited may be described as an optimistic Bildungsroman. Whereas the earlier novels were parodies of the Germanic fictional genre, *Brideshead* traces the growth of the hero from innocence through a long period of agnosticism to his final maturation which is expressed in terms of his conversion and of his submission to the will of God. The spiritual nature of the hero's quest can be fully appreciated if we compare it with the denied quest of the earlier heroes. Tony Last in *A Handful of Dust* moves from one enveloping kind of shadows into the far worse and denser opacity with no gleam of hope. Ryder, Julia, Sebastian and Lord Marchmain, on the other hand are, to use the phrase of G.K. Chesterton which is the title of third book of *Brideshead*, twitched back to God's love. In Chesterton's story The Queer Feet, God catches the sinners he loves with an unseen hook and an unseen line, which is long enough to let them wander to the end of the world and still to bring them back with "a twitch upon thc thrcad."

In mythico-religious terms, the crisis of the characters in *Brideshead* – Ryder, Julia, Lord Marchmain and Sebastian – is a crisis of self-definition and of perception. But the novel deals principally with Ryder, the narrator, who strives to achieve a validating contact beyond the self. His glittering success as a secular artist cannot free him from his subjective consciousness. It is through an epiphany that he experiences a sudden realisation of truth which ultimately sets him free. Such a moment of realisation is the moment of total surrender to God's will. The vision of the transcendent absolute in a moment of grace clarifies Ryder's outlook of the objective world not only as a person but as an artist and Ryder and Julia do not move any more in unknown worlds but thanks to the newly-acquired unifying idea of God are made aware of an organising and meaning-giving principle of the universe of which they are potent parts. From now on, it is going to be, to adapt Nathan Scott, "life together" as opposed to "life fractured and broken into isolateness, and solitude and loneliness."[28] The revelation of something 'wholly other' utterly transforms and enriches the lives of Ryder and Julia.

Such a profoundly religious theme as the transmutation of the whole individual being can only be expressed by means of what is called in theological epistemology, the 'principle of analogy' which acknowledges at once "the inadequacy and the inevitability of human language." This explains Waugh's use of a language highly charged with imagery and symbolism, in the novel as a whole and in particular the final part of the story. The artist Waugh has successfully endeavoured to render the Catholic themes in compelling imagery within the limits of the novelistic medium.

After "ten dead years" as a highly successful but in his own estimate, a shoddy architectural painter, Ryder goes in search of fresh artistic stimulus in Mexico. Now on his way back, he boards the luxury liner in New York where his wife Celia has been waiting to join him. The parodic function of the liner is indicated by the chief purser's invitation to Celia Ryder to "come on an expedition into the cold storage with me tomorrow" and see "whole Noah's Ark of such objects." An earlier reference to the Biblical Ark in the intriguing kingfisher image applied to Julia is worked out fully here. The vulgar liner is what Nicholas Kostis calls, "an isolated microcosm of human vanity."[29] In contrast to Noah's Ark which sheltered God's Elect from the deluge, the modern ship stands for the falseness and sterility of the upper class whose chief representative is Celia. Beautiful but shallow, Celia is a contrast to her husband who is genuine and has little patience with sham and appearances. Whereas Noah stored all things living, the sole animal aboard, the latter- day ark is a "life-size effigy of a swan moulded in ice and filled with caviar" at the party given by Celia, the accomplished modern hostess. There is nothing to distinguish between the aristocratic or partly aristocratic guests who "put out their cigarettes in the little pool ice water which now surrounded the swan" and Hooper's men in the epilogue who throw cigarette butts in the florid fountain in Brideshead. The wastelanders on board the liner are unaware of their sinful condition in stark contrast to the men and animals in Noah's Ark which were kept free from the stain of sin.

Julia's presence in the ship gives another dimension to the Ark imagery. In the violent three-day storm which hits the false and fragile liner, Julia and Ryder alone are able to maintain stability and health while nearly all other passengers are knocked all of a heap. Celia is the most ill of them all. As in the Old Testament myth only those on the Ark were preserved from death, now Julia and Ryder alone are preserved from harm. The storm itself is a symbol of purgation. Julia and Ryder who are soon to be lovers are purged of their old attachment and are to enter into an almost mystical union. Like her mother Lady Marchmain, Julia is a twitch upon the thread to win back Ryder to God: "It was as though a deed of conveyance of her narrow loins had been drawn and sealed. I was making my first entry as the freeholder of a property I would enjoy and develop at leisure." (297) The storm has the same Cathartic effect on Julia as it had on old Lear in Shakespeare's tragedy. It awakens in her a sense of the Last Four Things that her old catechism had taught her.

Julia grows in staure in proportion as she becomes aware of her sinfulness. In her wanderings in fields of nothingness, she resembles Ryder. But unlike Ryder, she as a cradle Catholic, cannot still the stirrings of conscience. After their meeting on the liner, Ryder and Julia live together for two years at Brideshead, planning to get married once they have obtained their respective divorces. She is struck with a traumatic sense of guilt, when suddenly Lord Brideshead, the grotesque matchbox collector who is the head of the family, announces his proposed wedding to the middle-aged Mrs. Muspratt but says rather rectitudinously that he is unable to bring her home on account of Julia and Ryder living in sin. Julia's hysterical outburst is directed less at Bridey's insensitivity than at her state of sin. Beside herself, she berates in anguished sobs and broken sentences for 'living in sin.' Her long monologue, somewhat in the stream-of-consciousness manner, carries within it a flood of memories of the past – the devotion to the Sacred Heart in her youth, her mother's Christ-like sufferings on her behalf. She is sick to death at her present worthless state: "No way back; the gates barred; all the saints and angels posted along the walls." (329)

In the strict theological terms of the novel, a sense of sin is an essential concomitant to an honest self-awareness. Julia's condition is of one who feels 'the past and future pressing so hard on either side that there is no room for the present at all.' From Ryder's psychological point of view, it is a pre-conditioning from childhood. Her violent outburst enables her to recover her equanimity momentarily but so haunting is her sense of guilt that a little later when the lovers are together in the moonlight in front of the fountain she is enraged at Charles's attempt at drollery and strikes him across the face with a switch. There is obvious symbolism in her throwing the switch into the water "where it floated white and black in the moonlight." Water has been one of the recurring symbols of purification throughout the novel. Her present gesture is one more feeble attempt on her part to cast aside the Church's teachings through ritual and liturgy.

Julia's references to herself and Sebastian as mere forerunners are meant to prepare the reader for Ryder's abandonment by her, before long. All of Ryder's attachments have been deceptive and they have inevitably to yield to something substantial and meaningful. In tones strongly reminiscent of T.S. Eliot, he muses: "perhaps all our loves are merely hints and symbols; vagabond-language sprawled on gateposts and paving-stones along the weary road that others have tramped before us." (345)

Ryder cannot remain untouched by Julia's experience of a gnawing sense of sin. The voice of Cordelia has added up to the sense of the mystery to things. Cordelia has been working with the ambulance and has just returned from North Africa after having seen Sebastian working as an under porter in a monastery. His homosexual companion has hanged himself in a German concentration camp. With characteristic assurance which has sprung from her purity of motives, Cordelia already thinks of Sebastian as a saint. Her description of Ryder's love for Julia as thwarted passion awakens in him a new awareness of the nature of things. The welling up of faith in Ryder is conveyed in one of the most striking images—that of the gathering avalanche outside the trapper's door in the arctic:

> And another image came to me, of an arctic hut and a trapper alone with his furs and oil lamp and log fire; everything dry and ship-shape and warm inside, and outside the last blizzard of winter raging and the snow piling up against the door, quite silently a great weight forming against the timber; the bolt straining in its socket; minute by minute the darkness outside the white heap sealing the door, until quite soon when the wind dropped and the sun came out on the ice slopes and the thaw set in a block would move, slide, and tumble, high above, gather weight, till the whole hillside seemed to be falling, and the little lighted place would open and splinter and disappear, rolling with the avalanche into the raving. (354)

The gathering avalanche outside the trapper's hut is the aesthetic correlate for the onset of faith in Ryder's life. Despite his long association with the Flyte family, Ryder has remained cynically aloof from their religion and shown nothing but contempt for it. But he can no longer ignore the haunting awareness of the transcendental forces peering through the cracks of his private universe. He has to take cognisance of the transempirical factor of human existence. Like the trapper who, secure and warm inside his hut, is struck with fear at the gathering avalanche, Ryder is growingly overwhelmed by the demands of faith which is building up within him. The only way that he can escape the blind alley of empirical positivism is to yield to the demands of the sacred. The image of the avalanche illustrates the Christian insistence that one must lose one's life in order to save it. Ryder will have to give up his temporal loves, if he hopes for lasting happiness. With its core of connotations, the metaphor of the avalanche describes not only the condition of Ryder but the whole sterile and unoriented post-war generation to whom Waugh was writing.

Ryder's gravitation towards faith, strikingly suggested by the imagery of the avalanche, marks a definite stage of his spiritual education and a wholly new orientation. Armed with his new-found faith, the quester will be able to make the leap over the ontological divide and on reaching the higher realms across the metaphysical abyss he will attain the integral selfhood which has been eluding him so long. All that Ryder needs is the final twitch upon the thread which is provided by the eleventh-hour conversion of Lord Marchmain in the old familiar surroundings of Brideshead Castle. Lord Marchmain's arrival after years of adultery and apostasy on the continent at Brideshead is the symbolic return of the erring human soul to the well-spring of eternal happiness. His death-bed repentance constitutes the novel's climax and its focal point, for on it hinges the salvation of two of the central characters – Ryder and Julia.

Lord Marchmain, the chief among the novel's waifs, returns to Brideshead to pave the way of religious redemption of the others who are in dire need. He represents, in the words of Nicholas Kostis the "formal summation of all the negative struggles"[30] that Ryder has witnessed since his Oxford days. The return of this Byronic character from the flesh pots of Venice to "the realm of the spirit" is one of the pivotal moments in the novel and of its fictional necessity. His arrival and eventual death in his old home in a state of grace synthesise all the loose thematic strands into a meaningful whole. What makes Lord Marchmain's death one of the most dramatic scenes in all literature is the old man's eventual perception of the true nature of things. His story is the story of what Jeffrey Heath calls one of Waugh's successful maturations.[31] The final moments of Hubert Duggan and Oscar Wilde are two of the probable models for the fictional scene. Lord Marchmain's death parallels those of Duggan and Wilde in several points, especially in their weak nod showing their assent to faith and rehabilitation.

Lord Marchmain's altered figure gives everybody a pang of pity. No longer the upright and stately figure they had known, he is now bent with age and sickness, already slightly symbolic that he is accepting his creatureliness. He yet retains his theatricality and love of panache. Accompanied by his Italian mistress, Cara whom he teasingly calls *Carissima* (emphasising her capacity for true love), Lord Marchmain comes to Brideshead Castle. He wishes to lie down in the "Queen's bed" in the garish Chinese drawing room. Like Lear, he asks his daughter Cordelia to minister to him in words heavy with Biblical overtones: "Cordelia, will you watch for an hour in this Gethsemane?" (364) His unwillingness to die is less on account of his strong will than of his inability to face the eternal "darkness." His obvious preference for Julia and Ryder to Bridey and his bride Mrs. Muspratt is a symbolic gesture of making Charles his spiritual heir. The approach of Lord Marchmain's death brings hidden domestic tensions to the surface. Julia's increasing fretfulness is an index of her ever-growing conviction that the moment of her own conversion is inevitably imminent. As Ryder remarks "the sense that the fate of more souls than one was at issue" and recalling the image of the avalanche, "the snow was beginning to shift on high slopes." Ryder himself, despite his bravado, begins to realise that his defenses are becoming weak. Lord Marchmain's rambling thoughts are centred on the notion of the quests of the ancient and medieval knights: "Aunt Julia knew the tombs, cross-legged knight and doubleted earl, marquis like a roman senator, lime-stone, alabaster, and Italian marble; tapped the escutcheons with her ebony cane, made the casque ring over old Sir Roger." (378)

Like the parched lands in the kingfisher legend waiting for spiritual rain, Lord Marchmain is beginning to open his soul to the revitalising gifts of grace. Soon, as he says, "the fountain will be dry till the rain fills it, setting the fallen leaves afloat in the basin." Father Mackay, the cheerful Glasgow Irishman, undeterred by his earlier failure with Lord Marchmain is willing to try once more, on Julia's insistence. He is the chosen instrument of the Church and ultimately of God, to win back Lord Marchmain. Brushing aside the doctor's fear that his presence will do Lord Marchmain harm, Father Mackay goes in to give the old man absolution. The most dramatically moving moment of the novel fraught with immense consequences, has arrived. With everyone, including Ryder, kneeling around the bed the priest gives him Extreme-Unction. The one who prays hardest for the sign of God is Ryder: "I suddenly felt the longing for a sign, if only of courtesy, if only for the sake of the woman I loved, who knelt in front of me, praying, I knew, for a sign." (384)

Spiritual growth demands unconditional surrender and enormous self-sacrifice. The manner of death of Lord Marchmain has such an electrifying effect on Julia that she gives up once and for ever the one thing that seemed to matter to her, namely her love of Charles Ryder. By sacrificing her creature comfort, she preserves her spiritual instinct. She has been irrevocably twitched back to God and Church as her closing words to Ryder movingly reveal: "Probably I shall be bad again, punished again. But the worse I am, the more I need God. I can't shut myself out from his mercy. That is what it would mean: starting a life with you, without him." (386) The cathartic purification by means of grace is total, embodied in the avalanche image. Ryder's quest is now complete. Along with Julia, he is utterly powerless before the transcendental power of the Church and of God. He is stripped of temporal possessions – his family, his secular art, his love for Julia – but he has gained himself.

Two among several entries on the subject made in his *Diaries* – the one dated 18 July 1961 and the other dated 9 May 1962 – show how profoundly Waugh viewed the idea of Catholic renunciation:

> In the time of our grandparents avarice was rewarded with popular esteem and with power: luxury took many delicate forms: the world wore so fair a face that the warnings of the prophets sounded archaic and neurotic. . . . It took heroic Faith to renounce the world and the flesh and fear the Devil. Now all we need for the renunciation is elementary common-sense. But that virtue has grown scarce lately.[32]
>
> *Abjuring the realm*: To make an *interior* act of renunciation and to become a stranger in the world; to watch one's fellow-countrymen, as one used to watch foreigners, curious of their habits, patient of their absurdities, indifferent to their animosities—that is secret of happiness in this century of common man.[33]

Ryder's progress to the Church marks the triumphant end to his quest. Out of a long journey in darkness he comes into a blazing light of grace and faith which enables him to see the unity of being. What seemed once so fugitive and fragmentary is now part of a harmony in which all opposites are reconciled. "Homeless, childless, middle-aged and loveless" he may be, as he describes himself to Hooper, he has, however, regained a lost world, the City of God. He finds his true identity by becoming a member of the Church of Rome, the Universal Church, "the paradoxical *complexio oppositorum*"[34] in which nature and grace, faith and reason, tradition and progress, cross and glory, are brought into a "dynamic synthesis." It is through the strength that he derives from the sacraments of the Church which are the true channels of grace that Ryder is able to cope with the absurdity, the horror and the boredom of the phenomenal world.

What distinguishes Ryder's quest from mere adventure is the fact that he attains to full spiritual stature, able to make proper evaluation of the world in which he lives. He muses, echoing the words of the Preacher, "Vanity of vanities, all is vanity." One of the recurring liturgical phrases in the novel, "Quomodo sola sedet civitas" which Cordelia quotes to Ryder to make him understand the "mysterious Other" reality beyond the three-dimensional world epitomises the war-time condition of not only Brideshead but of the world in general. The full verse from the book of Lamentations is translated thus in the authorised version: "How doth the city sit solitary, that was full of people! how is she become as a widow! she that was great among nations and princess among the provinces, how is she become tributary!"

Brideshead which once ranked high among county families is now fallen in the hands of the soldiers of the war whose mindless spoilation has left it as desolate as the Great Jewish Temple in ruins. The world in general of which Brideshead in its present state is a macrocosm, is dominated by an inferior race of men devoid of all moral and ethical scruples.

In the engulfing chaos however shines the red flame of the sanctuary lamp in the little derelict *art-nouveau* chapel of Brideshead Castle. Coming at the very end, the symbol of this flickering flame carries within it many vectors of theological meaning moving within the novel. It stands for the vindication of faith in a chaotic world. Within the novel's aesthetics the flame serves the function of the objective correlative of the hero's self-transcendence which enables him at the end to rise above the illusions of the past and to circumvent despair.

NOTES

1. Sean O'Faolain, *p. 66.*
2. *The Critical Heritage,* p. 247.
3. *Ibid.*, p. 253.
4. *Ibid.*, p. 259.
5. *Ibid.*, pp. 270-71.
6. *Evelyn Waugh, A Reference Guide*, p. 70.
7. Evelyn Waugh, *Brideshead Revisited* (Penguin Books, 1987), pp. 9-10.
8. John L. Hutchins, *New York Times, Book Review,* 930, Dec. 1945.
9. *Evelyn Waugh, A Reference Guide*, p. 27.
10. Giovanni Cechim, "Echi Di Eliot Nei Romanzidi Evelyn Waugh" in *Evelyn Waugh, A Reference Guide*, p. 87.
11. Jeffrey Hart, "A Touch of Chrism," *Triumph*,1970.
12. Evelyn Waugh's warning on the inside of dust jacket quoted in *The Critical Heritage*, p. 36.
13. *Ibid.*
14. Jerome Meckier, "Evelyn Waugh," p. 102.
15. T.S. Eliot, "Tradition and Individual Talent," *Twentieth Century Literary Criticism; A Reader*, ed. David Lodge (London: Longman, 1972), p. 73.
16. David G. Brailow, "'My theme is memory'; The Narrative Structure of *Brideshead Revisited,*" *Evelyn Waugh Newsletter*, vol. 14, no. 3 (Winter 1980), p. 1.
17. William J. Cook, Jr., pp. 193-235.
18. A phrase taken from Krumm's discussion of T.S. Eliot in John McGill Krumm, "Theology and Literature; The Terms of the

Dialogue on the Modern Scene," *The Climate of Faith in Modern Literature*, ed. Nathan. A. Scott Jr. (New York: The Sudbury Press, 1964).

19. The relevant passages are: Paul's Epistle to the Ephesians 5:22 and John's Apocalypse 21:2, in the New Testament.
20. Rodney Delasanta and Mario L. D'Avanzo, "Truth and Beauty in *Brideshead Revisited*," *Modern Fiction Studies*, XI, no. 2 (Summer 1965), pp. 140-52.
21. Quoted in John Reley, "Two Waughs at War: Part 2 – A Reassessment of *Brideshead Revisited*," Evelyn Waugh Newsletter, vol. 12, no. 3 (Winter 1978), p. 4.
22. William J. Cook, Jr., p. 222.
23. Francis S. Heck, "Brideshead or Proust and Gide Revisited," *Evelyn Waugh Newsletter*, vol. 9, no. 2 (Autumn 1975), p. 6.
24. *The Picturesque Prison*, p. 169.
25. Rodney Delasanta and Mario L. D'Avanzo, pp. 140-52.
26. Quoted in Charles Hutton-Brown, "Sebastian S. Saint; The Hagiographical Sources of Sebastian Flyte," *Evelyn Waugh Newsletter* vol. 11, no. 3 (Winter 1977), p. 2.
27. Charles Swainson, *The Folklore and Provincial Names of British Birds* (London: Elliot Stock, 1886), p. 105.
28. Nathan Scott, "Faith and Art in a World Awry," Nathan Scott, ed., *The Climate of Faith in Modern Literature* (New York: The Sudbury Press, 1964), p. 14.
29. Nicholas Kostis, "*Brideshead Revisited:* The Saga of Water and Spirit," *Evelyn Waugh Newsletter,* vol. 19, no. 3 (Winter 1985), p. 3.
30. *Ibid*., p. 5.
31. *The Picturesqure Prison*, p. 181.
32. *The Diaries of Evelyn Waugh*, p. 784.
33. *Ibid.,* p. 787.
34. A phrase adapted from S.J. Avery Dulles, "The Essence of Catholicism: Protestant and Catholic Perspectives," *The Thomist,* vol. 48, no. 4, October 1984, p. 630.

In Quest of the Unique Self: *Helena*

Although Waugh had conceived the idea of writing *Helena* in 1935 it took him nearly fifteen years to have it ready for publication. He began the actual writing of it in 1945 but had to put it aside for one reason or another. He was distracted in his work firstly by the voluminous critical attention that his *Brideshead* had generated and secondly by the election result which proved a disaster to the conservative party. Christopher Sykes in his biography[1] notes that Waugh worked long at the novel, doing painstaking research on the life of St. Helena whose origins were lost in legend. The enormous labour is evident in the author's superb style marked by economy, wit and irony. His diary entry for 6 May 1915 points both to the seriousness with which he approached the saint's life and to his own high sense of calling as a writer:

> I have done enough reading to start tomorrow on *Helena.* All day there was expectation of VE Day and finally at 9 it was announced for tomorrow. . . . It is pleasant to end the war in plain clothes, writing. I remember at the start of it all writing to Frank Pakenham that its value for us would be to show us finally, that we were not men of action. I took longer than him to learn it. I regard the greatest danger I went through that of becoming one of Churchill's young men, of getting a medal and standing for Parliament; if things had gone, as then seemed right, in the first two years, that is what I should be now. I thank God to find myself still a writer and at work on something as 'uncontemporary' as I am.[2]

In working on the 'uncontemporary' subject of St. Helena Waugh in fact finally resolved the antithesis between "the mystical [and] the romantic habit of mind" that he had described long ago in his *Rossetti* (1928).[3] Like his doughty heroine who went in quest of the True Cross in her eighties, Waugh had realised rather late in life he is not a man of action and that he had the unique vocation of a writer. This theme that salvation arises from an individual's acceptance of the particular task that God in his merciful providence calls him to fulfil is prominent in *Helena* and in the war-trilogy later.

In his essay entitled "St. Helena Empress' which he wrote in 1952 Waugh expatiated on this theme:

> It is said that great popularity in fiction and film is only attained by works into which readers and audience can transpose themselves and be vicariously endangered, loved and applauded. This kind of reverie is not meditation. . . . There are evident dangers in identifying ourselves with Saint Francis or Saint John of the Cross. We can invoke the help of the saints and study the workings of God in them, but if we delude ourselves that we are walking in their shoes, seeing through their eyes and thinking with their minds, we lose sight of the one certain course of our salvation. There is only one saint that Bridget Hogan can actually become, Saint Bridget Hogan, and the saint that she *must* become, here or in the fires of purgatory, if she is to enter heaven she cannot slip through in fancy-dress, made up as Joan of Arc.[4]

Described by Waugh in the Preface as a legend, *Helena* is the author's only historical novel. But it is not only a historical reconstruction but is at the same time a literary metaphor for the confusion of the political and moral issues of his own times. Waugh's aim in writing the book is quite overt. It is his most explicitly apologetic work of Catholic fiction. As in *Brideshead Revisited* and the war-trilogy, the faith of his adoption provided him in *Helena* a most functionally "useful symbolism of order and goodness as against the besieging forces of chaos and the irrational."[5]

Ever since its publication *Helena* remained Waugh's favourite for as he maintained it was his best written book and had at its core a subject very dear to him, namely Catholicism. But it was precisely the doctrinaire nature of the novel that many reviewers found distasteful. Critics fault the book with a lack of firmness of touch that one associates with Waugh. His humour and satire in places become diffuse and overly obvious. Moreover, Waugh uses his novel as a vehicle for moral instruction.

Frederick J. Stopp is one of the few critics who sees the novel as being successful in conveying in an aesthetically satisfying way the intersection of the timeless on time. The book shows an intimate fusion of the historical and the personal in a unique act in time and the no less intimate consonance of the supernatural and the natural which made this act a miraculous and saintly one.[6] *Helena* articulates through subtle and complex means some of Waugh's familiar leit-motifs: Vulgar love of distortion of sacred truths and "abuse of right properties of things, in this case,

Christian doctrine itself."[7] Rome of Helena's day had to contend with a multitude of schisms and rival religious factions as England in Waugh's day. With all its strong fortifications, Rome was still vulnerable. Waugh endows Helena with a true insight into the nature of things. She fears that brutal and barbaric forces are bound to break open the walls of the Holy City of Rome.

It is easy to see why Waugh prized *Helena* above his other books and why he was disappointed with the hostile reaction that it met with on its publication. Waugh believed that the blunt message of St. Helena embodied in the novel that it was a matter of plain historical fact that God became man and died on the cross at a particular geographical place was relevant to all times, and especially urgently so in the times in which we lived. One of his concerns as a novelist was to defend the good against corruption and evil, the beautiful against the ugly and the unholy. The views of Lactantius the tutor to Crispus Helena's grandson a Christian echo Waugh's own:

> It needs a special quality to be a martyr—just as it needs a special quality to be a writer. Mine is the humbler role, but one must not think it quite valueless. One might combine two proverbs and say: 'Art is long and will prevail.' You see it is equally possible to give the right form to the wrong thing, and the wrong form to the right thing. Suppose that in years to come, when the Church's troubles seem to be over, there should come an apostate of my own trade, a false historian, with the mind of Cicero or Tacitus and the soul of an animal, and he nodded towards the gibbon who fretted his golden chain and chattered for fruit. A man like that might make it his business to write down the martyrs and excuse the persecutors. He might be refuted again and again but what he wrote would remain in people's minds when the refutations were quite forgotten. That is what style does—it has the Egyptian secret of the embalmers. It is not to be despised.[8]

Helena conceived her life's mission as one of clearing the mists of futile speculation surrounding the Christian doctrine and impeding people's beliefs.

Waugh's role as a humble man of letters was to tell the life of a woman who is known for her one supreme and constitutive act, namely the "invention" of the True Cross, "a solid chunk of wood" for people to knock their "silly heads" against. All the religious speculations of Arius, Donatus and the rest of them were wide of the mark. Her whole early life had been a preparation and prefiguration of this constitutive act of her life which was to sustain the faith of the people for ages to come.

An anagogic interpretation of the novel yields a fresh dimension to the discovery of the True Cross which is the core of the novel. The anagogical level of interpretation in Dante's four-fold method has to do with the divine life. Helena has shown right from her childhood a questing, questioning mind. At the outset of the novel, Helena, the young daughter of Old King Coel, tells her eunuch tutor Marcias (who is later to become a well-known gnostic) that she wants to find the real Troy. Since her father traces his descent far back to Troy, young Helena feels bound to go in quest of that city which according to her tutor exists only in poetry. With what Marcias has called her "masculine mind" she stubbornly insists on marrying Constantius who has promised to take her to the City of Troy: "I must go with Constantius. After all, papa, we Trojans are always in exile, aren't we-poor banished children of Teucer?" (31) Throughout the book, she is seen inquiring. When she becomes a baptised Christian very late in life, she subjects practically everybody to her persistent interrogation. But it is no longer about the City of Man, but that of God. Her one obsession in her old age is the whereabouts of the Cross on which the Saviour hung. When asked, Pope Sylvester can only reply that no one has even asked that question before.

Her entire life seems patterned by Providence. Married to Constantius when still young, she is abandoned by him when he rises to imperial power. She bears him a son, Constantine, who is later to become the first Christian Emperor of the Roman world. She herself becomes a Christian and in her old age sets out on a long and arduous journey in quest of the True Cross to the Middle East. Helena is one of Waugh's most informed questers in the sense that she is ready to heed the promptings of grace which pulls her at the end towards the Divine Life. Despite repeated discouragements from people including those in religious life, she persists in the mission of her life, fully conscious that she is moving towards blessedness.

Although endowed with "an innate and unshakable realism,"[9] to echo Stopp, Helena conforms to what she clearly knows is the Divine will. Hers is not the spurious mysticism of the Gnostics or the raving pietism of non-conformists who in their egotistic individualism mistake appearance for reality. Plain, rugged common sense characterises her entire life. Her natural honesty has made her fearless even in the august company of elders, as her behaviour as a young bride at Ratisbon shows:

> The religious, too, confounded her. In her own country the Gods had been honoured in their seasons; Helena had prayed, year by year, devoutly and at ease at the altars of her household and her

> people, had greeted the returning Spring with sacrifices, had sought to placate the powers of death, had honoured the sun and the earth and the fertile seed. But the religious ladies of Ratisbon spoke of secret meetings, passwords, initiations, trances, and extraordinary sensations, of Asiatics who floated about the room in half-darkness, of enigmatic voices, of standing stark naked in a pit while a bull bled to death on the lattice above them. (43)

She betrays the same impatience, when in her eighties and in search of the True Cross, she comes across extravagant stories of the cross. She dismisses as 'bosh' the story of Lady Maxmilla with her clothes bursting into flame while sitting on the tree that King Solomon had reputedly cut for use in the temple. But what is extraordinary is that plain-speaking women like Helena in this legend and Cordelia in *Brideshead Revisited* are gifted with an acute sense to distinguish the power of nature from that of Grace. With her supernatural insight and immensely practical common sense she stands in complete contrast to her husband, her son and in general to all the men of secular politics. She is quick to detect the weakness of her son, now Emperor: "I know I am human. In fact I often feel that I am the only real human being in the whole of creation. And that's not pleasant at all." (122) Anagogically speaking, Helena who is constantly pulled Grace-ward, is in contact with the mystery of eternal life. She is terrified of the future in which a whole world would be possessed of Power without Grace. Constantine, yet an unbaptised Christian, can never ever hope to retain his power over his Empire without the sanctifying grace of baptism which alone can wash away all the sins of his life. There is little to differentiate Constantine from his father who likewise is ecstatic about secular power and splendour. To the young pagan bride Constantius describes the wonders of the Imperial city when he returns from Aurelian's triumph. Lack of good taste is in evidence: "I felt sometimes they treated us as if we were part of the wild animals from the procession but they gave us some staggering dinners. Everything was got up to look like something else, partridges made of sugar, peaches of mincemeat; you couldn't tell what you were eating." (55) Constantine's Labarum, that sumptuous product of the jeweller's art epitomises, in Stopp's words, "that falsification of the past in the spirit of myth which is the mark of pseudo-religions."[10] In its secular vulgarity, it is the exact antithesis of the True Cross of which Helena goes in quest.

Waugh's St. Helena essay provides us with an invaluable gloss on the nature of Helena's quest by connecting her with Mary Queen of Scots whose motto was said to be: "En ma fin est mon commencement–In my end is my beginning." This motto incidentally is the leitmotif of T.S.

Eliot's "East Coker," the second of his *Four Quartets.* Helena's final journey ("my end") gave not only her fame but gave Christendom its much-needed spiritual impetus. In a world which was becoming spiritually disoriented and moving further and further away from Christ, the true Centre, Helena while accepting a state of life full of dangers to the soul in which many have foundered, yet remains fixed in her purpose. At the anagogic level, Helena's quest is the soul's relation to the destiny. Helena's search for the baulks of old, worn-out timber is determined by her moral vision which aids her in making her major option and in her ultimate participation in God's redemptive mercy.

But struggle for redemption entails a painful and individualistic journey. In undertaking a journey to the East, not unmindful of all the perils of the way, Helena is making a metaphorical exit from the City of Man which to her was embodied in the Rome of her husband Constantius: "Rome, where all the treasure of the world flowed and was squandered, has despoiled Constantius . . . that large shadow of him which Helena had glimpsed, pursued, briefly enjoyed, was lost for ever. He was a man unschooled in courtesy; no inherited veil of kindliness hid his small, cold soul. Helena saw all this in the first days of his return and accepted it." (54) "In stark contrast to her former tutor Marcias whose pursuit of the City of Troy has led him to the false doctrine of Gnosticism, Helena gives up her romantic dream of her youth and goes steadfastly to the one, true City of God. Charles Ryder in *Brideshead Revisited* had similarly to give up the alluring charms of the City of Man magnificently epitomised by the Brideshead House.

In the face of the material and quantitative values of her age, of secularization and of demythologization of the Christian events, Helena is unshakable in her resolve that Good is "just waiting for one of us to go and find it [the Cross]—just at this moment when it is most needed." (128) The implicit objective of her quest, like that of the Grail, is to reaffirm the spiritual values of life for which the Saviour died on the "baulks of timber" and of which her times were in most dire need. A later age might regard Helena's "invention" as mere relic, nothing more than aid to devotion, but in an age such as hers when Christianity was precariously vulnerable to the forces of barbarity and disorder outside the City walls, it seemed to Helena that she was God's chosen instrument to find the piece of wood which could give direction and significance to people's lives. In a spiritual quest, the moment of realization is the moment of total surrender to God's will. When her task is done, Helena is justifiably proud that she has heeded God's call: "No one who watched that day, while the Empress calmly divided her treasure, could have discerned her joy. Her work was finished. She had done what only the saints succeed in doing; what indeed constitutes their patent of sanctity. She had completely conformed to the will of God." (156)

Helena's spiritual quest deals with God and what he represents for man, unlike the secular trips of the early Waugh characters (for example *Vile Bodies*) who undertake a journey from unclarified motives and for dubious rewards. The heroine's long journey to the East becomes a potent metaphor for self-actualization which is the predominant aspect of the spiritual quest. Helena's supreme moment is at once the recovery of the muddy wood from total extinction and of the discovery of her true self. What her son the great Emperor of the Roman world only dimly perceived when with the sign of the Cross he miraculously won the action at Milvian Bridge, Helena now sees with absolute clarity. The Cross has the power to transform one's life. Neither the wisdom of Longinus, nor the physical prowess of the Roman sapper-paragons of her adolescence would have sufficed her. Unless illuminated by the Christian Cross secular wisdom and action cannot prevail against the onslaughts of barbarism. There can be no self-discovery without a loss of the illusions of youth: "Longinus had become invested in her mind with the legends of her race, identified with those white-robed men of the sickle and the mistletoe whose garbled lore was still whispered in the kitchen quarters." (21) But as Stopp remarks, these two "deities of her adolescence" are the forerunners[11] of the wisdom and strength of the godhead whose incarnation in Christ marks the summation in human history.

Waugh's own growing sense of humanity is evident in his treatment of Helena's quest through which she achieves selfhood. Her latent potentialities for hyper-personal social unity with her fellowmen are fully realised. She is gifted by nature with easy affability and a capacity for homely intimacy with men and women of varying social ranks. Constantius has nicknamed her 'stabularia, the ostler' for he finds her with a bit in her mouth and is on homely intimacy with the men in the stables. Though reputedly the daughter of a British King, she mixes freely with people far inferior to her in birth. To such a one, the meaning of the Incarnation in which the tendency towards finality is elevated to the supernatural order does not present an insuperable problem in cognition. Her anagogic vision (and Waugh's) must be embodied in the concrete world of experience. To her synthetic mode of thinking, there can be no separation of spirit and matter. Spiritual concerns can and must be inextricably related to the teeming physical world of men, of anguish and failure. Where pious and pietistic men like Pope Sylvester fail to see, Helena sees the Cross, a mere piece of junk cast away by the early Jews, as a symbol of the union of the flesh and spirit. Since grace of which the Cross is an ever-contemporary symbol, operates through the material world, any attempt to separate the natural and supernatural orders would have seemed unthinkable to Helena. It is a religious necessity that Grace has to be coupled with human needs both physical and spiritual. This theme that human needs cannot be divorced from one's quest for spiritual perfection is a shaping factor of the structure of the war-trilogy. Recognition of the supernatural implies an acceptance of the material forces and existences of the universe in which the mystery of the supernatural godhead is grounded.

After her baptism, performed privately, Helena emerges a new woman, one seed in a vast germination. The strong, questing will has found its object; the exile her home. Already past seventy, Empress Helena is a transformed human being. In the years prior to becoming a Christian, Helena has always cherished her privacy, whether at Nish or Dalmatia or Trives. But once she is a Christian, she is obliged to take the whole humanity as one vast family of which she is a potent member, God's vehicle.

People who thought that all that remained for the Dowager Empress was to nestle down in her cradle of universal respect and prepare her soul for the day when she would find herself wafted to heaven and royally received, were mistaken. She gladly agrees to go to Rome when Constantine invites her to his jubilee celebrations. There forfeiting her solitude she mingles with the teeming, throbbing multitude. Coming out of her curtained litter, she tirelessly follows the tourists' round and daily sees more men and women than ever before in the total sum of her lifetime. The unbeautiful City, gross and haphazard, is always over-crowded and especially now for the Emperor's jubilee, there is added a huge press of officials and sight seers, hucksters and crooks, paying anything for a roof, sleeping every where, a motley crowd, grasping and pushing and peering every where, "Levantines, Berbers, blacks, amid the etiolated and stunted progeny of the slums." A few years earlier she would have shrunk from them and would have asked her guards to clear a little cloister for her to breathe in. But now she is a member of the whole crowded humanity for whom the Saviour died. Not for her the Horatian exclusiveness any more:

> There was no hate in her now and nothing round was quite profane. She could not dispense with her guard but she mitigated their roughness, and always her heart was beyond them, over their big shoulders, in the crowd. When she heard Mass at the Lateran basilica – as she often did in preference to her private chapel she went without ostentation and stood simply in the congregation. . . . The barrow-man grilling his garlic sausages in the gutter, the fuller behind his reeking public pots, the lawyer or the lawyer's clerk,

> might each and all be one with the Empress Dowager in the Mystical Body. And the abounding heathen might in any hour become one with them. There was no mob, only a vast multitude of souls, clothed in a vast variety of body, milling about in the Holy City, in the See of Peter. (92-93)

This is Waugh's own concept of the Christian community which is ungrudgingly inclusive of all sorts and conditions of men. Helena's eager kinship with the throngs is in emphatic contrast to her old ideas of social exclusivity and jealous sense of privacy. Christianity has established a new order to which she must conform.

It is one of the novel's ironies that even before she becomes a Christian, quite unconsciously but with her characteristic naivete, she expresses a Christian conception of the City. On their way to Ratisbon, soon after their wedding, Constantius is exhilarated at the sight of the Swabian wall, but all that stirs him only falls flat for Helena. To complacent Constantius the wall, mile upon mile, from snow to desert, a single great girdle provides a safe retreat from hostile barbarism; peace, decency, law and order within the savagery and bloody mumbo-jumbo outside. Helena, however, is doubtful. She wonders whether Rome will not ever go beyond the wall into the wild lands, beyond even the ocean whether they may be more and still more people. With her keen insight she provides a perception which is central to the orthodox Catholic faith. The idea that the present wall is a natural division in the human race seems to violate reason: "I didn't mean that. I meant couldn't the wall be at the limits of the world and all men, civilized and barbarian, have a share in the City?" (40)

The road "so smoothly metalled, so straight, so devious that led to Nish, to Rome and beyond" very soon palls. True happiness comes only when she enters the bustling world of human beings and confronts the world of corruption symbolized by Empress Fausta. Helena's readiness to settle in a single small room among the nuns of Mount Zion where she does her own housework and takes her turn in waiting at table is motivated by the same clear-sighted recognition of human worth. The violence and evil that Helena confronts in Constantine's Empire and the Eternal City, instead of deflecting her from her quest has a positive effect on her. Self-discovery in fact begins with spiritual struggle against the forces of brutality and evil. Distortions and violence in the physical world serve to deepen the heroine's moral perceptions.

It is one of the tenets of Waugh's faith that Grace uses the purely human, often times imperfect, as its medium. Helena sees the force of Lactantius's arguments about the credibility of the Christian faith but is yet unwilling to take the plunge, finding excuse in her advanced age. But to Lactantius, age can never be an impediment to the pursuit of an ideal, especially a Christian ideal. The verdant world of nature seems to him to offer hope not only to the young as Wordsworth asserted but to the old and the fragile:

> In the dawn, reflected Lactantius, to be old was very heaven; to have lived in a Hope which defied reason; which existed, rather, only in the reason and in the affections, quite unattached to common experience or calculation; to see that Hope take substantial and homely form near at hand and on all sides, as a fog, lifting, may suddenly reveal to a ship's company that, through no skill of theirs, they have silently drifted into safe anchorage; to catch a glimpse of simple unity in life that had seemed all vicissitude – this, thought Lactantius, was something to match the exuberance of Pentecost; something indeed in which Christmas, Easter and Pentecost had their royal celebration. (88)

Underlying Lactantius's optimistically exultant reflection on the nature of Christian faith is the basic Christian perspective in which the idea of God leads to a unified view of reality. By dying on the cross Christ elevated matter and mankind by transforming them to Himself. The novel closes on a similar note of hope. Helena who once thought that she was "too old to pass the point" eventually goes far beyond the point, surpassing all expectation, goes in search of the True Cross, the familiar piece of wood, yet a most sacred object, with a singleness of purpose and with indifference to all considerations of personal comfort and security. She leaves the world clattering about the hypostatic union and with the approval of the pious Pope Sylvester turns to the East for the solid chunk of wood.

Helena starts on her pilgrimage in the early autumn of the year 326 and like the Magi some three centuries ago reaches Aelia Capitolina in Palestine after a long and weary journey. On being told that the marble steps to the lavishly upholstered Government House, where she is to be lodged, were the staircase which Christ descended on his way to death, the aged empress kneels down there and then in her travelling cloak she painfully and prayerfully climbs the steps on her knees, ordering the whole suite to follow her example. Later she orders the sappers to crate the marble staircase to the Pope. She is grateful when the Holy Coat is presented to her but makes it plain that that is not what she really wants. She goes about her quest of the True Cross with determination, questioning everybody. But peoples, men of deep scholarship – the Jews, the Coptics – give her "precious stones of symbolism and pure meaning"[13] where she has expected the bread of plain objectivity. Briskly dismissing the phrases and analogies of these men of the academics, spiced with spurious logic, she turns to questions of human probability, of carpentry and the likely places where the Jews, who in their meticulous observance of their laws of cleanliness might have cleared away the baulks of timber and thrown them out of reach of Christ's disciples. All that remains for Helena is to search the hiding places round Calvary. Macarius, the "innocent Bishop" who accompanies the Empress to the site full of builders and people busy at the basilica that Helena has ordered is plainly sceptical of the enterprise. Helena, however, though physically exhausted, is certain of finding a hole in the vast site where is hidden the timber.

Everyone in Jerusalem remarks on Helena's vigour but she is in fact, weary. Winter in the damp convent of Mount Zion where the First Lady of the Roman world does the housework seems hard to cope with. She is so weak that she has not the strength to ride out with the procession to Bethlehem at Christmas. But by Twelfth Night she rallies and on the eve she sets out by litter along the five rough miles to the shrine of Nativity which is free of the pilgrim throngs. There an hour before dawn she is led to the stable-cave where in the packed congregation she finds an obscure place for herself. If Helena is to find the True Cross it can only be by direct supernatural aid, not by archaeological reasoning. When practically every one seems hopeless and helpless to her, it is to the manger that she goes, like the Magi of old. Her own acts of charity in the ordering of churches in the Holy Land seem to matter little to her: "It was like a masque of oriental magic, this utterance of a spell, this materialization from the clouds of domes and colonnades. Helena said the word, the complex machinery of imperial engineering was set into motion and she returned to help wash dishes in the convent scullery." (139)

Helena's "Second Spring" begun with her baptism is now in need of rejuvenescence if she is to succeed in her final quest. Without the interaction of the supernatural on the natural order of things, which is what Epiphany is all about, human efforts, however well-intentioned will eventually prove futile. Prayerful participation in the serene liturgical ritual of the feast of the Epiphany deepens Helena's sense of spiritual reality in the familiar physical world. The "epiphany" connotes a sudden revelation, a spiritual manifestation, something that the object of one's environment rising above themselves, and transfigured, can yield. To Helena as to the Magi, the figure of the human child is an epiphany of a transcendent absolute. James Joyce's use of "epiphany" in his *Ulysses* and *Stephen Hero* in a highly specialised sense, has won it enormous literary prestige. Like "objective correlative," "negative capability" and "inscape" the term epiphany has become a useful symbolist vehicle for writers. For Stephen

Dedalus, the whole naturalistic world with its tedious vulgarities is still a store-house of epiphanies capable of infinite expansion of meanings. But Waugh, who had no patience with Joyce's secularization of art, wishes to retain the implications of the term in its pristine theological purity. The assertion of the idea of Incarnation which is central to the Christian faith becomes the focal point in Helena. While the gnostics of the world are blinded by selfishness and intellecutalism, Helena in that mystical moment in the low vault of the chapel that she too like the magi, the patron saint of late-comers, has emerged from a kind of "outopia" or nameless realm and will vanish like them in the "sinking nursery fire-light among the picture books and the day's toys." For her as for them, the primordial discipline of the heaven is relaxed and a "new defiant light" blazes amid the "disconcerted stars." Her intensely moving prayer to the three kings proceeds from an unshakable confidence in the power of God whose redemptive mercy is wide and inclusive. There is room enough in her own prayer for her poor overloaded son Constantine, for the great as well as the lowly, including the souls of her "wild, blind ancestors, and for the sly foe Odysseus and the great Longinus." The "learned, the oblique and the delicate" are as much dear to God as the simple and the naive. Helena has reached the most crucial stage in her long and painful pilgrimage. The feast of the Epiphany has been an exploration of her soul in her relation to God and to the world. With the coming weeks of Lent comes the robust realization that she has exhausted all the natural means of finding of what she has set out to seek. This has been not only a quest for the lost timber but also a pilgrimage of self-discovery. In personal humility and a sense in the power of grace lie the discovery of the Cross. Although exempt by her age from all obligation of fasting, Helena undertakes to follow the austere Lenten regulations of the diocese of Macarius. Fasting seems to her a matter of practical expediency and despite the nun's pleading, she adopts a strict dietary regimen. By the beginning of Holy Week she is barely recognizable as the formidable woman who not long ago cross-examined the archaeologists. Helena's question about the exact spot of the True Cross can only be answered in a mode very different from what is natural, that of the dream. At the end of the strenuous office of the Good Friday, Helena withdraws in solitude with thoughts of the bereaved women long ago. Accepting a syrup of opium from one of the nuns, she lies down relaxed after an almost sleepless week.

From the point of view of craftmanship *Helena* has a highly wrought structure. Scenes and incidents which parallel and contrast each other carry the thematic resonance of the novel and contribute to its over-all design. Unity of theme is brilliantly achieved by means of stylistic integrity and a sense of symmetry. Ironic juxtaposition of episodes, an unfailing stylistic device of Waugh, serves to emphasise the novel's theme. The stable in the Church of Nativity where Helena is moved to pray eloquently to the Magi is undoubtedly meant to recall Helena's adolescence in the stable of Colchester. There is a similar structural significance in Helena's dream in which the Wandering Jew gives her the miraculous news of the True Cross. Helena who is an exile in quest of the Cross meets the Wandering Jew who is an eternal type of a homeless exile. That Waugh has been fascinated by the figure of the Wandering Jew is evident in the enquiries he makes of him in his letter to Robert Henriques, "the only religious Jew of my acquaintance"[13] and to Nancy Mitford.[14] There is a deepening sense of irony in making the Wandering Jew, who is under a curse, the only source of information about the sacred object of Helena's quest. This figure moving in timeless eternity but excluded from Grace is providentially instrumental in Helena's achievement.

The Jew who reviled the "Galilean" when the latter stumbled under the weight of the cross in front of his shop was told by Christ to "tarry till I come." Despite his years, with his smooth basalt skin and hair barely tinged with grey is a stocky and robust middle-aged man. There is a curious similarity in the conditions of Helena and the Jew. Still living within the exigencies of time, Helena however has "tarried" long enough to make her life's one true discovery. The Jew then gives a graphically amazing picture of the events of the day of the crucifixion. For a stiff price from Helena he shows her the place where the cistern in which the three crosses were thrown away lies buried. Without hesitation he takes the Empress to the western edge of the new platform and judging the distance carefully from the summit of Golgotha he comes to a spot, where digging in his heel, he suggests Helena might try to look for the lost treasure.

Not doubting for a moment that the revelation has divine origin, Helena presides over the daunting, historical undertaking. The work is done by the men, who doubt the wisdom of the excavation, not cheerfully but nevertheless with "Roman method and discipline." Helena has an ivory chair carried down and sits attended by a nun, hour after hour in the flare and smoke and dust, watching the men at work. She disdainfully dismisses suggestions that her dream may not be genuinely authentic and persists that one is entitled to expect miracles from God in matters of such momentous importance as the Cross. The discovery of the True Cross along with other fragments and the Nail towards the end, is meant to be, as Stopp observes, neither an attempt at conversion nor an explanation on the author's part but rather "a perception of the workings in human life of a kind of comic analogy never to be fully resolved in life."[15] Helena's pedestrian performance of the discovery of the Cross is played out against "gigantic" supernatural background, under the aspect of eternity. Unglamorous as it may seem in comparison with the daring deaths of other martyrs of the Church, Helena's discovery, done in humility and faith, has had a vital impact on the men of her times and of the generations that are to come.

On the literal level, Helena's quest for the True Cross is a search for the lost piece of wood which makes contact with the eschatological mystery of life. Just as Galahad's quest leads him to the mystic ecstasy which stems from his vision of the Holy Grail and as Dante's story of her achievement dramatizes the mystical marriage of the human soul with its Divine Maker. For the True Cross points beyond itself—to the meaning of deliverance of the human soul from the thraldom of corruption to its destined liberty of eternal glory. This universal truth with enormous transcendental implication is most effectively conveyed by the imagery of the horse and the rider which runs through the entire narrative surface. The horse theme is first stated in Chapter ("Court Memoir") of the novel. During the epic recital at King Coel's banquet at which is present Constantius who is soon to present his suit to Helena's father. Helena, an attractive adolescent, passionate about horse riding, indulges in an elaborate fantasy:

> Helena was playing horses, a game which began with her first pony; a breathless, wordless steeplechase across impassable superequine obstacles, splendidly leapt, and endless stretches of resilient sward. Helena had galloped thus in solitude hours without number, but of late years, as her womanhood broke bud, a keener excitement infused the game. Two played it now. There was the will of the rider that spoke down the length of the rein, from the gloved hand to the warm and tender tongue under the bit; articulate, coaxing, commanding, now barely sensible . . . now steel-hard and compelling. . . . And there was the will of the animal to shrink and start, to toss aside the restraint of bridle and saddle and the firm legs across her, to shake the confident equipoise, awake him to the intense life and the will to combat under him, . . . Then at the height of the play, in sweat and blood-flecked foam, came the sweet moment of surrender, the fusion, and the two were off together, single, full-stretch over the resounding earth, as they had raced in childhood with none but the wind to oppose them. (24-25)

Overtly erotic, the imagery of the horse and the rider has at its core a deep religious meaning central to the novel. Helena's surrender, analogous to that of the horse to Constantius is a precursor to the greater surrender to God's grace which is fraught with immense consequence for Helena as an individual and for the entire world. This young girl of high adolescent spirits is to be checked in her course first by Constantius who marries her and later by God himself. The symbol of the horse brilliantly conveys both the fusion of two natures – those of Helena and Constantius and of meek surrender to the will of God.

One of the ways in which Waugh achieves stylistic concision and clarity in his fiction is the use of refrain. The overpowering sense of God which subdues the intractable human will is pointed by Waugh's recurrent use of the horse imagery. Imaginative variations are played on the horse theme, sometimes explicit and sometimes wildly idiosyncratic. As a young woman Helena is a horse with a bit in her mouth. During his ride to Rome, Constantine is seen forging one of the nails that she has discovered along with the Cross, into the snaffle for his horse. In all this, the horse functions as a symbol of God's will and purpose in general. However it has a particular relevance in Helena's case. This young British girl with plenty of horse sense is going to be one of God's chief instruments in reinforcing His message to a world which is sadly vulnerable to the forces of barbarism and pagan seduction. But in the first place He has got to subdue her over-assertive will, as a rider tames his horse, before she can undertake the great mission of her life. The earlier erotic fusion between the two lovers – Helena and Constantius – prefigures the merging of the divine and human natures signified by the grotesque use that Constantine the Emperor finds for the holy nail. Jeffrey Heath's quotation in his notes to the chapters on *Helena* "Will is to grace as horse is to the rider"[16] succinctly epitomizes the idea of the human "hubris" being crushed by the power of God.

Counterpointed against the story of Helena's discovery of the True Cross is that of her celebrated namesake, Helen of Troy. In contrast to Aphrodite's call to Helen of pagan antiquity to "come" to the carved bed of Paris, which brings the long war and the consequent ruin of Troy, stands the mystical call of God, quiet and serene, to Helena the Empress Dowager. Helena's answer to that call was an act of heroic virtue. The horse imagery connects both the stories. Marcias's reference to the wooden leg of the great horse ironically undercuts the values that Helen of Troy stood for. For all the supposed divinity of her origin, Helen has become a byword for marital infidelity. Helena of Colchester, however, has been Providentially predestined to go not in quest of Troy, which is man's city but of the True Cross, the symbol of the eternal City of God.

The conclusion of *Helena*, than which there can scarcely be a better example of Waugh's metaphorical language, calls back the horse theme connected this time with hunting. Although Helena passes out of authentic history and the miracles that she is alleged to have performed in Cyprus on her way back to her son's new capital in Constantinople part of the growing Helena-myth, her enterprise of the discovery of the chunk of wood is something life-giving. By her one constitutive act, Helena has brought the true faith riven by the moral and philosophical confusions of her age back to its simple, unadorned foundations. With the quiet authority derived from God, Helena puts back the entire humanity onto the right path:

> Hounds are checked, hunting wild. A horn calls clear through the covert. Helena casts them back on the scent.
> Above all the babble of her age and ours, she makes one blunt assertion. And there alone lies Hope. (159)

Helena with its audacious apologetic tone has curious affinity with Waugh's *The Loved One* which he had published two years earlier. Regarded usually as a biting satire on the burial habits of the Californians, *The Loved One* has at its core the same mystical element as *Helena*. It is, as Desmond MacCarthy pointed out long ago, a "ruthless exposure of a silly optimistic trend in a modern civilization which takes for granted that the consolations of religion can be enjoyed without belief in them."[17] Both *Helena* and *The Loved One*, the one with the devotion of a practising Christian and the other with a surface flippancy which hides the author's true intent, explore the nature of existence. To Waugh Catholicism was the rock-bed of the fundamental truth of life, which claimed precedence for the supernatural over the rationalism of the modern age. Waugh's aim in the two novels, as in *Brideshead Revisited* was to establish theological truths rather than social or political ideologies. Anagogically speaking these three novels have for their theme the dynamic principle of grace and the relation of the human soul to God. Despite his cool and cynical realism, Dennis Barlow, the protagonist of *The Loved One* demonstrates that he is capable of growth and moral maturity. It is truly a tragedy insofar as the characters fail to recognise their creatureliness and the profound theological truth that man without God is less than man, a truth central to Waugh's faith as an artist and an individual.

NOTES

1. Christopher Sykes, *Evelyn Waugh* pp. 318-21.

2. *The Diaries of Evelyn Waugh*, p. 627.
3. Quoted in Jeffrey Heath, "Concluding *Helena,*" *EWN*, Autumn 1976.
4. *A Little Order.*
5. *The Critical Heritage*, p. 335.
6. *Ibid.*, p. 43.
7. *The Picturesque Prison*, p. 199.
8. Evelyn Waugh, *Helena* (UK: Penguin), p. 80.
9. Frederick J. Stopp, in *The Critical Heritage*, p. 327.
10. *Ibid.*, p. 330.
11. *Ibid.*, p. 331.
12. Christopher Derrick, "The Times," 1974, *The Critical Heritage*, p. 335.
13. Mark Amory, ed., *The Letters of Evelyn Waugh,* p. 334.
14. *Ibid.*, p. 221.
15. Frederick Stopp, p. 334.
16. *The Picturesque Prison*, p. 310n.
17. Quoted in *The Critical Heritage*, p. 41.

An Introduction to the War-Trilogy

In his dedication of *Officers and Gentlemen*, the second volume of the war-trilogy, to Major-General Sir Robert Laycock, who "every man in arms should wish to be," Waugh stated with some exaggeration that the novel was "pure fiction, that is to say of experience totally transformed." Two of his life-experiences provided Waugh with stimuli to his creative imagination, travel and war. Even as his travels in Abyssinia, the Artic and South America, arduously undertaken and which would have daunted men younger than himself, provided him with material for his journalism, travel books and fiction, his first-hand experience of the Second World War proved invaluable in his later career as a writer. The Second World War called forth two different kinds of response in the writer. Lesser writers whose war novels were immensely lucrative used their experience to write the popular genre of heroic adventure fiction. The more serious writers, on the other hand, like George Orwell and Evelyn Waugh were easily disenchanted with their war experiences. To them World War II seemed a grim conclusion in its time, confirming their fear accumulated through the decades preceding it. When the war began, Waugh believed that it would provide him with an opportunity, even if belated, to find his vocation as a man of action. But within four years of entering the army, he was deeply disheartened to find himself called upon to do dishonourable things. Where he had expected to find devotion to such just causes as honour and heroism, he only found treachery, cowardice and sheer incompetence. He recorded his disillusionment in his diary for 29 August 1943:

> I have got so bored with everything military that I can no longer remember the simplest details. I dislike the Army. I want to get to work again. I do not want any experience in life. I have quite enough bottled and carefully laid in the cellar, some still ripening, most ready for drinking, a little beginning to lose its body. I wrote to Frank [Pakenham] very early in the war to say that its chief use would be to cure artists of the illusion that they were men of action. It has worked its cure with me. I have succeeded, too, in dissociat-

> ing myself very largely with the rest of the world. I am not impatient of its manifest follies and don't want to influence opinions or events, or expose humbug or anything of that kind. I don't want to be of service to any one or anything. I simply want to do my work as an artist. (547-48)

Waugh's extraordinary love affair with the army like Ryder's in *Brideshead Revisited* had come to an abrupt end. However his early romantic idealism of war and enthusiasm for the military were reflected in the war novels he was to write later. The disillusion with the army that the hero of the trilogy parallels that of his creator's, although to the protagonist himself the ordeal was to be an initiation into authentic manhood. A process of disillusionment leads to a new awareness.

Based closely on the author's personal experiences in the war, there is a near-identity of the novelist with his hero, Guy but his well-developed irony enables Waugh to distance himself from the protagonist when he is out of sympathy with the latter's viewpoint. Jeffrey Heath, in fact, has argued that the voices of three distintct aspects of Waugh contribute to the war-trilogy's "curious harmonies."[1] There is the voice of Waugh's persona Guy Crouchback, the voice of the narrator, who sometimes pretends to share Guy's naivete and occasional undertones from the real-life Waugh. Since the trilogy was Waugh's attempt to do all he could with his own war experiences and observations, a brief summary of Waugh's career would help us more easily to follow the fortunes of the trilogy's hero. Waugh's acutenesss of observations of the ostentatious incompetence of the officers and of other trivialities recorded in the *Diaries* make delightful reading. Keeping diary on service was incidentally, a serious military offence.

Waugh joined the Royal Marines as a second lieutenant and after further training he was posted in July 1940, to Haverfordwost where he and his men embarked in a steamer to forestall any German invasion of Eire. The threat however fizzled out. In August 1940, Waugh became battalion intelligence officer. After assault training round Scapa Flow, he sailed to West Africa as part of the Free French, undertaken with General de Gaulle, the French leader, to seize the part of Dakar in French West Africa. The expedition was a fiasco. At his own request, on his return, he was transferred to Combined Operations, under Colonel Robert Laycock. In February 1941 Waugh sailed with No. 8 Commando from the Isle of Arran to the Middle East. In April he took part in a night raid on the German-held coastline of Libya, at Bardia. At the end of May he fought in the rearguard action that preceded the evacuation and loss of Crete. In July when the Commandos in the Middle East were disbanded, he was transferred back to the Marines and returned to England in a liner that went round the Cape. The years 1942 and 1943 were spent entirely in the United Kingdom. During the absence of Laycock who had left for North Africa, Waugh was expelled from Special Service Brigade. In December 1943, he went on a parachute course. In July 1944 he went with Major Randolph Churchill to join a British Military Mission to Tito's Partisans in Yugoslavia. After a recuperative jaunt in Italy following the crash of the aircraft in which he was travelling with Churchill, he returned to Yugoslavia in September. Waugh stayed in Croatia with the Mission until early December. He was then posted to Dubrovnik on the Dalmatian Coast, as liaison officer between British troops and the Yugoslav authorities. He was expelled from Dubrovink by Partisan pressure. In February 1945 he returned to Italy, where in March he had a private audience with the Pope about the Partisan's treatment of the Catholic Church in Yugoslavia. Later he returned to London. In May his application to return to Yugoslavia in a diplomatic capacity, as British Consul in Dubrovnik, was turned down. On 18 September he was demobilised. Waugh's 'Memorandum on LAYFORCE'[2] gives a full account of his experiences in the Commandos, including his part in the Battle of Crete.

Such huge and amorphous lump of real-life experience as Waugh's would have daunted a lesser writer. Right from the beginning of the trilogy, Waugh's sense of design, in which the aesthetic form and moral meaning are perfectly blended, is immediately apparent. In returning to his war experiences Waugh was returning to his old familiar themes of God's mercy and man's acknowledgement of His mastery. Through irony, comic grotesque and parody Waugh makes us see that he does not share the amorality of the characters in the trilogy. The three-part saga which told the story of the progressive realisation of an uncharacteristic Englishmen of aristocratic lineage that "no good comes from public causes, only private causes of the soul" was Waugh's most ambitious fictional enterprise yet in his career.[3]

The first volume *Men at Arms* appeared in 1952 with Waugh's announcement on the dust jacket of the novel that he hoped to complete the trilogy, each complete in itself, recounting the phases of the life of a civilian in the army. When however the second volume, *Officers and Gentlemen* appeared in 1955, Waugh seemed to have abandoned the idea of a trilogy. He thought that two volumes instead of three, would do the trick. *Unconditional Surrender* did not appear until six years later, with the admission from Waugh that he had realized all along that a third volume was needed. Finally in 1965, there appeared a "recension" under the title of *Sword of Honour*. In his preface Waugh admitted that he had been less than candid in assuming that each novel was to be regarded as a separate, independent work. The "product" was intended to be read as a single story.

The trilogy form is eminently suited to the theme of exploration of the hero's quest for self-definition. The three-volume novel, as Kathleen Tillotson has argued[4] is convenient for authors as it gives them a structural framework for their narratives which allows the novelists to impose order on a large body of material. Each of the novels deals with a separate aspect of war and each forms a distinctive experience. Yet the three books are linked by narrative continuity, recurrence of images and the reappearance of the characters. A structural parallelism is also noticed in the three novels; they begin in a light spirit in England and conclude with events abroad. At the conclusion of each instalment Guy suffers some kind of shock either of betrayal or of loyalty. Contrapuntalism and recurrence of themes in different keys characterise the trilogy's structure as a whole. Readers and critics of Waugh have regretted the cuts that Waugh made in the recension, intended as he put it "to remove repetitions and discrepancies" which were "tedious." But such cuts not only removed some of the hilariously enjoyable pieces such as the Prince Bonnie film, the Housey-housey game organised by the fire-eating Ritchie-Hook and the episode of the Loanshire officers suspected as spies but the cuts also seriously undermined the structural and thematic unity of the whole. For instance the removal of the references to Captain Truslove, Guy's childhood hero and the English composer who announced that Guy had the "death wish" are serious aesthetic losses. The most important change however comes at the end of the story, but from the point of view of theme, the decision to change seems a wise one. It relates to Guy's children. In *Unconditional Surrender* Guy and Dominica are said to have children of their own. Waugh decided not to let Guy have children of his own in the recension, and make Trimmer's child the sole heir to Broome. This change places emphasis on the spiritual nature of the novel's closure. We have used the three novels of the trilogy rather than the one-volume edition, for the division of the trilogy into three parts correspond to the three phases of Guy's search for wholeness and self-hood.

NOTES

1. *The Picturesque Prison*, p. 212.
2. *Diaries*, pp. 484-547.
3. Frederick Stopp, *Evelyn Waugh: Portrait of an Artist*, p. 46.
4. Quoted in Andrew Rutherford, *The Literature of War*, p. 120.

The Wrong-Headed Quest: *Men at Arms*

Since its publication in 1952, *Men at arms* has been considered Waugh's most mature work which combines the author's shrewd power of observation, high polish and profound comedy. De Vitis called it the best of Waugh's works. It presents the trilogy's hero, Guy Crouchback, the romantic crusader preparing for his quest of glory. The notion of the crusade however proceeds less from the hero's sense of personal honour and a need for authentic selfhood than from a sense of religious commitment which issues in social action. *Men at Arms* shows the impact of the Second World War on a youngish Englishman, fastidious and narcissitic, who is looking for an opportunity to cover himself with glory. In the course of the trilogy, Waugh demonstrates that Guy's crusading idealism renders him inadequate to face the cynicism and anarchy of the modern age. With his obsessive devotion to the ideals and values of the Middle Ages, the hero of *Men at Arms* is a figure of fun and an anachronism in the world of mid-twentieth century. Waugh's aim is to cure his hero of his excessive romanticism. Guy is set adrift in a chaotic world of conflicting aims and interests, a world which is shamelessly bereft of the sense of the Incarnation. Such muddling through a series of "military limbos," is essential for the hero's ultimate realisation of spiritual fulfilment and personal worth. Waugh's secure sense of irony enables him to perceive the contradictions inherent in the situation; the dichotomy between Guy's high idealism and the means by which he hopes to attain it. The hero is yet unaware of the goal that awaits him at the end of his life's pilgrimage. A wide gap separated Guy's intentions and his actual performance. As in Jane Austen, irony in Waugh is the neutral discoverer and explorer of incongruities.

The story of Guy's original misconceived idealism and his final disillusion resembles closely Crevantes' *Don Quixote*. There is at bottom of both the tales a recognition of the contradictions in human experience. Both the heroes may in some sense be regarded as being the loci of positive value. They may both be taken as men of good intentions who require purification under the pressure of modern reality. What is emphasised in both cases is the impurity of their ideals. Like Don Quixote, Guy Crouchback exhibits a tendency to dictate an irrelevant idealism out of the past onto his own world which has entirely different orientations. In the course of the novels, the two heroes are brought face to face with the painful realities of their times. At the beginning, both the protagonists are woefully out of step with the values of their times. Like Cervantes, Waugh stresses that imperfection and utter meaninglessness point towards a fuller and more meaningful whole. Guy Crouchback undergoes an identity crisis similar to that of Don Quixote. Their stories are stories of self-appraisal and self-definition. Basically, the two novels separated by centuries are parodies of the romance of chivalry. What Trisode Molina said of Cervantes that he was the "implacable expeller of errant knight"[2] might be said with some justification of Evelyn Waugh. Beneath the veneer of parody lie the philosophical problem of appearance and reality, of truth and illusion, and of intense subjectivity and objective knowledge. Underpinning Guy's quest for honour through hardship and danger that is witnessed in *Men at Arms* is the ironist's quest for meaning in the universe. The obsessive chivalric code of Guy and his urge to shape the world according to his pattern are called in question. What is pointedly zeroed in is the utter folly of men like Guy and Quixote to lay claim to the ultimate meaning of reality. At the same time, however, Waugh retains some measure of admiration for his hero who inspires in the readers a complex mixture of emotions.

Guy's imagination is fired by the tales of adventure, such as those of Captain Truslove which he enjoyed as a school boy, so much so that the war seems to have provided him with an opportunity not only to prove his mettle but to reform the world by force of arms. The quest-motif is, as B.W. Wilson has remarked, overlaid for Guy "by romantic associations with chivalry."[3] This romantic crusader is in dire need of acclimatization or in mythic terms, "initiation."

Men at Arms is not only a critique of unexamined and romantic chivalry, it is also a deeply religious novel. Mr Crouchback, Guy's father with his impeccable orthodoxy and high moral rectitude suggests a realistic standard of values and is the novel's constant point of reference like the Priest, the Canon and the Man in Green in Cervantes' masterpiece. What Guy experiences in the pages of *Men at Arms* and in the later books, is a kind of spiritual birth. The spiritual dimension is suggested by the repitition of rubrics from the Roman Catholic mass at various structural levels of the novel. As Vincent Sherry has noted, Guy's training programme which ends at Easter "becomes a form of Lenten preparation for the Resurrection."[4] Not only Guy but everyone in the novel's wasteland is deprived of spiritual zest. Apparently comic, *Men at Arms* is really a bitter saga of men and women who are hemmed in by waste, warfare and aridity.

In his Preface to *Sword of Honour* (1964) Waugh stated that the story of the trilogy was the description of the Second World War "as it was seen and experienced by a single, uncharacteristic Englishman." A Catholic aristocrat, nearly thirty-six years of age (Waugh's own age when the latter entered war service), emotionally and spiritually withered, Guy Crouchback is a bit of a grotesque for a protagonist of a war novel. The war in Guy's mind is an equivalent to the Holy Crusade in which all wrongs ought to be righted. With the detachment of an ironist, Waugh traces the stages in the development of his hero's character and the process of his "humanization." Entry into several social areas in the course of the narrative provides Guy with the necessary education which strips him of his illusions about the war and opens his eyes to the harsh glare of the modern anarchy which the war epitomises. Guy is Waugh's most rounded character and yet in his plight as refined "Innocent" in an "alien" environment, this three-dimensional figure shows kinship with his fictional forbears, for example, Paul Pennyfeather and Adam Fenwick. Guy's quest is an achieved quest, far more than that of Charles Ryder in *Brideshead Revisited.* In *Men at Arms*, the quest is undertaken with optimism and although at the end of the novel, he has still not realised himself, capable of actualizing his unique potentialities.

Guy's characterisation is invested with palpably poetic ambiguity. Guy simultaneously approaches the solidity of a three-dimensional figure and is suggestive of Everyman of the morality play. His experiences in a world of horror and cultural and moral decadency dramatise the hopeless isolation of the twentieth-century man. *Men at Arms* has at its core the twin wasteland theme of alienation and quest for existential meaning. Rooted in its hostility to the modern age which has repudiated God and has denied man of meaningful human relationships, *Men at Arms* in its synthesis of comedy and seriousness, is a very human study of a sensitive individual who finds it hard to come to terms with modernity. The protagonist has perforce to undergo the processes of shock, suffering and traumatic growth before he attains selfhood. Andrew Rutherford's judgement that each of the three novels contributes to the unique felicity of the trilogy[5] as a whole seems most apposite. The recurrence of the motifs and themes of *Men at Arms* in the later books contributes to the unity of tone of the trilogy. However, "complete in itself" (to adapt Waugh's own statement) *Men at Arms* recounts the phases of the hero's (as well as the author's) long love-affair with the army, full of vicissitudes.

In plotting the process of what Carl Jung calls "the individuation" of the protagonist the author moves him through clearly marked stages of development. Such neatly marked progression is discernible within each of the novels. The narrative surface of *Men at Arms* is wrought to perfection. Background information regarding Guy's character and his life preceding his entry into the war is provided by the Prologue. This is followed by the hero's zestful entry into the gaiety of army life and his eventual disgrace following upon the unauthorised raid upon Dakar.

The story of Guy is that of alienation par excellence. Nowhere in Waugh's oeurve is the complete alienation of an individual from his time and environment rendered in such poignantly aesthetic terms as in his war-trilogy. Eight years of agony and loneliness have to pass before Guy decides to enter the war. In all these years of intensely bleak spiritual aridity, Guy has been living in 'Castello Crouchback' in Santa Dulcina in Italy. The castle had been built by Guy's illustrious and gracious grandparents, Gervase and Hermione. A scion of an old Catholic family of the pre-Reformation days in England Guy's sense of isolation is given a further religious dimension. He is cut off and driven away from a debased society with which he has little in common. Like Guy Fawkes (the unwitting victim of the notorious gunpowder plot) whose name he bears, he has wished to be aloof from his unsympathetic countrymen. He "crouches back" from all human contact. Waugh's ironic double vision becomes apparent. While debunking the ideals of the society which his hero finds abhorrent, Waugh at the same time lampoons Guy's total withdrawal from humanity. His spiritual isolation in Italy has followed the shattering divorce from his promiscuous wife Virginia. Their marriage and early life in Kenya have been happy enough but Guy was not spiritually equipped to face emptiness after his wife's desertion. The years in Italy are years of paralysis in which Guy is "too immersed in angst"[6] to attract sympathy from anyone. His life is characterised by what is known in Thomistic theology as "accidie" or spiritual sloth which incapacitates an individual: "He was not loved, Guy knew, either by his household or in the town. He was accepted and respected but he was not *simpatico*."[7] "While gross vulgarians like the Wilmots and the Musgraves were simpatici, Guy alone "who they had known from infancy, who spoke their language and conformed to their religion, who was open-handed in all his dealings and scrupulously respectful of all their ways . . . Guy alone was a stranger among them." During those years of "nothingness" Guy has felt no brotherhood even in his religion. He has merely observed from the forms prescribed by his religion but has withdrawn from active participation "in the moral realities which these forms and rituals symbolise."[8] Release from the wasteland where his soul has languished for eight years seems to him to be offered by the Russian-German alliance and the war that such an alliance is to make inevitable: "The enemy at last was plain in view, huge and hateful, all disguise cast off. It was the Modern Age in arms." (12)

With the fervour of a knight-errant who believes that he is the last one left to defend the fortress of faith, Guy prefers to seek the blessings of Sir Roger of Waybroke rather than St. Dulcina, titular partroness of the town. Within the ambience of the novel's rhetoric, the figure of Sir Waybroke in the Italian Church is meant to generate in the reader contradictory emotions. Reference to Waugh's "interested objectivity" and with both aspects of the contradictions he perceives has already been made. This concern leads to an "ambivalence of attitude to one side and to the other – to both at once."[9] Sir Roger of Waybroke embodies the ideals of chivalry and traditions which endure. The sword on the knight's tomb is to Waugh, as much as to the hero, the "sword of honour" in sharp contrast to the Sword of Stalingard which is exposed for veneration in the last novel of the trilogy. The latter symbolises the loss of honour and the cynical power politics of the present century. Sir Roger who left his manor to fight in the Second Crusade was shipwrecked on the Italian Coast. He entered the service of a local count but died while fighting the count's neighbour. But Waugh's irony is directed against Guy who identifies his cause with that of a man who died not in the Holy Crusade but in a private quarrel. Sir Roger therefore, as Jeffrey Heath has argued, is a false idol[10] as Guy's motivation for going to war is as spurious and dubious as Sir Roger's death in an unworthy cause in an Italian neighbourhood. Waugh's double ironic vision is thus closely linked to the theme of the novel, namely the hero's quest for awareness and spiritual regeneration and of his ultimate ability to discriminate between "confusing appearance and ambiguous essence."

Guy's alienation is both sociological and ontological. An "atomic" man, typical of our times, Guy feels he has no place in the scheme of things. He feels no brotherhood either among members of his own family circle or among people who profess his religious faith. So cut off is he that he sometimes "imagines himself serving the last mass for the last Pope in a catacomb at the end of the world." Such psychological disjunction or malintegration seems to be rooted in his incapacity to act in accord with the goals or rather the lack of goals, the social chaos, the disintegration of value systems and the moral confusion of the society in which he finds himself thrown. Vague hints of deterministic aetiology are also provided. Guy belongs to one of the recusant families who have looked upon themselves as martyrs to a deep sense of dispossession and as social outcasts in a predominantly Protestant ethos. A strain of eccentricity in the Crouchback family seems to have complicated matters further. Guy's father, Mr Crouchback with "mysterious and tranquil joy" is a lonely figure lost in the deterioration of the spiritual terrain of the times:

> He had like many another been born in full sunlight and lived to see night fall. England was full of such Jobs who had been disappointed in their prospects. Mr Crouchback had lost his home. . . . He had rather early lost his beloved wife and been left to a long widowhood. He had an ancient name which was now little regarded and threatened with extinction. Only God and Guy knew the massive and singular quality of Mr. Crouchback's family pride. . . . He was quite without class consciousness because he saw the whole intricate social structure of his country divided neatly into two unequal and unmistakable parts. On one side stood the Crouchbacks and certain inconspicuous, anciently allied families; on the other side stood the rest of mankind. (34)

The family has known other tragedies: Guy's elder brother Gervase was killed in the first war. Ivo, only a year older than Guy, the oldest in the family, died mad when he was only twenty six. Angela, the eldest, married a Protestant, Arthur Box-Bender whose life's ambition was to make a mark as a politician. Their son, Tony, who has entered the Second World War is an unsocial recluse who later becomes a monk. To Guy, his brother Ivo's death "sometimes seemed a horrible caricature of his own life which at just that time was plunged in disaster." His marriage with the giddy-headed non-Catholic Virginia has further disoriented Guy. Tony and Guy each in his way, exemplifies the anomie of the times: "Tony was from another world; their problems were not his. Guy belonged to neither world." (30)

The questing action of such an oddly withdrawn protagonist dramatizes man's futile attempts to return to a prelapsarian state of Adamic innocence – the recurring Waugh-theme of "Man in Exile." There is more than a hint of irony in Guy's "medieval" attempts to recover the innocence and unity of being which existed in the Garden of Eden. War, of all things, seems to him the way to self-regeneration. Through what seems a remarkable stroke of luck, Guy enlists as a Halberdier through the good offices of the genial Major Tickeridge, the "kind and hairy man" to whom Mr Crouchback introduces his son. Major Tickeridge has come down to the Marine Hotel, Matchet to be with his family. Guy himself has come to the hotel where his father has taken up lodgings, after leaving Broome. The hotel is kept by the old servants from Broome. The Prologue ends with Mr Crouchback presenting his son with the medal of Our Lady of Lourdes which belonged to Gervase as a protection against the perils of war.

Inchoate romanticism in Waugh's mind is synonymous with late adolescence and a refusal to grow up. The characters of Waugh's later fiction betray the same bondage to adolescence and an incorrigible nostalgia of a childhood in a fallen, sinful world as those of the Bright Young Things of the earlier books. Guy can claim kinship with Paul Pennyfeather, Adam Fenwick, Basil Seal and Tony Last by virtue of his doomed attempt to recover to the 'unreal perspectives of childhood.' That Waugh was always fascinated by the adolescent notion that life was a frivolous game is evident in his treatment of Father Ronald Knox, one of the friends whom he admired: "Ronald had no desire to grow up. Adolescence for him was not a process of liberation or of adventure. Manhood threatened him with tedious duties and grave decisions. His mind had flourished and matured while his heart was still a child's. He grew up slowly. Each stage of his growth imposed a burden: each enlargement of spirit, the loss of something fond."[11] At thirty-five, Guy Crouchback seems an overgrown child who is terrified by adulthood. War, like the school room or nursery, seems the most alluring refuge from the painful realities of adulthood. His fellow Halberdiers are even more infantile, who expect ever to enjoy the licence of childhood. Significnatly, the Halberdiers have their training in the old school rooms at Kut-al-Imara. Such a setting is a correlate for the re creation of past boyhood of these officers and gentlemen.

Archetypically, the process of questing leads to enlightenment that can be achieved in no other way. An achieved quest is one at the end of which the explorer has grown out of his unrealizable illusions and has attained an awareness of accommodation with the real world. Guy, who at the beginning of the trilogy, quests for just causes and true wars has to be taken along the path of disillusionment. Such a road that he travels is one that is as confusing as the dark wood that Dante had to travel once. Guy is no picaroon like Basil Seal. He is a man of lofty albeit unrealistic ideals; yet, the picaresque mode is present in the environment of several of the peripheral characters who are little better than pseudo-crusaders. The sterility of the environment in which Guy is trapped is a metaphor for the condition of a pilgrim in the amoral world of twentieth century. Morally stunted men—Apthorpe, Ben Ritchie-Hook, Frank desouza, Trimmer, Sarum-Smith—inhabit the wasteland world which Guy enters. Chief of these in *Men at Arms* is Apthorpe. The division of the novel into three parts named after Apthorpe—"Apthorpe Gloriosus," "Apthorpe Furibundus" and "Apthorpe Immolatus"—underlines the parodic function of the character essential to the novel's meaning. Apthorpe, about whom there is a fundamental implausibility serves as the parallel and parody of Guy who is himself "at best a burlesque crusader."[12] Jerome Meckier's article on Evelyn Waugh contains some of the most penetrating insights into the novelistic function of Apthorpe. The rise and fall of

Apthorpe find their inverted correspondence in the fortunes of the protagonist. In his fradulence and as a symbol of bogus life-force, Apthorpe resembles Grimes in *Decline and Fall*. Apthorpe is Guy's double and doubles and dopplegangers, as Waugh notes in his *Diaries* "don't recognise each other." Apthorpe is the alazon or the *miles gloriosis* as the title of the first part of the novel suggests. Like Shakespeare's Falstaff, Apthorpe establishes what Meckier calls the "novel's concern with separating myths from reality."[13] Apthorpe represents the phoniness of the phoney war,[14] a theme that Waugh has already treated in his *Put Out More Flags*. Guy and Apthorpe complement each other. Whereas the one is overly shy and withdrawing, the other is pompous and inventive. They become a pair of twins, when temporarily immobilized by injured knees, they support each other when going to the dining hall. The motif of mistaken identity of the earlier novels is present again. The fire-eating enfant terrible Ben Ritchie-Hook, soon to be Brigadier, consistently mistakes Guy for Apthorpe at the mess entertainments. Emphasised throughout is the non-identity of the hollow men. Apthorpe is described as one who tends to become "faceless and tapering the closer he approahced." He becomes increasingly "surreal" as the story proceeds: "Guy treasured every nugget of Apthorpe but under assay he found them liable to fade like faery gold. Only so far as Apthorpe was himself true, could his enchantment work its spell. Any firm passage between Apthorpe's seemingly dreamlike universe and the world of common experience was a thing to cherish." (107-8) Guy is easily "impressed" with his double's background and "bechuana tummy" but he yet thinks that Apthorpe's claims as goal-keeper at Staplehurst's and his High-Church aunts mere fibs. He is, however, reassured on these points by Ambrose Godall, a late Catholic convert of St. Augustine's church. Through his ability to master the P.T. exercise from which he has been exempted on account of his age, and through other acts of authority, Apthorpe gains ascendency over Guy.

His "scatological" obsession with personal hygiene and elimination of waste places Apthorpe is among Waugh's least developed primitives. His energies, in Kiley's words "are concentrated on simple, biological needs which have been settled or put out of the centre of civilized minds for thousands of years."[15] The "mysterious Bust Thunder Box" which is part of Apthorpe's vast and cumbersome gear performs a complex symbolic function. Not only does it summarise Apthorpe's own character, it also creates, as Meckier has shown, the "archteypal negative epiphany,"[16] one that accentuates Guy's experience even as he parodies it. In externalizing the hollow and romantic idealism of Guy, the "thunder box" is functionally similar to the sword of Sir Roger which Guy is seen to venerate in the parish Church of Santa Dulcina. They are both "reification" of Guy's self-image and illusory ideals. As Guy's Jungian "shadow," Apthrope cherishes his portable latrine much the same way as Guy envisions the war as a holy Crusade. Just as Apthorpe hopes to keep himself uncontaminated by the chemical closet, so Guy hopes to keep his ideals pure and alive. The "biffing" by Ben Ritchie-Hook of Apthorpe's latrine symbolises the shattering of Guy's military and crusading ideals.

It is of some aesthetic significance that the "tense personal drama" involving Apthorpe's chemical closet begins in the central point of the novel's narrative, in Book II subtitled "Apthorpe Furbundus." Apthorpe's conflict with Ben Ritchie-Hook over the "Thunder Box" begins two days after the news of the fall of Finland. Guy's reaction to the news is one of dismay: "For Guy the news quickened the sickening suspicion . . . that he was engaged in a war in which courage and a just cause were quite irrelevant to the issue." (142)

The madcap antics of the protagonist's grotesque double are counterpointed against the protagonist's own crisis of perception, and his growing disillusion with military life with accompanying self-awareness. Guy is at a critical stage of his life, for although the news of the Finnish disaster has nearly shattered his morale, his life values are still shallow and are in need of Lenten purification. He is still bound by the "spell of Apthorpe" and as the narrative proceeds, Guy finds himself a fellow conspirator and "joint custodian" of the "Thunder Box." The backdrop of the austere liturgical season of Lent provides the necessary Waughian irony. To Waugh, the impassioned moralist, literature or art is ambiguously involved with the sacred and the profane. As Guy is developing into a serious soldier with "genuine Christian motivation," his comrade-in-arms, through Falstaffian amorality becomes increasingly devalued. The persistent Dionysiac-Apolline polarity of Waugh's early fiction continues to be operative in the last novels. Frequent allusions to the rites of the Church give *Men at Arms* and the other novels of the trilogy their religious weight and vision. The ritual element is essential to Waugh's purpose for it is the ritual content which enables him to dramatise in fiction the intersection of the timeless and the temporal. Allusions to the liturgy of the Lent and of the Holy Week entitle *Men at Arms* and its sequence as modern liturgical novels. They not only contain the Catholic rituals but generate in the characters feelings of an extra-temporal nature, so that we may speak of a ritual ambience"[17] in these war novels. The latter lose little in their interpretation as quest narratives insofar as they have the same end in view as the rituals of the Church, namely enabling the protagonist/participant achieve inner harmony and establish dynamic, meaningful relationships with others. It is the same belief that ritual is a prediction that underlies Guy's prayer at the beginning of Book II, of *Anima Christi*, one of the most devotional oft-said medieval compositions: "Southsand was a place of solace. Hotel and Yacht Club would shelter him, he thought. Giuseppe Pelecci would feed him and flatter him; Mr. Goodall raise him. Mist from the sea and the melting snow would hide him. The spell of Apthorpe would blind him, and gently bear him away to the far gardens of fantasy." (135) Mark L. Gnerro's explication of the passage and its rhetorical function in the novel is brilliantly convincing.[18] He has argued that this transitional passage placed at the midpoint of the novel suggesting ambivalences in Guy's make up, it at the same time forecasts meaningful changes about to take place in the novel's structure. Coming as it does after the protagonist's crushing humiliation from his former wife, the passage, says Gnerro, contains hints of future changes in theme and narrative.

Aided and abetted by Guy, Apthorpe succeeds in preserving his property for his own use until the last day before Easter. Least suspecting the stratagems of his opponent (Ritchie-Hook), Apthorpe thinking himself as a lieutenant with his tin-hat, goes to the playing field where he has believed his closet to have been out of his enemy's sight. The quotation "He nothing common did or mean" referring to King Charles I is mockingly recalled in order that the reader may conjure up the figure of a well dressed and pompous buffoon enthroned on his closet only to be exploded out of his royal seat within a few minutes. With the destruction of the "Thunder Box" the 'Apthorpe spell' loses its potency. This is the beginning of Guy's healthy disillusion with army life. However, Apthorpe continues to be absurd before he retreats completely from the world of living men into a realm of fantasy. Since the loss of his thunder box, he has become "impervious to shock" of any kind. It was a time the army was not troubled by psychiatrists. "Had it been, Apthorpe would no doubt have been lost to the Halberdiers. He remained – to the great comfort of his fellows." (180-81) At Penkirk, he begins "his one man war with the Royal Corp of signals." He misunderstands his duties set out in the military manual, and insists that the regimental signallers come under his command for administrative purposes. This leads to his direct confrontation with Lt. Dunn, the signals officer. Things come to a head when Apthorpe enters the signallers' lines and begins destroying one of their boots. Then back in his own office he pens a "challenge to Dunn to meet him, armed with a heliograph, before their men for a Trial by Combat in proficiency in Morse." (184) Apthorpe's ego is further inflated with his promotion as Captain. There follows schoolboy ragging for sometime from the junior officers when the new Captain insists on being saluted. Structurally, Apthorpe's fooleries are meant to parallel as well as contrast with the reverses that the Allied forces suffer at the moment at the hands of the mighty enemy. In death as in life, Apthorpe is surrounded by otiose ostentation. As he is borne along on the stretcher to an obscure hospital in West Africa, he resembles a "victorian woodcut from a book of exploration." In the hospital he brags to Guy of his "High Church aunt" of whom he now confesses there has been only one and in an aura of mystery, he asks Guy to carefully deliver his gear to his crony Chatty Corner, the "man of the wilds" who has succumbed to the advance of civilization." The incompleteness of Apthorpe's life is more than hinted in his name with associations of the ape.

Two of the events more than others afford Guy knowledge of the irony inherent in the affairs of man: Apthorpe's elevation as Captain when he himself remains a mere platoon commander and Apthorpe's death of which he has been an unwitting cause. Guy is mortified when Apthorpe and worse a man like Hayter have been found fitter for promotion. But at no previous stage has Guy expected success: "Guy felt no resentment; he was a good loser – at any rate an experienced one. He merely felt a deep sinking of spirit such as he had felt in Claridge's with Virginia, such as he had felt times beyond number through all his life." (168)

An awareness of life's irony is a mark of growth in Guy. Kierkegaard's definition of irony as the "confine between the aesthetic and the ethical stage in life"[19] seems an accurate description of Guy's situation. Irony tends to establish a sense of responsibility in a style of life which would otherwise remain on the "aesthetic" (that is, romantic, unrealistic) level of existence in the world. However absurd it might seem to a person of Guy's mental and intellectual make-up, irony educates him to face the absurdity and to accept the patterned ways of thinking and acting. As a result of such an experience of irony, to continue to follow Kierkegaardian philosophy, an individual is stimulated to examine his life-style in the light of the life-goal he has set for himself. In making his protagonist face life's ironies, Waugh hopes to trick him out of his pride. Humility will be the mark of the ethical stage which Guy has not reached yet. What Waugh is doing in *Men at Arms* is to involve his hero in a comic sense of shame through which he will ultimately achieve a tolerance for an "absurd discrepancy."[20] The Christian virtue of humility alone can guarantee a serious alteration in one's outlook on life, without the loss of ontological import. Such a realization that one's patterned ways of thinking is not adequate to realise one's life goal is not a negative experience, but rather a compelling positive epiphany. Irony, according to Frye, along with comedy, romance and tragedy, is an "episode in a total quest myth."[21] When irony is as thoroughgoing as in the narrative of *Men at Arms*, it imitates the theme of the quest.

Of the other hollow men in *Men at Arms* who claim Guy's loyalty, Ben Ritchie-Hook ranks next to Apthorpe. If Apthorpe personifies Guy's romantic yearning for sentimental comradeship, Ritchie-Hook exemplifies the hero's adolescent love of military ferocity. Guy's inner being is in perpetual conflict caused by the simultaneous attraction of these two men. With a single terrible eye, "black as the patch which hung on the other side of the lean skew nose," set in a steel-rimmed monocle, and with his bared teeth, the Brigadier is clearly one of the primitives of the modern wasteland. He was the great Halberdier *enfant terrible* of the First World War and the youngest commander in the history of the Crops. Guy is readily impressed by his military record of war wounds, decorations and disobedience followed by acquittal. "Where lesser men collected helmets Ritchie-Hook once came back from a raid across no-men's-land with a dropping head of a German sentry in either hand. The years of peace had been years of unremitting conflict for him. Wherever there was blood and gunpowder from Country Cork to the Matto Gasso, there was Ritchie-Hook. Latterly he had wandered about the Holy Land tossing hand-grenades into the front parlours of dissident Arabs." (66) For this remarkable warrior, "the image of war was not hunting or shooting; it was the wet sponge on the door, the hedge hog in the bed; or rather, he saw war itself a prodigious booby trap." (72)

The creation of Ben Ritchie-Hook provides Waugh with ample ammunition to make his own satiric assaults on the spiritually chaotic contemporary life. One of Waugh's aims (as in the case of Apthorpe) is to debunk the military idealism of Guy Crouchback who sees it embodied in the Brigadier. Guy readily identifies Ritchie with the intrepid Truslove, one of the heroes of his boyhood reading. His adolescent admiration for the "biffer" blinds him to the inner vacuum of the man. Guy's hero-worship of a wholly disoriented man is one of Waugh's ways of dramatizing the inability of the modern man who in his solipsistic fantasy is unable to distinguish between subject and object. Such inability makes Guy a failure both in his marital and military life. Guy will have to escape the hold that this symbol of ferocity and brute strength has on him if he is to attain selfhood. That Ritchie Hook is no more than an over-sized grotesque capable of betrayal, Guy realizes at the end of *Men at Arms*. He realises at great cost to himself, that Ritchie-Hook, despite his daring, is inadequate as an individual and can never lead him in a Crusade, and that Ritchie-Hook and Sir Roger of Waybroke are worlds apart.

Guy volunteers to lead the unofficial Dakar Expedition at the end of the book which Ritchie-Hook organises in the "true Truslove spirit." This seems the only chance of combat to the "Hookforce" which after several delays has reached the West African coast. In its futility and the disgrace it brings to the men involved in the mission it foreshadows another expedition in a later book of the trilogy ("Operation Popgun") by means of which Ian Kilbannock, the "arch impostor" and Trimmer, his stooge, cover themselves with undeserved glory. Unknown to Guy who leads his men to Beach A in Dakar, Ritchie-Hook, in disguise conceals himself in the party. While the operation is nearly over, the disguised Brigadier goes deep into the shore in order to decapitate a Negro sentinel. His conduct puts the lives of the men in great peril and the entire operation brings discredit to Guy and Ritchie-Hook. Guy is once again taught the bitter lesson of life's irony. The expedition, instead of helping him win a military cross, merely has his copy book blotted. This added to his implication in Apthorpe's death further alienates him from his superiors and fellow army men.

Ambrose Goodall of St. Augustine, an Anglo-Catholic converted not long ago to Catholicism is one other 'eccentric' who misleads Guy through his advice on a crucial theological point, that of his claim of his former wife Virginia. An "enthusiast who lacks a well developed sense of sin,"[22] Goodall is well-read in the history of English Catholic aristocracy. Slightly flown with wine, Goodall relates the story of one of Guy's Catholic kinsmen, who even after his divorce, met his former wife ten years later and had a son by her. He convinces Guy that theologically the original husband committed no sin in resuming sexual relations with his former wife. So impressed with Goodall's account of the "blameless and auspicious pseudo-adultery" is Guy that he goes to London the following day to see Virginia, now Mrs. Troy. At first Virginia is touched by his forlornness and is willing to comply with Guy. But when he hints at his claim on her as his one-time wife, Virginia loses her composure which has already been ruffled by three calls from Apthorpe to Guy. She rightly rebuffs him: "I thought you'd taken a fancy to me again and wanted a bit of fun for the sake of old times. I thought you'd chosen me specially, and by God you had. Because I was the only woman in the whole world your priests would let you go to bed with. That was my attraction. You wet, smug, obscene, pompous, sexless, lunatic pig." (133) "Simply another inhabitant of the twentieth century jungle" as Robert Kiley describes her, Virginia's "retrogression is sexual."[23] She moves from marriage to marriage, from lover to lover with no apparent discrimination. Her present appellation of Mrs. Troy mockingly evokes her classical counterpart who forsook her husband for the sake of new love. This vacuous woman, however, is gifted with keen perception of human affairs. Guy who is in search of identity begins to masquerade as a dashing soldier and lover and his attempts to change his outward appearance make him doubly ridiculous. In order to make himself impressive with Virginia, he wears a moustache and a monocle, thus becoming a combination of Apthorpe and Ritchie-Hook, the two men he admires. But the hard-headed Virginia remarks on how comic his disguise makes him: "After disguise, his whole new calling a masquerade." (124) It is the Waughian theme of non-identity of the earlier novels. Heartless and amoral Virginia may be but she keeps her identity, unlike Guy who constantly thinks of getting under someone else's skin. It is one of the novel's dominant ironies that this woman whose conversation is replete with the "then unprintable words" should be (to use Aristotelian terminology) the efficient cause in the process of "humanization" of Guy in the trilogy later. Living in a world of shadows, Guy reflects in himself and shares with others some of the traits of character of the other wastelanders, who all lack a stable sense of security. All these characters are 'Comedians' (to borrow the title of one of Graham Greene's novels) on the great stage of fools, impersonating and playing roles which sometimes suit them but often do not. Guy has joined the army because the uniform seems an appropriate disguise to hide his identity. Apthorpe is described as being "gloriously over-technicoloured like Bonny Prince Charles in the film" and Ian Kilbannock, the journalist-peer as "an arch-imposter in his Air Force dress." In his quest to find himself, Guy takes on shifting roles but his efforts at role-playing end in mortifying disillusion. Trimmer and Ian Kilbannock play a significant part in the lives of Guy and Virginia in the subsequent novels of the trilogy.

Mr Crouchback, Guy's father, alone among the characters in *Men at Arms* and in the other novels affirms the traditional Catholic values which Waugh, the man and novelist entirely approved and defended throughout his life. There is no satire in the portrait of this affable old man but only playful comedy. With his steadfast faith and stable identity, Mr Crouchback is the novel's positive point of reference. In his serenity and extraordinary love of charity he radiates the same element of love as the Sanctuary lamp at Broome. Like Sir Roger who exemplifies the chivalric code, Mr Crouchback is a living embodiment of the tenets of the Church and like the visible Church itself, is the rock of stability in the novel's world of flux. His function in the novel, Waugh told Frederick Stopp, was "to keep audible a steady undertone of the decencies and true purpose of life behind the chaos of events and fantastic characters."[24] But as the novel proceeds, he is also seen as a victim of the rapacity of the modern age. In his humility and tolerance, Mr Crouchback becomes easily identifiable with the "suffering servant," a Christ-like figure "bowed under the cross."[25] It is the spirituality that his father embodied that eventually saves Guy from despair and helps him see the error of directing his quest towards outmoded chivalry and adventure. The most mature of Waugh's fictional fathers,[26] Mr Crouchback is an unfailing source of inspiration to Guy. Mr Crouchback's benign influence stands in contrast to, say, the father of John Plant in *Work Suspended* whose influence cripples his son's creativity. Guy comes to respect more and more as the story proceeds his father and the high tradition he represents. Reduced to near poverty, but fortified by a memory "which kept only the good things and rejected the ill," Mr Crouchback has long learnt to accommodate himself to the reality of the temporal world.

Guy joins service after eight years of intense soul-searching and self-communing hoping to find in the army glamour in military action and adventure. His acute shyness innate to him and his age set him apart from his fellows. All through the novel, whatever the circumstances, Guy suffers from intense isolation. His heart is said to be "lonely" and that he is "different from the rest of the crowd." He wonders why he is unable to say "here's how" that seems to come easily enough to others. Disillusion comes quite early. To be fighting a war alongside inexperienced youths straight from public schools, such as Frank desouza seems unprofessional:

> He wondered, sometimes, what system of selection had produced so nondescript a squad. Later he realized that they typified the peculiar pride of the Crops, which did not expect distinguished raw materials but confided instead in its age-old methods of transformation. The discipline of the square, the traditions of the mess, would work their magic and the *esprit de crops* would fall like blessed unction from above. (44)

Guy is particularly piqued by Trimmer's presence. With his golden hair which he tries to conceal under a cap, and his cockney accent, Trimmer seems to epitomise the theatrical vulgarity of the times. So enraged is Guy by Trimmer's cockiness that he makes a menacing gesture which would have easily earned him a court-martial.

Only much later in his army life does Guy realise that his love-affair with military is fraught as in any real marriage, with "familiarity, annoyance and discord." His "grim initiation is marked by frustration. During the training in which his colleague Apthorpe comes off fairly well, he himself gets nearly killed. The commonness of the atmosphere is revolting: "Was it for this that the bugles sounded across the barrack square and the strings sang over the hushed dinner table of the Copper Heels? Was this the triumph for which Roger de Waybroke took the cross?" (104-5) But what, despite this, makes him still pride himself in his undertaking is the joyous celebration of British regimental life (based upon Waugh's own experience in the Royal Marines). It is this that sustains him in moments of chagrin. Just back from his humiliation at Virginia's hands, the voice of the Brigadier infuses new vigour into him:

> He ceased for the time being to be the lonely and ineffective man—the man he so often thought he saw in himself, past his first youth, cuckold, wastrel, prig—who had washed and saved and dressed at Claridge's, lunched at Bellamy's and caught the afternoon train; he was one with his regiment, with all their historic feats of arms behind him, with great opportunities to come. He felt from head to foot a physical tingling and bristling as though charged with galvanic current. (136)

Weeks of alternating chaos and order and the ineptitude of the officialdom would have convinced anyone less romantic than Guy that the Halberdiers have not lived up to their putative reputation as an effcient organization with impeccable aristocratic traditions. His disenchantment is often temporary and he marvels the capacity of army men to be cohesive against odds: "He was thinking of this strange faculty of the army of putting itself into order. Shake up a colony of ants and for some minutes all seems chaos. The creatures scramble aimlessly, frantically about; then instinct reasserts itself. They find their proper places and proper functions. As ants, so soldiers." (164) It is hard for him to believe that his country would lose the war. "There was in romance great virtue in unequal odds." (174) The war that he is engaged in has the two moral requisites for a lawful war—a just cause and the chance of victory. But as days pass, his faith in the justness of the war is increasingly eroded. His platoon spends its days doing absolutely nothing. The monotonous, liturgical incantation of the signallers near whom his platoon is working echoes the emptiness of feeling of his own men. The thought of his nephew with perhaps five years cut clean out of his young life brings home to Guy the pointlessness of it all. Like Scobie in Greene's *The Heart of the Matter* he begins to ponder on the nature of evil and of injustice as a fact of life:

> at this very time "Scobie" was close at hand, demolishing partitions in native houses, still conscientiously interfering with neutral shipping. If they had not the services of the new Catholic Chaplain, Guy might have gone to Father Rank to confess increasing sloth, one dismal occasion of drunkenness and the lingering resentment he felt at the injustice he had suffered in the exploit to which he had given the private name of 'Operation Truslove.' (232)

Waugh's hero has similar stirrings of Catholic conscience like Greene's. Both damn themselves with their generosity. Guy's giving stolen whiskey to his friend in the hospital only hastens his death as Scobie out of his overwhelming sense of 'Pity' for those around him unconsciously brings about the death of his servant.

In *Men at Arms* there is "no consummation of the quest" but there are enough indications that disenchantment with war and with his private crusade has already begun. A Waughian circularity of theme is evident at the end of the novel. One sort of alienation is replaced by another. Army life and war, instead of aiding the hero in establishing meaningful relations with his fellow men brings merely a sense of frustration and a feeling that he is, in the nature of things, destined to be cut off from his fellow men. He has blotted his copy book by the disgraceful Dakar raid and of his part in his own friend's death: "Already the Second Battalion of the Halberdiers spoke of Guy in the past tense. He had momentarily been of them; now he was an alien; someone in their long and varied past, but forgotten." (246)

NOTES

1. B.W. Wilson, "*Sword of Honour*; The Last Crusade," *English*, Autumn, 1974, p. 89.
2. Manuel Duran, *Cervantes* (Boston: Twayne, 1974), p. 6.
3. B.W. Wilson, p. 89.
4. Vincent B. Sherry, Jr., "Literary Effects of World War II," *Dictionary of Literary Biography*, no. 15 (Michigan: Gale Research Company, 1983), p. 622.
5. Andrew Rutherford, *The Literature of War*, p. 121.
6. Paul Doyle, "Evelyn Waugh," *Dictionary of Literary Biography*, No. 15, p. 581.
7. *Men at Arms* (UK: Penguin, 1965; rpt. 1985), p. 15.
8. Marston La France, "*Sword of Honour;* The Ironist Placatus," *Dalhousie Review*, no. 55 (Spring 1975), p. 33.
9. Andrew H. Wright, "Irony and Fiction," *Journal of Aesthetics and Art Criticism*, p. 12.
10. *The Picturesque Prison*, p. 220.
11. Evelyn Waugh, *Ronald Knox* (London: Campman and Hall, 1959), p. 79.

12. Jerome Meckier, "Evelyn Waugh," p. 108.
13. Evelyn Waugh, *Diaries,* p. 783.
14. Jerome Meckier, "Evelyn Waugh," pp. 107-8.
15. Robert Kiley, "The Craft of Despondency—The Traditional Novelists," *Deadalus*, Spring 1963, p. 224.
16. Jerome Meckier, "Evelyn Waugh," p. 108.
17. The idea of "ritual ambience" is an echo from Richard F. Hardin, "'Ritual' in Recent Criticism: The Elusive Sense of Community," *PMLA*, October 1983, pp. 846-62.
18. Mark L. Generro, 'Echoes of the Anima Christi in a pivotal paragraph of Evelyn Waugh's *Men At Arms,' EWN*, Winter 1986, pp. 3-6.
19. Jeffrey C. Sabosan, "Irony and the Unexpected," *Cross Currents*, no. 4, 1977, pp. 429-34.
20. Stanley R. Hoipper, "Irony—The Pathos of the Middle," *Cross Currents*, no. 12, 1969, p. 36.
21. *Ibid*., p. 39.
22. *The Picturesque Prison*, p. 224.
23. Robert Kiley, p. 225.
24. Quoted in Andrew Rutherford, p. 124.
25. David Lodge, "Evelyn Waugh" in *Six Modern British Novelists,* p. 79.
26. The father-son relationship is one of the central topics of discussion in Jeffrey Heath's *The Picturesque Prison.*

The Second Stage of the Protagonist's *"Pilgrimage"*: *Officers and Gentlemen*

Officers and Gentlemen, the second novel of the trilogy, which Waugh had originally thought would conclude the story begun in *Men at Arms* traces the progressive disillusionment of the protagonist Guy. "Elaborately lucid"[1] as Igoe described the novel, *Officers and Gentlemen* continues the story of the journey of a man of high ideals towards despair. The novel shows that Guy Crouchback, "the virtuous prig"[2] is doubly deceived by political and personal values. Waugh's aim is to further deflate his hero's illusions about war, military routine and about life in general. At the end of the novel, Guy is bitterly disillusioned by the decline of aristocracy and the death of tradition. Guy pursues his ideals in much the same way as in *Men at Arms*, fired by the code of chivalry which seems to him to be embodied by Sir Roger of Waybroke. As the story of his personal quest proceeds, however, his growing disillusionment deepens and the novel very nearly acquires the dimensions of tragedy. To his utter chagrin, Guy gradually realises that not all officers are gentlemen and that most of them are capable of deceit, betrayal and cowardice. Set against the historically real background of Second World War, *Officers and Gentlemen* tells the story of a "real" person whose illusions of temporal justice and honour are shattered by the disvalues of the modern age in which war has been refined to an incredibly lethal degree. Guy is appalled by the discovery that the individual does no longer count in such a world of carnage and amorality: he has become a mere name or number among millions of names and numbers.

Guy's quest takes the form of a journey. The forms of Classical stories of quest for example *The Odyssey, The Aeneid* and *The Divine Comedy*, are structured by a journey. In these stories the journey takes on the significance of a quest in which the protagonist searches for a goal of some importance for himself and his society. Guy's search, like that of his classical counterparts covers ground geographically but as the trilogy proceeds, it also probes the psyche of the hero. What gives depth to Waugh's later heroes is the novelist's concern in plotting the geography of the human soul. Unlike the picaresque heroes who move through a series of adventures in a haphazard manner, Guy becomes increasingly introspective in the course of the trilogy. The progression inward is an important feature of quest narratives from the story of Homer to the novels of the present day. The several classical allusions in the story while providing continuity with the literatures of the past also raise Guy's existential situation to universality. Discursive and episodic as *Officers and Gentlemen* is, it yet raises issues fundamental to the nature of man, such as the problems of war and of evil. War in *Officers and Gentlemen* as in *Men at Arms* is an image of man, in which the forces of good and evil are in perpetual combat for dominance. However, in presenting the dilemma of Guy's plight in a chaotic world, Waugh makes his sympathies with his hero quite explicit. The narrator's identification with the hero increases in proportion as the latter becomes more and more disillusioned with war and the way of the modern world. But Waugh makes it clear that in the destruction of Guy's cherished illusions lies his salvation and self-knowledge. One after the other of the hero's idols fall. Major Hound, is like the man in the Old Testament story who sells his soul for a mess of pottage. Ivor Claire who embodies to Guy the finest spirit of England, "the flower of the nation" turns out to be a craven coward and a traitor. Standards of aristocracy seem crudely compromised when its members cover up the disgrace of Claire. The final blow comes with Cretan debacle at the end of the novel. Reality seems so vicious and terrible that for a time he is rendered speechless. The moral and military chaos accompanied by the horrors of war, and of shameless incompetence kill off all his crusading zeal: "Now that hallucination was dissolved, like the whales and turtles on the voyage from Crete, and he was back after less than two years' pilgrimage in a Holy Land of illusion in the old ambiguous world, where priests were spies and gallant friends proved traitors and his country was led blundering into dishonour."[3] Guy's marital and military experiences leave a deep scar in his soul, not unlike the physical wound of Odysseus that symbolically reaches deeper than the surface scar.

Not only does *Officers and Gentlemen* trace the private quest of Guy, it at the same time reflects Waugh's view of contemporary civilization. As in the classical quest narratives, the protagonist of *Officers and Gentlemen* represents the society through which he blunders along in search of his goal. The novel's war-torn landscape is similar to the sterile wastelands of Dante's *Inferno* and some of the Arthurian romances. Guy moves through alienated world where the normal laws of causality break down. Moral blindness seems to infect the whole society. The world of *Officers and Gentlemen* is a world of grotesques whose condition accentuates the need for spiritual redemption. A world where fixed values have ceased to exist is fit only for grotesques and distorted moral beings. The ontological incongruity suggested by these grotesques is part of Waugh's vision of human experience. There is all-round deterioration. Trimmer who becomes a hero in spite of himself, Virginia who is become increasingly amoral, the eccentric Ludovic, the author of *Pensees* and the incompetent army officers represent the dislocation of values of the world of the Second World War and after. However, through total modulation, Waugh makes it plain with whom his sympathies lie. As William Cook has noted, while the novel is pessimistic and negative regarding civilization, it is positive in its assertion of the superiority of the hero's values.[4]

It is by approaching Waugh as a religious artist, especially in the books after *Brideshead Revisited*, that we can best perceive that principle of order and development which affords his *oeuvre* a sense of coherence and unity. Implied in the quest of the hero in *Officers and Gentlemen* is the quest for the sacred, as references to the Church's liturgy indicate. When the novel opens, Guy, who is watching a group of progressive novelists in firemen's uniform squirting a little jet of water into the morning room, is reminded of "Holy Saturday at Downside." Mr. Goodall is seen praying in the Church on All Soul's Day and assiduously "releasing *toties quoties* soul after soul from Purgatory." The theme of modern man's quest for re-integration is inevitably intertwined with the search for meaning which only an authentic kind of religion can provide. It was one of the cardinal acts of faith with Waugh, the artist, that literature must combine both the spiritual and empirical aspects of life and must deal with man's concrete existential situation. Guy recognises that his friend Ivor Claire who becomes his beau-ideal is quite different from him and yet they have both a destiny to fulfil. In describing their condition Waugh uses one of his favourite philosophical phrases: "As for Guy, he had recognized from the first a certain remote kinship with this most dissimilar man, a common aloofness, differently manifested – a common melancholy sense of humour; each in his way saw life *sub specie aeternitatis.*" (87)

Waugh has deplored, time and again, the aesthetic norm of our age which, with its positivist approach has rejected meaningful interpretation of the aesthetic object. Religion for Waugh is the ultimate ground of our being. His later creation, Gilbert Pinfold viewed the world the same way as Guy and Ivor and "found it flat as a map."[5] In his analysis of the novel *The Ordeal of Gilbert Pinfold* (published two years after *Officers and Gentlemen*) Jeffrey Heath observes that Pinfold is at last able to liberate himself from the bestial forces of the regions of his own mind only when he returns to Christendom after his nightmarish experiences on "S.S. Caliban."[6] Heath suggests that in his obsessive love of privacy Guy in the earlier novels of the trilogy resembles Pinfold and that the latter's uncharitable pursuit of privacy finally gives way to the hero's compassionate wisdom in *Unconditional Surrender*, published four years after the Pinfold novel. It is ultimately the Church that is to provide Guy with the ability to circumvent despair, and help him rise above the illusions of a romantic past.

The futility of the quests of the hero and of the other characters is dramatised in appropriate, concrete imagery. In the evocation of the names of Achilles, Hector, Philoctetes, Miltiades and Jason, is implied an ironic contrast with a happier and a more heroic age. Guy's own quest is a Gothic parody of the Medieval quest which was inspired by a truly religious sense. Quotations or half-quotations from the writers of the past are used for the same purpose, namely to illustrate the pseudo-heroism and trumpery decor of a sordid age – an age in which clowns like Trimmer and opportunists like Ian Kilbannock can thrive. The romance of the early enthusiasm of Guy in *Men at Arms* gives place to a gradual tone of disenchantment in Guy's war-experiences in *Officers and Gentlemen.*

As early as *Decline and Fall* Waugh has shown himself master of the ironic techniques of juxtaposition and counterpoint. This technique of ironic contrast and parallel reaches its culmination in *Officers and Gentlemen*. It heightens and magnifies the absurdity of the quests of the hollow men in the novel and specially that of the protagonist. The parody of the Grail quest in Book One ("Happy Warriors") and the passage of the dead soldier in Book Two ("In the Picture") underscore the theme that the hero's notion of modern crusade is based on a misconception. These incidents illustrate Waugh's conviction of the inadequacy of romanticism and the folly of men who set store by it. At the same time, however, after the fashion of T.S. Eliot, the parody of the quest implies a contrast between a past which embodied a genuine sense of chivalry and the sordid present in which orthodoxy and good manners are suspect. The contemptible episode of Trimmer's raid on a friendly coast further heightens the absurdity of the modern situation devoid of judgement and scruples.

Similarities in thematic design and narrative technique link *Officers and Gentlemen* to *Men at Arms.* Apthorpe with his gear was an externalization of Guy's longings, is replaced by Ivor Claire. The two novels contain some of Waugh's biting indictment of military mismanagement and irresponsibility. Guy traverses different strata of society in much the same way. But purification and growth, as Cordelia in *Brideshead* had posited, entail suffering. Consequently, therefore, *Officers and Gentlemen* which is the dramatic middle of the Crouchback saga, is marked by a certain toughness. The first stage of Guy's quest has been easy enough but the landscape at the "second stage" becomes increasingly threatening. Faced with the horror and boredom of modernity, Guy begins to question its value systems and shows signs of new awareness. An entirely new orientation and a fresh evaluation of life seem most in need. Waugh's complex artistry in *Officers and Gentlemen* is evidenced in his ability, to quote Didion, to "deal simultaneously with an individual, his God and his society, neither slighting nor magnifying the subtle delicate pressures each exerts upon the other."[7] By the end of *Officers and Gentlemen* Guy recognizes the futility of his ideology and his disillusion with the modern age sets the tone of *Unconditional Surrender*. Guy's pilgrimage becomes, at the end of the epic, a painful self-discovery and an accompanying sense of accommodation with reality.

As much of the trilogy is a parody of Medieval chivalry, it is patterned on the quest-motif, associated with it. In particular the quest of the Holy Grail is parodied in the episode of Guy's search for Apthorpe's friend, "Chatty" Corner who is ensconced in a lugubrious castle on the isle of Mugg. This mock-quest is replete with snatches of old songs and chivalric metaphor.

Back in England after the Dakar expedition at the end of *Men at Arms* Guy is sent to X Commando force training on the island of Mugg. But before going to Hebrides, Guy has to collect the gear Apthorpe has bequeathed to Chatty Corner:

> Now, as then, an act of pietas was required of him; a spirit was to be placated. Apthorpe's gear must be retrieved and delivered before Guy was free to follow his fortunes in the King's service. His road lay backward for the next few days, to Southsand and Cornwall. 'Chatty' Corner, man of the trees, must be found, somewhere in the trackless forests of war-time England. (21)

Of the series of burlesque episodes of which the novel is full, Guy's search for Chatty Corner and his discharge of Apthorpe's kit as a sacred duty is ironically the most effective. The account is one of Waugh's finest pieces of writing and serves to deflate the hero's extravagant idealism. After inserting an advertisement Guy waits for response from Chatty Corner. His call to Chatty has gone like Roland's bugle call from the gorge of Roncesvalles in the Arthurian legend. Chatty's real name is James Pendennis, an echo of Arthur Pendragon from Malory. Guy's approach to Chatty's "lair" in Mug is described in recurrent images of classical chivalry. But the triviality of the enterprise is all too plain. He has had to wait for a signal from Chatty a long time "like the Russian sentry . . . the guardsman who was posted daily year in, year out, until the revolution, in the grounds of Tsarskoe Selo on the spot where Catherine the Great had once wished to preserve a wild flower." (40) The desolate residence of Chatty is a travesty of Grail castle where Guy, the latter-day knight goes to seek out Chatty. The bleak surroundings of the island complete the Waste Land theme. Chatty is the sick old king waiting for the knight who will restore him and his land to former health. Mugg has had no fame in song or story and Chatty of whose description Waugh in *Men at Arms* makes him an embodiment of animalism and degeneration: "a brown with grizzled hair. . . . It was easy to see how he had gained a footing among the gorrillas. . . . He swung his head from side to side, gazing about him from under shaggy brows as though seeking some high path by which he could swing himself aloft and lie cradled in solitude among the rafters."[8]

Like Hetton Abbey in *A Handful of Dust* Chatty's lair has a Gothic facade he himself has not inherited any of the ideals or values of the former age. As Guy approaches the unfriendly place he is reminded of the refrain "Child Roland to the dark came," celebrated in Robert Browning's poem. It conjures up at once the medieval romance in which Roland goes in search of personal fulfilment. The incongruity of the lone inhabitant in the "old Castle" of medieval structure is at once striking:

> Guy . . . was prepared, as he entered the room, to find a tableau from some ethnographic museum, some shaggy, prognathous hypothetical ancestor, sharpening a flint spear-head among a heap of gnawed bones. . . . Instead he found a man, bulky and hirsute indeed . . . and plainly far from the well, wrapped in army blankets, seated before a peat fire on a commonplace upright chair, with his feet in a steaming bucket of mustard and water. At his hand stood a whisky bottle and on the hob a kettle of water. (56)

In his illness he resembles the old sick king of the Grail story. Apart from being known as Chatty, James Pendennis is also known as "Kong," thus suggesting a lack of identity, one of the recurrent themes associated with quest-motif.

The crucial moment arrives when Guy asks Chatty to sign on his field note book in token of the receipt of Apthorpe's gear. Guy, like the Grail knight, has a sense of personal fulfilment when Chatty sings: "Suddenly the wind dropped. It was a holy moment. Guy rose in silence and ritually received the book." (59)

In truly Waughian manner, the scene quickly shifts to the seat of Colonel Hector Campbell of Mugg known locally as the New Castle to distinguish it from the ancient and more picturesque edifice occupied by

Chatty Corner. Campbell's residence has a far more sinister aspect than Chatty's. With the six dogs ranging in size from a couple of deer hounds to an almost hairless Pomeranian, and named after the heros of Greek mythology Mugg's palace seems a veritable modern-day Hades. This piece of Gothicism represents a manifestation of the diabolical reversal of myth and archetype. The dominant symbol of Gothic fiction is that of the ruined palace, the great Gothic castle. Its major plot line is that of the quest-motif which owes much to medieval romances and Grail legends. The Grail quest is diabolically reversed. Campbell, his wife and Katie their great-niece from Edinburgh are horrible grotesques who are not products of a stable value-system. Waugh has superbly caught the dream-like unreality of the scene, with its mixture of horror and buffoonery. The whole atmosphere is an expression of the dissonance of human experience, its total irrationality: "The exterior was German in character, Bismarckian rather than Wagnerian, of moderate size but designed to withstand assault from all but the most modern weapons. The interior was pitch pine throughout and owed its decoration more to the taxidermist than to sculptor or painter." (60) Expressions such as "armorial decorations obscured by smoke," "baronial severity of the furniture" establish the burlesque nature of the situation. The colonel "much bedizened with horn and cairngorms" mistakes Guy for Angus Anstruther-Kerr whom he has been expecting for dinner. Guy's "probable destiny," according to the narrator, seems manifest: "to be blinded by smoke among arm chairs, to be frozen to death in wider spaces, or to be devoured by the dogs where he stood." His voyage has been a voyage into darkness which cannot provide him with the spiritual nourishment of which he is sorely in need. There follows a ceremonious repast grotesquely redolent of the meal in the days of chivalry. The Colonel "hacks away at the haunch of venison" and the butler follows his own devious course "with a tray of red-currant jelly and unpeeled potatoes." Katie, the Natzified great-niece, with a fanatical Scottish fervour strikes Guy as the most mysterious of all. Some ten or twelve years younger than Guy, she plays the role of the classical damsel in distress. She passes him a piece of paper with the cryptic message "POLITICAL PRISONER" marked on it. Throughout the dinner she violently asserts her nationalism until at last, Mrs. Campbell asks her to leave. Dinner over and as Tommy and Guy get into their car, they see a storm-lantern waving from a upper window from where a friendly challenge 'Heil Hitler' reaches their ears. The following morning Guy discovers in his car a bundle of printed papers on which is written in large letters, "Call to Scotland. England's Peril is Scotland. Why Hitler must win." This further provokes Waugh's risibilities. The absurd document sends the most clownish spy-catcher in

Waugh's fiction, the man with a much hyphenated name, Colonel Grace-Groundling-Marchpole, on a false scent. This is one of the episodes in which Waugh runs away with himself. On their way back home, Guy and Tommy, the "two men who have loved the same woman" namely Virginia, are seized by a fit of laughter. They seal their friendship on a place "rarer and loftier than normal human intercourse."

Waugh's love of fantasy and of Dickensian distortion of reality proceeds from the writer's comic prejudice. Such comic sense coupled with the satirist's predilection for distorted focus affords him a mode of perception, which as Andrew Rutherford has pointed out, is the basis of Waugh's wit as the Pope's.[9] Apart from providing the reader with an "amoral delight," this kind of fantasy has another dimension. Grotesque comedy has been worked with a moral pattern. Guy the Christian stoic is made to inhabit the same universe as Chatty Corner and Colonel Campbell and his high-spirited daughter. While Waugh presents the oddity of human nature with obvious relish, he at the same time refuses to compromise with his own set of values with which he judges the world. It is this unblinking confidence in his own moral values that gives his comedy a sharp albeit distorted focus.

The difference between Guy and the picaros of Waugh's earlier fiction lies in the purpose of the novel. Guy's adventures are not so much self-contained satirical episodes as positive steps in his quest. In contrast to Chatty Corner and Colonel Campbell who are unable to maintain any meaningful contact with the world of teeming reality, Guy is searching for a fate which will include both a full realisation of self and of love of other human beings. The picaresque form is a reliable vehicle which offers Waugh certain advantages in the portrayal of modern life in all its variety and in the search of the central character for values by which modern man can live. On the level of the parable, the occupants of the two castles are the besetting demons whom the protagonist has to subdue in order to succeed in his quest. Guy, the modern pilgrim is cut adrift in a world of endless encounters and of inhabitants who live without the least eschatological perspective. The point of the whole adventure of Guy is to make him see the need to restructure his own life which will conform to the Christian idea of self-knowledge and self-control. Guy's separateness from a world in which physico-moral order is disrupted and confused is sought to be insisted upon. Set apart from other men, Guy must learn to transcend the Nothingness which resides within modern man. Dr. Glending-Rees, the staunch advocate of sea weed who comes to Mugg for demonstration of a balanced diet is another eccentric like Colonel Campbell.

But these are lesser clowns compared with the ones in the theatre of war and those who are entrusted with the civil administration. Guy alone among the knights of the parodic chivalry is inspired by lofty ideals. The rest are cowardly, incompetent and disloyal men who place expediency above honour. Chief among them who figure in *Officers and Gentlemen* are: Fido Hound, Ian Kilbannock, Ivor Claire, Trimmer and Ludovic. Structurally, these characters play a significant part in providing the ironic contrast, one of Waugh's chief literary devices. In terms of the underlying quest-myth, Guy offers example of how the difficult goal is to be achieved. As he does this, he at the same time defines the very qualities which keep the other knights in the story from achieving the goal. They have nothing of the heroism that Winston Churchill lauded in the glowing rhetoric:

> The knights of the Round Table, the Crusaders, all fall back into the past . . . these young men going forth every morn to guard their native land and all that we stand for. . . .
>
> Every morn brought forth a noble chance. And every chance brought forth a noble knight.[10]

Throughout the trilogy, Waugh undercuts the misplaced and grandiloquent military fervour of the Prime Minister during the war years. In *Men at Arms* Guy is said to find Churchill's war broadcasts painfully boastful. He "knew of Mr. Churchill only as a professional politician, a master of sham-Augustan prose, a Zionist, an advocate of the popular Front in Europe, an associate of the press-lords and of Lloyd George."[11]

The title of Book Two "In the Picture" epitomises Waugh's attitude to the men who "misconducted" the war. Disorganization is of the very essence of the military life to Guy. It is always, in the words of the Adjutant, "order, counter order, disorder." Waugh puts the military catchphrase, "In the Picture" to telling ironic use. Every one who enters the army is put in the picture, "when all the painters of the world had finally abandoned lucidity." (130) Such disorganization while generating a great deal of farcical humour, is a correlative of the spiritual perversity of contemporary life as a whole. Waugh indicts modern civilization for its burying of personality. By attacking the characters who have no fixed identities and the physical reality in which the faceless creatures have their being, Waugh demonstrates the necessity of relying on a spiritual order. Aimless and disoriented, they rely upon their own puny and frail reason instead of upon Divine Reason.

Guy's double, Apthorpe, in *Men at Arms* long since dead, his place is taken by Ivor Claire, the cavalry officer to whom Guy transfers all the values of nationalism and honour. Ivor Claire in *Officers and Gentlemen* seems to Guy the living embodiment of the aristocratic ideal which alone can sustain his nation in its hour of trial. Guy's romantic euphoria at the thought of his good fortune in sharing the great enterprise of war with his brother officers is summarised in the closing passage of the "Interlude": "He could not yet mourn Ritchie-Hook. . . . Guy thought instead with deep affection of X Commando. . . . Ivor Claire was another pair of boots entirely, salty, with-drawn, incorrigible." (114)

Claire's abject cowardice and his desertion of his men in the battle of Crete shatters Guy's ideals of war and of life. This occasions a thorough reappraisal of his own life's values. He recognizes with shame his own dishonourable participation of war which has so far been conducted by men of unheroic temper as Ivor Claire. The recognition of the bankruptcy of what once seemed an impregnable ideology is hard to bear. Ivor's desertion is the final stage of Guy's disillusionment. With this, as Bergonzi has noted, "Guy's self knowledge is complete and the domination myth of much of Waugh's work is deflated."[12] Guy's aphasia in the hospital after his escape from Crete is caused as much by the physical rigour he has had to endure as by the thought of self-serving conduct of Ivor Claire and his ilk. Claire Hopley compares Guy's silence in the hospital to that of Angela in *Put Out More Flags* and argues that both Guy and Angela become alienated and silent because they both understand the significance of war.[13] At first it looks that the experiences in Crete have made Guy speechless (but it is clear before long that he is physically able to speak) but, as in the case of Angela in *Put Out More Flags*, words are hopelessly inadequate to express his disillusionment with war. Utterly disenchanted, he has to stay silent in his hospital bed like Angela who prefers to be all by herself in her apartment. Guy has to face a reality which is beyond the reach of words. Betrayal of a noble cause is far more appalling than the discovery of the British troops terrorized by the German bombers in Crete. In literalizing the truth that war is unspeakable, Waugh proves himself one of the best War novelists who can subtly explore the moral and psychical issues raised by the war. Guy is unable to talk about their perceptions because of a profound psychic trauma. He is temporarily deranged like Hamlet: "SILENCE was all. Ripeness was all. Silence swelled lusciously like a ripening fig, while through the hospital the softly petulan north-west wind, which long ago delayed Helen and Menelaus on that strand, stirred and fluttered." (226)

But such an ordeal as Guy has endured is inevitable in the process of self-realization. Not only are there echoes from Hamlet but there are implicit references to King Lear. Guy is the modernized version of King Lear who acquires wisdom through madness. Julia Stitch, the novel's Cleopatra, a carry-over from Waugh's *Scoop* commits the last act of betrayal in the novel. With her seductive attitudes and "her hypodermic needle of her charm," the ubiquitous political hostess wheedles out of Guy the true events surrounding Claire's desertion of his men in the Battle of Crete. She knows that Claire's alibi that he was ordered into the boat and was made to believe that his men were following him in another is far from credible. Yet in her eagerness to cover up his disgrace and for fear that Guy might meet the fierce Ritchie-Hook she ships Guy home by the slowest means of transport. Guy is thus prevented from joining his old battalion and his old fire-eating Brigadier who will surely court martial Claire for treason. Hardly has Guy left when Mrs. Stitch throws away the envelope containing the red disc of the dead soldier, which Guy has asked her to deliver. A composite of Shakespeare's Cleopatra and of Jose-Maria de Heredia, Julia with her eyes "one immense sea, full of flying galleys" is a true representative of modern degeneracy.

Of the pseudo-knights in Guy's "Crusade," the most despicable is Major Hound who calls himself Fido. The author makes his contempt for Hound known in constant canine analogies that he associates in the description of him. The rise and fall of Hound contains some of Waugh's finest prose, characterised by allusiveness and parodic parallels. Hound is presented as a quester of the post-lapsarian world with its irreconcilable ambiguities and paradoxes. His quest for food and drink is an index of the perversion of priorities in an age of spiritual vacuum, dramatizing as it does the fact that modern man is a victim and plaything of terrible coincidences. A latter Noah, Hound is "sure in his righteousness." Whatever strange tides were flowing round him Major Hound is still kept afloat.

A paper soldier whose maxims include "In bumf lay salvation" and "sauve qui peut," it falls to Major Hound to be in command of the Hook force when Tommy Blackhouse breaks his leg and is made immobile. He has graduated from Sandhurst whose traditions he is hopelessly unable to live up to, under the stress of evacuations in Crete. The efficiency of the military machinery of the commandos is called into question when Tommy hands over the responsibilities of the commander to Fido Hound. This is in sharp contrast to the efficiency of the Halberdiers who would not take Guy into action on account of his age.

His duties as acting commander of Hookforce include keeping his brigade headquarters in constant touch with his men and with Creforce. The strain of moving back and forth between his men and the shifting Creforce headquarters proves too much for him. Like Judas, he falls victim to sensual appetite: "Fido stood at the parting of the ways. Behind him lay a life of blameless professional progress; before him the proverbial alternatives: the steep path of duty and the heady precipice of sensual appetite. It was the first great temptation of Fido's life. He fell." (177) In bartering his cigarettes for the tin of beef and a single biscuit, Hound barters away a precious piece of his manhood and his soul: "Fido took his price of shame in his hand, the little lump of the flaky, fatty meat and his single biscuit. He did not look at Guy but went away out of sight to eat. It took a bare minute. Then he returned to the centre of his group and sat silent with his map and his lost soul." (177)

Hound's moral degradation is contrasted with the high-mindedness of the aged Greek General of the name of Miltiades, a name meant to evoke the ancient Athenian warrior who defeated the Persians at Marathon. General Miltiades is seen burying his driver. His young aide tells Guy that the General would not leave the driver of the truck which was shot at the Germans the previous night. General Miltiades is the custodian of the values and chivalric ideals that both Waugh and Guy greatly cherish and which no longer inspire the British army men: "Barracks, boarding-houses, palaces, English country houses stricken battlefields—all were the same to General Miltiades." (186) General Miltiades, to quote B.W. Wilson,[14] is allied with forces of light and reason against those of pagan vulgarity typified by Ivor Claire, Mrs. Stitch and Sir Ralph Brompton. But as Corporal-Major Ludovic notes in his diary gentlemen like General Miltiades "are now very old."

Waugh relentlessly traces the weary and degrading quest of Hound. Rationalizing his flight as a flight from thieves Hound is ever in search of food to allay his growing hunger. The path is strewn with barriers such as caves, culverts, mountains and bodies of water—all archetypically associated with quest in works of Classical literature. Like his more respectable forbears, Hound must wade across water and leap through the forest trees in order to reach the safe retreat of the green valley. But instead of the spiritual rejunvenation which awaited the classical quester, Hound is merely looking for gratification of physical appetite. At the Creforce headquarters (where the "men are huddled on their haunches like chimps in a zoo") Hound receives two great bundles of 1,000 drachma notes. But frightened by a rifle shot he loses his way among the boulders and scatters the Greek currency and borne along by a "benevolent zephyr of classical myth," he lands on mossy ground. He awakes in the Arcadian valley only to be challenged by an old Cretan, his bearing patriarchal and his costume phantasmagoric. The old man in trousers strips Hound of his possessions in a most balefully unceremonious manner. "Fido wept." Jeffrey Heath notes a reversal of the Prelapsarian repose in the episode of the green Cretan valley. The Adamic theft of his children's rectitude is reenacted by the menacing old man.[15] Instead of regaining the lost Paradisal splendour, Hound is fated to absolute and irretrievable moral and spiritual degradation. After a symbolic dip in the fountain Hound moves along a gorge until at last he is picked up by Ludovic who refreshes him with wine and is led to a cave where a group of defectors are making an aromatic heterogeneous stew. In a language charged with mock-chivalric imagery, the quest-motif is recalled once again:

> Ludovic strode on. Fido stood with hanging head and closed eyes, out on his feet. And in that moment of prayerless abandonment, succour was vouchsafed. Tiny, delicious, doggy perceptions began to flutter in void. He raised his bowed nose and sniffed. Clear as the horn of Roland a new note was recalling him to life. Unmistakable and compelling, above the delicate harmony of bee-haunted flower and crushed leaf a great new smell was borne to him: the thunderous organ-tones of Kitchen. (202)

The "proletarian solidarity" in the cave, of which Major Hound has become an integral part bespeaks the displacement of the leadership of aristocracy which has been accelerated by what Ian Kilbannock, the journalist-peer has earlier in the novel called the "people war." Hound makes a most servile gesture to the company in the hope of obtaining a succulent fare. The image of the bats completes the *Waste Land* theme of aridity, spiritual blindness and eeriness: "Suddenly, for no human reason, a great colony of bats came to life in the vault of the cave, wheeled about, squeaking in the smoke of the fire, fluttered and blundered and then settled again huddled head-down, invisible." (204) The menacing scene foreshadows the liquidation of Hound at the hands of Ludovic.

Among the anti-heroes whose fates closely touch that of the protagonist, Trimmer occupies a unique thematic position. With his soulless predatory amorality and cautious cowardice Trimmer represents the destructive force which threatens to engulf all norms of order and decency. His many aliases – Gustave, Ali, Trimmer, Captain Mac Tavish, briefly Major Mac Tavish – suggest his total lack of self-identity. A nomad in a desocialized world, Trimmer stands for the values of an increasingly materialistic society which has no consciousness either of good or of evil. Loss of personal history or identity is the most common condition in an ethos which prizes worldly success above moral concerns or personal rectitude. Individuals like Trimmer who lack self-identity thrive in a society in which there is an absence of guiding or governing norms.

The name of Trimmer has had, as Thomas A. Gribble has shown in his article,[16] a long albeit debased lineage. As far back as the seventeenth century, the term "Trimmer" has denoted uneasy, cowardly compromise.

Dryden gave it a more sinister and pejorative connotation, describing "Trimmer" as "damn'd neuters" who were "neither fish, nor flesh nor good red-herring." In T.S. Eliot's *Waste Land* the inhabitants, who like Dante's souls in the vestibule of the inferno, exist without blame or praise and are unwilling to make a choice between God and the devil.[17] Waugh's Trimmer becomes a hero through total misapprehension and mendacity. Through Trimmer Waugh is making once more a scathing attack on a civilization in which people cannot ever hope to transcend or comprehend their finitude.

The operation "Popgun," the ridiculous raid designed chiefly by the "arch impostor" Ian Kilbannock rockets Trimmer to undeservedly dizzying heights of fame. Planned as a Commando assault by the department of General Whale, a lighthouse on an uninhabited island, the operation is at once aimed at boosting the sinking morale of the public and raising American opinion of the war. Captain Trimmer with his twelve men is sent on the mission. The party, however, by mistake lands on a friendly French coast, Trimmer is wholly unnerved but the Sergeant blows up a railway line. Kilbannock's drunken misquotation of Hugh Latimer's words from John Foxe's *Book of Martyrs* establishes the unchivalric character of the entire episode: "Be of good comfort, Master Trimmer, and play the man. We shall this day light such a candle by God's grace in England as I trust shall never be put out." (149) As with several of Waugh's key-quotations this has contradictory connotations. While it implicitly contrasts the abject cowardice of Trimmer with the Protestant martyrs of the sixteenth-century England, it makes Kilbannock heir to the tradition of false propaganda. John Foxe, considered by some as an "arch fabricator of Protestant Propaganda," is said to have distorted parts of the religious history of England in order to sow dissensions between the Catholics and the Protestants of his day, in much the same way as the modern press-peer in the story is going to falsify history and make Trimmer a national hero.

Waugh makes sound artistic use of the ironical implications of the episode of Trimmer's raid. The acclamation that follows the hair dresser-turned-captain is counterpointed against Guy's growing sense of failure and disillusion with his chosen vocation. A parody of Guy's raid on Dakar at the end of *Men of Arms* Operation Popgun is associated with the explosion of thunder box of Apthorpe with whom Trimmer has spiritual affinity. Guy's characteristically courageous action which merited a Military Cross brought him only disgrace and dishonour whereas Trimmer is promoted to Colonel. There is double irony in Trimmer winning Virginia, as his mistress. This liaison has far-reaching consequences on Guy's career. Operation Popgun performs a further rhetorical function of foreshadowing the Cretan debacle at the end of *Officers and Gentlemen.*

Played against the cosmic overdrop of the Holy Saturday the episode of the popgun raid demonstrates the distortion of the Christian rituals by men of a degenerate, secularized age. By implication, Waugh emphasises that fulfilment of man's moral and aesthetic potentialities is far more important than the creation of opportunities for rising in the world. Trimmer and, in a far greater degree, Kilbannock are expositors of the so-called philosophy of self-made manhood for which Waugh has ferocious contempt, for such a philosophy fails to take account of the cosmic issues of life and man's need to search for his soul and spiritual and moral existence. From the perspective of Eternity the temporal defeats and victories are bound to appear trivial. Disasters in the Middle East happen in the Holy week. On Maundy Thursday the Australians in Greece had been attacked on their open flank. Belgrade had been bombed on Palm Sunday. The momentous proposals for an operation to impress American opinion are made by General Whale alias Sprat at a moment when "all over the world, unheard by Sprat, the *Exultet* is being sung that morning." (117) It finds no echo in the hollow hearts of Sprat, Trimmer and Kilbannock in general, in the men of the age of modern technological war fare, who have no awareness of the heavenly or infernal importance of man. A loss of the sense of sin has meant inevitably the loss of the sense of redemption.

The ancient Christian theme of the "fortunate fall" which the medieval hymn of *Exultet* most poetically and movingly embodies has formed part of the Holy Saturday Mass. Teetering on the verge of heresy, as R.W.B. Lewis says, the hymn seeks to solve the problem of the existence of evil.[18] Adam's sin was necessary in the scheme of the Atonement and Redemption. It is as a consequence of sin that the world has been enlarged and enlightened through the figure of the Redeemer. Furthermore the *Exultet* points to the transforming power of human experience with its tinge of sin, shock and suffering. It is through errors that we humans reach to maturity and identity. The ancient theme of the "Felix culpa"[19] rectifies the inadequacy of the philosophy which put a premium on human innocence. Struggle against an ineffable and "absurd" affection is presupposed in any attempt for the full reach of human personality. An irrational world ruled by players and jokers such as Trimmer has to be taken into full account.

If Trimmer and Kilbannock are a couple of rugged entrepreneurs in quest of fame and fortune, Corporal Major Ludovic is an affected enthusiast and a pedant. He is another parody of Guy, a representative of what he himself describes in his *Pensees* as the "Age of Purges and Evacuation." His intellectual aberrations are intentionally magnified beyond normal credibility so that they are more effectively exposed. The measure of Waugh's stature as a comedian, as Christopher Sykes remarked in 1955,[20] is that the jottings of this mysterious man with sepulchral aspect are, for all their absurdity, often aptly impressive. In a sharp contrast to Guy whose struggle against existential odds culminates in a creative act of faith, Ludovic best illustrates the "death-wish," one of the novel's recurring themes. Unlike the "foenix culprit" in Joyce's *Finnegans Wake*,[21] who though related to the devil and nothingness yet is reborn like the legendary bird from out of the ashes, Ludovic is congenitally disabled to transcend his finitude and negativity. Ludovic is the novel's symbol of blight and murder. His capability in the death of Fido Hound is more than slightly hinted. Ludovic's psychotic obsession with death and purgation is to be associated later in the trilogy with the Sword of Stalingrad from which he is to seek inspiration for his literary magnum opus, to be called the "Death Wish."

As the trilogy proceeds, the role of Guy's father gathers an increasingly positive significance. There is none of Waugh's irony in his portrayal of Mr. Crouchback, whose function as Waugh is reported to have told Frederick J. Stopp, is "to keep audible a steady undertone of the decencies and true purpose of life behind the chaos of events and fantastic characters"[22] although he is a 'typical victim in the war against the Modern Age.' Reduced to poverty, and teaching the Classics at our Lady of Victory's preparatory School, Old Crouchback nevertheless, symbolises the reassertions of the spiritual values of the twin-traditions of aristocracy and the Catholic Church. Waugh's affectionate approval of good old Crouchback is evident in the school scenes and in his treatment of the nasty and ingrate Cuthberts who plot to turn him out of his lodgings. Doubt "is a stranger to him," as the devoted Miss Vavasour is perceptive enough to observe. He is the novel's Christ-figure, the holy idiot of Dostoevsky, whose mind the Cuthberts are obliged to admit "seems to work differently than yours and mine." His familial pride in Father Grevase, who has been a victim of treachery, like Waugh's Edmund Campion, is touching in its simplicity. Some of Waugh's affirmative, social criticism is found in his attitude towards Mr. Crouchback, who with his extraordinary kindliness and concern for his fellow human beings stands as the finest exemplar of traditional values and of shaping powers of the past. His treatment of the gross Cuthberts is typical of his nature. He is an odd man in a society which is value-free and has no respect for religion or tradition: "A week or two ago you said there was someone in need of a room here. . . . I came to give a week's notice that I shan't need the sitting-room in future, not in the immediate future, that is. After the war, I shall be very pleased to take it on again, . . . I'll stay of course, until you find a suitable tenant." (38)

Old Crouchback sees no dichotomy between service to the monarch and his faith as a Catholic. His reaction to the news of Trimmer's raid is one of pride in his country's military prowess. Waugh's irony in Crouchback's misplaced praise does nothing to discredit the essential goodness of the old man. What sustains Guy in the later stages of his quest is his growing trust in his father's moral sense and the values he has stood up for all his life. Like his father, he will begin to accept the necessities of mundane law and yet admit the existence of God.

Even before the novel is half-way through, a few pages after the opening of Book Two, the narrator describes Guy as having "begun to dissociate himself from the army in matters of real concern." (122) Already war-weary, Guy sees the futility of his endeavour and of the chivalric idealism which he once so ardently associated with modern warfare. Experience of war has indeed "transvalued all values."[23] Such a sense of early disenchantment is an indication of the measure of maturity in the moral perception of Waugh's hero. This moment of disillusion is the prelude to the self-discovery that Guy achieves at the end of the trilogy. One after the other Guy's idols begin to fall. Hound and Trimmer are men of straw but it is when "the finest flower of them all" – Ivor Claire – begins to stink that the collapse of Guy's idealism becomes complete.

Guy's experience of treachery of the man of God is set in Alexandria, which Waugh the travel-writer-turned-novelist describes as the "ancient asparagus bed of theological absurdity." Alexandria the seat of ancient heresy is a most appropriate setting not only for the defeat of the military aspirations of the Western world which has turned away from the path of the true faith but also for petty ecclesiastical betrayals. Guy is rudely shocked when the German priest at the confessional tries to obtain secret military information from him. For a moment, the Church, like the army, seems to have failed him. It is not until his father's insistence on the Church as a mystical body, in the last novel of the trilogy (the "Church of sinners" as Virginia refers to it), that Guy regains his old faith.

The collapse of illusion receives its most striking expression in the image of the dead soldier in the third book of the novel. In Crete, Guy is wandering alone seeking information when suddenly, he comes upon a young soldier, stiff and dead.

> The young man was dead, undamaged it seemed. He lay as though at rest. The few corpses which Guy had seen in Crete had sprawled awkwardly. This soldier lay like an effigy on a tomb-like Sir Roger in his shadowy shrine at Santa Dulcina. Only the bluebottles that clustered round his lips and eyes proclaimed that he was flesh. . . .

> Meanwhile, lacking words the three of them stood by the body, stiff and mute as figures in a sculptured Deposition.
>
> To bury the dead is one of the corporal works of charity. There were no tools here to break the stony ground. Later, perhaps, the enemy would scavenge the island and tip this body with others into a common pit and the boy's family would get no news of him and wait and hope month after month, year after year. A precept came to Guy's mind from his military education: 'The officer in command of a burial party is responsible for collecting the red identity discs and forwarding them to Records. The green disc remains on the body. If in doubt, gentlemen, remember that green is the colour of putrefaction.'
>
> Guy knelt and took the disc from the cold breast. He read a number, a name, a designation, RC. 'May his soul and the souls of all the faithful departed, in the mercy of God, rest in peace.'
>
> Guy stood. The bluebottles returned to the peaceful young face. Guy saluted and passed on. (206)

The anonymous dead soldier symbolises the collapse of Guy's lingering illusions of the war. "This episode," as Kiley has said, "stands out among hundreds of pages of farce and irony as a simple, almost sentimental, statement of the dignity of death in the midst of one of the most futile battles of the war."[24] The calm and statesque serenity of the dead man is in sharp contrast to the roar and confusion of disorganised warfare. In the highly-charged symbolic language of the passage heterogeneous elements are brought together to generate semantic tension. As in Waugh's best writing, the scene of the three spectators standing by the corpse "stiff and mute, as figures in a sculptured Deposition" is meant to evoke contradictory perceptions. The chivalry metaphor associates the dead soldier with Sir Roger in the shadowy Santa Dulcina. In his dignity and repose, the obscure soldier might be the figure of Christ himself, bowed under the weight of sorrow. The association of the dead soldier with Sir Roger, the medieval martyr might suggest the novelist's affirmation of the positive values which Guy set out to defend. But the sudden intrusion of realism is signalled by the disagreeable bluebottles which cluster round the lips of the corpse. Guy's own euphoria is to be replaced (or has already been?) by stark realism of the war. Rupert Brooke has inevitably to be replaced by Wilfred Owen.[25] The dead man is a remainder of the inadequacy of Guy's ideals embodied in Sir Roger who died long ago not in the war of the Crusade but in a village brawl.

Symbolic events or situations such as this have a functional effect in the story. Their appearance affects in some way the tone of the story or the mind of the character. The disc on the soldier's body indicates that he is a Catholic, like Guy. The latter's duty as a Christian asserts itself immediately and he mutters a prayer for the faithful departed, salutes and passes on. Mrs. Julia Stitch, who is a "mine of indiscretion," to whom Guy later gives the red identity disc, throws it into a waste paper basket, thus signifying the futility of Guy's crusading mission in an unheroic age. The tossing of the disc by Mrs. Stitch is also a rhetorical reminder that Guy has received just treatment at the hands of the woman for not having done his duty to the young solider. He neither cared to bury him nor attempted to console the crying girls. Guy's inability to have the soldier's death recorded symbolises the ineffectuality of his personal quest which has taken no account of his fellow men. The conflation of the disc with Gervase's medal in Guy's overwrought mind is symptomatic of his dimness of perception and confusion of values. On his way back to Egypt after the ordeal in Crete Guy is so exhausted that he holds the disc of the dead soldier and invokes the aid of Sir Roger. While at one level, the serene posture of the dead soldier is that of the crucified Christ, at another level, it epitomises the inadequacy and unreliability as an ideal for a twentieth century quester.

True illumination is possible only when the quester experiences the pentecostal purification which is predicated on total self-surrender. This is suggested at the novel's opening. In a passage of apparent frivolity Waugh contrasts the fruits of materialism with the lasting treasures of wisdom of the Holy Spirit: "A crescent scream immediately, it seemed, over their heads; a thud which raised the paving-stones under their feet; a tremendous incadescence just north of piccadilly; a *pentecostal wind*; the remaining panes of glass above them scattered in lethal splinters about the street." (10) This idea of transfiguration through purgatorial sanctification with the aid of the divine spirit is strongly reminiscent of the "Pentecostal fire" in line ten of "Little Gidding" in T.S. Eliot's *Four Quartets*. The blitz reminds both writers of the power of "the dark dove with the flickering tongue"[26] which proclaimed the coming of the Holy Spirit on the distraught disciples of Christ.

From the vantage point of the Biblical ethos the modern war and the cause they pretend to espouse are seriously suspect and are lacking in that crusading spirit by which the quester-protagonist has so mistakenly set such great store: "In training, Guy had often wondered whether the exercises at Penkirk bore any resemblance to real warfare. Here they did. This was no Armageddon." (221)

Guy, like his creator, is beginning to question the moral and political assumptions behind what Waugh called in *Vile Bodies* the greatest battlefield in human history. Far from being the Armageddon, terrifyingly described in the *Apocalypse* (or more commonly called *The Revelation*)[27] in which the forces of unrighteousness and the allies of the anti-Christ are roundly routed, the present war is fought from sheer self-interest and in which the participants are willing to make unholy alliances. Guy's cup of bitterness is full when after he is told of the details of Ivor's desertion, news comes of the British alliance with the war and of the causes he has all along believed to be just and honourable seems complete and final. He symbolically burns the incriminating documents which could have brought about Ivor's court-martial and disgrace: "That afternoon he took his pocket book to the incinerator . . . and thrust it in. It was a symbolic act; he stood like the man at Sphakia dismembered his Bren and threw its parts one by one out into the harbour, splash, splash, splash, into the scum." (240)

As in T.S. Eliot, allusions to pagan and Classical lore give universal implications of the hero's existential predicament in Waugh. Guy may be modern Theseus lost, like his Classical counterpart, in the Cretan labyrinth without an Ariadne's thread and Ivor is thought of as "that young prince of Athens sent as a sacrifice" to Crete. Guy's hardship and privation in Crete and eventual escape in a bug-infested fishing boat are comparable to the destructive forces that Theseus has had to contend against. Similar references to Classical figures such as Heraclitus earlier in the novel, at the "heterogeneous" luncheon of the socialite Mrs. Stitch and of her husband Algernon, the man with a look of "blank benevolence" perform a similar function, namely to contrast the debased latter times with the genuine cultural heritage of the ancient Greek civilization. Julia is like the women in T.S. Eliot's *The Love Song of J. Alfred Prufrock*, who "come and go/Talking of Michelangelo."[28] Such allusiveness is particularly appropriate in the situation of Waugh's novel which persistently parodies the quests of heroes of a more meaningful past.

Guy's own search for values has not been entirely fruitless. Lying in the basement of Julia's sumptuous apartment and stripped of his chivalric illusions, he is taking stock of his career:

> Guy lacked these simple rules of conduct. He had no old love for Ivor, no liking at all, for the man who had been his friend had proved to be an illusion. He had a sense, too that all war consisted in causing troubles without much hope of advantage. Why was he here in Mrs. Stitch's basement, why were Eddie and Bertie in prison, why was the young soldier lying still unburied in the deserted village of Crete, if it was not for Justice? (239)

The process of humanization of the protagonist has begun. With his illusions pierced, Guy grows out of his innocence into experience which has taught him to come to terms with the world of scum in which he has to live. With the sense of the need for accommodation comes also the need to commit himself to an *active* cause. Only such a commitment will enable him to recreate in his life the values of the past of which his saintly father old Mr. Crouchback is a living embodiment, and make him grow out of the stasis, the state of unactualised potentiality in which he has hitherto existed.

Waugh's deepening sense of commitment of Catholic tenets finds a corresponding artistic correlate in his later works. In the epilogue to *Officers and Gentlemen* Waugh offers his protagonist what he thinks a viable way himself. Behind the oblique irony characteristic of Waugh lies an unmistakable seriousness of tone. Arthur Box-Bender, Guy's brother-in-law shows him the list of religious books that Tony has sent for from prison:

> *The Spiritual Combat by Francis de Sales Christ the Ideal of the Monk by Abbot Marmion. Spiritual Letter of Don John Chapman. The Practice of the Presence of God by Lawrence.*
>
> 'I think it ought to be "Dom John" not "'Don John," he said.
>
> 'Yes, yes, very likely. My secretary copied them. But what d'you make of it?'
>
> 'Most edifying. I can't say I've read them much myself. Are you thinking of becoming a monk, Arthur?'
>
> The effect of the little quip was remarkable. (247)

Waugh is defending what would seem to secular writers an untenable religious position. Guy protests against his brother-in-law's description of young Tony's vocation as monk as "religious mania," for after all madness runs in the Crouchback family. The narrator's close identification with Guy is explicit. In Guy's argument that "lots of quite sane people read books like that" one can detect the author's approving nod. Waugh once said that "the cloister offers a saner and more civilized life than 'the world.'[29] One of the assured ways of salvaging the old values and beliefs and of escaping the time-compulsiveness of the modern world is the life of a monk or of a religious recluse. Sebastian in *Brideshead* chose the way of a porter in a monastery and now it is Tony Box-Bender.

Waugh, however, firmly subscribed to the Augustinian view of the uniqueness of an individual's vocation. Sebastian and Tony Box-Bender have found their true monastic vocations. But Guy is destined for a very different sort of vocation. His chivalric quest is ended. He has now to begin a mission in which he has to reclaim his personal honour.

There is irony in the novel's conclusion. Guy is back with the Halberdiers, which seems to him to still uphold the elitist values in an age of more confusion.

> That afternoon Guy paraded on the square with a mixed squad of recruits and officers in training under Halberdier Colour-Sergeant Oldenshaw.
>
> '. . . I'll just run through the detail. The odd numbers of the front rank will seize the rifles of the even numbers of the rear rank with the left hand crossing the muzzles – all right? – magazines turned outward – all right? – at the same time raising the piling swivels with the forefinger and thumb of both hands – all right? . . . All right, Halberdier Colour-Sergeant Oldenshaw. All right.' (249)

But Guy's optimism is short-lived and he is soon going to realise that his certainties about his corps are in fact unfounded as the opening of *Unconditional Surrender*, the final volume of the trilogy is to show.

NOTES

1. *Evelyn Waugh, A Reference Guide*, p. 57.
2. Evelyn Waugh, *Letters*, p. 443.
3. Evelyn Waugh, *Officers and Gentlemen* (UK: Penguin, 1965; rpt. 1985), p. 240.
4. William J. Cook, Jr., p. 289.
5. *The Ordeal of Gilbert Pinfold*, p. 14.
6. *The Picturesque Prison*, p. 262.
7. Quoted in William J. Cook, Jr., p. 283.
8. *Men at Arms*, p. 75.
9. Andrew Rutherford, *Literature of War*, p. 133.
10. Quoted by B.W. Wilson in "*Sword of Honour*: The Last Crusade," p. 91.
11. *Men at Arms*, p. 176.
12. Bernard Bergonzi, "Evelyn Waugh's Gentlemen," *Critical Quarterly*, 5 (Spring 1963), p. 35.
13. Claire Hopley, "The Significance of Exhilaration and Silence in *Put Out More Flags,*" *Modern Fiction Studies*, no. 30 (Spring 1984), p. 92.
14. B.W. Wilson, p. 92.
15. Jefffrey Heath, p. 237.

16. Thomas A. Gribble, "The Nature of a Trimmer," *Evelyn Waugh Newsletter* (Autumn 1981), pp. 1-3.
17. *Ibid.*, p. 1.
18. R.W.B. Lewis, *The American Adam: Innocence, Tragedy and Tradition in the Nineteenth Century* (Chicago: The University of Chicago Press, 1955), p. 61.
19. From the *Exultet:* "O Felix culpa! quae talem et tantum meruit habere redemptorum." The paradox of the necessity of Adam's sin is contained in the verse, "O Certe necessarium Adae Peccatum."
20. *The Critical Heritage*, p. 368.
21. James Joyce's brilliant parody of the theological paradox of the "felix culpa" in his *Finnegans Wake* ("O foenix culprit! ex nickylow malo comes mickle massed bonum") is deservedly well-known.
22. Quoted by Andrew Rutherford, *The Literature of War*, p. 124.
23. Curtis Bradford, "New Republic" (1955), *The Critical Heritage*, p. 378.
24. Robert Kiley, "The Craft of Despondency – The Traditional Novelists," *Daedalus* (Spring 1963), p. 233.
25. B.W. Wilson, p. 91.
26. Line 28, "Little Gidding II," T.S. Eliot, *Four Quartets.*
27. The Revelation in the Authorised Version of the Bible, Chapter 16.
28. T.S. Eliot, "The Love Song of J. Alfred Prufrock," ll. 35-36, *Understanding Poetry*, ed. Brooks and Warren (NY: Holt, Rinehart and Winston, 1938; rpt. 1960), p. 387.
29. Evelyn Waugh, "Kicking Against the Goad," *Commonweal*, XLIX (1949), p. 534. Quoted in Marston LaFrance, "*Sword of Honour*: The Ironist Placatus," p. 43.

The Consummation of the Quest: *Unconditional Surrender*

Unconditional Surrender (1961), the last instalment of the trilogy written some six years after *Officers and Gentlemen*, brings Guy's quest to a conclusion. In the "synopsis" at the beginning of the novel, Waugh states that beneath the moral collapse and social outrage of the war, "personal honour alone remains."[1] But even before half-way through the novel, the protagonist learns that even his "personal honour" has to be sacrificed for a greater ideal, the ideal of compassion for one's fellow human beings.

Unconditional Surrender records what Patrick O'Donnovan has called the "epochal defeat of Christian civilization[2] which Waugh thought was clearly implied in England's alliance with the Russians which provides the novel's opening. A change of tone from the preceding novels is however noticeable. Waugh has mellowed in the years intervening *Officers and Gentlemen* and *Unconditional Surrender*. The deep note of gloom on which the previous instalment ended yields to a more positive assertion of human worth which is contained in the ironic ambivalence of the title of the present novel. Modern age has surrendered to the universal anarchy resulting from atheism and gross materialism. The protagonist, however, who is conscious of his noble calling does not have to make such an abject surrender to the decadence of the contemporary society; the noble personal quest of the hero, in fact increasingly emphasises the degeneracy of the times.[3] Waugh maintains in the novel that an individual sustained by a vision of Christian humanism can survive the social and moral outrage that the war has been instrumental in generating. What began in *Men at Arms* as the Quixotic quest for an impossible ideal has now become a realistic quest for personal identity. Guy Crouchback emerges victorious at the end of the trilogy insofar as he discovers his fulfilment on a "new ideological, personal lever."[4] Such a shift in emphasis might be said to proceed from the author's own growing sense of realism and ability to come to terms with a world that no longer has any ethical or moral code to follow. Far worse than Hitler's Armageddon is the Marxist revolution which has caused more deaths, in Waugh's view, than the

Second World War in Yugoslavia, where part of the novel's scene is laid. Such revaluations have led to the author's attraction of humanism which stressed the value of the individual. *Unconditional Surrender*, is thus a novel made of sterner stuff than the preceding volumes of the way trilogy and indeed the other earlier works of Waugh. Marked by gritty optimism the book gives the resounding message that it is possible for the individual to achieve personal wholeness and goodness in an ethos of ongoing evil.

More specifically than the other volumes of the trilogy, *Unconditional Surrender* explores the nature of evil in the world, a theme inextricably linked with the quest-motif. The novel contains one of the most memorably moving passages on evil, when Guy tries in vain to help the displaced Jews in Yugoslavia. Maturation marked by compassionate wisdom comes only after the hero-initiate has been confronted with raw evil. Guy, like Lear, has to learn through suffering which is an inevitable concomitant of the knowledge of evil. His whole quest is a painful movement through darkness of ignorance to the light of knowledge. The passage from a single view of life to a "complex, multi-faceted awareness" of existence, as Isaac Sequeira perceptively remarks,[5] is predicated upon an acquaintance with evil. No redemption is possible in the absence of suffering which is an inevitable concomitant of evil in the post-lapsarian universe. The contrast between the earlier Waugh heroes and Guy Crouchback is the contrast in their attitude to evil. Paul Pennyfeather is a helpless victim of evil circumstances whereas Guy attains maturity through confrontation with evil and overcoming it. The knowledge that Guy has gained about himself and the nature of evil results in a decisive change of behavioural attitudes and of character. Such a process of self-understanding enables the protagonist gain a clearer insight not only into the nature of evil but helps him achieve a measure of identity especially in relation to the society of which he now realises he is an inalienable part. It is a process of self-awareness, of recognition of one's weakness and strengths that marks one's maturation. Guy's story is the story of the realisation of this potential wholeness. Step by painful step, Guy is led from innocence to experience and from illusion to reality. His rosy notions of chivalry have to give place to a complex knowledge of existence which is compounded of evil and injustice. Guy at the end of *Unconditional Surrender* integrated into his society, domesticated and contented, maritally well-matched with the rustic Dominica, and proud of Gervase, the legitimised off-spring of Trimmer is a far-cry from the isolated figure at the beginning of *Men at Arms*, who feels no kinship even with men of his faith. His earlier lack of understanding of humanity and of the true nature of religion resulted in his death-wish and anomie.

The type of humanism that is exemplified by Guy is certainly not the atheistic anthropocentrism that Waugh has already repudiated in *A Handful of Dust* but theocentric humanism. Without faith humanism is but barbarism, anthropocentric humanism with its unbridled individualism and its dictum that "man is the measure of things" can never, if at all, try to cope with the engulfing evil. On the other hand, from the perspective of theocentric humanism, evil is finite whereas good is infinite. Anthropocentric humanism, "man-centered and earth-bound is a dreary utilitarian ethic that obstructs the flight of the human soul towards the spiritual radiance which is its destiny."[6] Blinded by egoism and self-love, anthropocentrism can never truly serve the spiritual needs either of an individual or a society. One of Waugh's consistent claims as an artist and man was that religion was the most important of all agents that formed a man's character. It follows therefore that it is theocentric or divine-centred humanism which can see life bound by a divine principle that ensures human beings of spiritual progress and evolution. Theocentric humanism is in other words, religion whose essence is man's relation to God. Evolving man has intuitively recognised that divine reality leads him out of the mists and shadows of empirical reality. Contact with evil inevitably leads such an individual to reach out for the divine which is equated with the supreme cosmic God.

Guy is aided in his search for qualitative and higher values of existence by his father the saintly old Mr. Crouchback who with his charity, piety and unbounded devotion to the Church's teachings, helps Guy perceive the true nature of reality. In Folk-lore terms, Mr. Crouchback performs the function of the "mystagogue" who entrusts the symbols of office to his son "who has been effectually purged of all inappropriate infantile cathexes."[7] Mr. Crouchback's advice on the mystical nature of the Church which does not strike attitudes effects a change of heart in Guy. The father's timely warning that "quantitative judgement don't apply" when it comes to the salvation of even one single soul saves Guy from despair. Guy's faith in the Church and in humanity is restored by Mr. Crouchback's Christ-like love and unreserved charity. Guy's pet illusions are stripped away by his own experience and by the example of his father.

Mr. Crouchback dead exercises an even more potent and transmogrifying influence on Guy than Mr. Crouchback alive. A change in his attitude to the Church and to God is signalled in his ability to pray at his father's funeral. His apathy towards Church exacerbated by his discovery in *Officers and Gentlemen* the imperfection of the men of God is on the wane and is to be replaced by an enthusiastic and intelligent integration into the community of saints. There is a Waughian touch in making the amoral Virginia talk about the Catholic Church as the "Church of Sinners," (138) a vital concept in Catholic dogma, although for the most part, very briefly treated. Sensitive people like Guy who have an acute sense of right and wrong very often confuse the holiness of Church with the rectitude of her ministers. Ironically enough the Reformers themselves who emphasised the corruptibility and sinfulness of human nature accused the Catholic Church of unholiness because of the weakness of some of its members, including the clergy. While alive Mr. Crouchback, affirmed by his example and precept, that the Church had at all times in a sinful world stood for the holiness of God and of his Christ. He had obviously been alert to the criticism that the sinfulness of her members cast a spot on the Church but had humbly acknowledged that the "contradiction" (to adapt Karl Rahner[8]) between the preaching of the Church's Gospel and the human practice of her preachers "not so much a scandal but as very proof of the effectiveness of the Spirit of God working a holy Church." It was this perception that the Church was the living Body of Christ, vitalized by the Holy Sprit of God to whose reality belonged "the divine life, the grace and the power of future aeons,"[9] the imperfection of her officials notwithstanding that had evidently sustained the old man in the face of life's odds. What Mr. Crouchback wanted his son to realize was the fact that the sacraments of the Church, independently of the worthiness of their ministers possessed objective validity and effectiveness; in themselves holy and sanctifying their recipients. When Guy protests about the lapses of the Church including her undignified compromise of the Lateran Treaty, Mr. Crouchback is quick to point out that his son conspicuously lacks in charity, obviously basing his argument on the premise that the Church herself was the prime sacrament and that one cannot abandon the Church "without in some measure losing that which one pretends to wish to preserve."[10] Guy's later unselfish acts of charity—first towards his ex-wife whom he marries and then towards the displaced Jews—proceed from this realization that he ought to put up with the disgrace of the Church's "sins," and love her in humility and silence.

Unconditional Surrender contains Waugh's emphatic rejection of romanticism. With his priggishness Guy is as absurd a figure as Tony Last in *A Handful of Dust*. Guy's disdainful sense of apartness in secular life and his inability to find fellowship with members of his own faith have a common source. He is a victim of romantic delusion. His attitude towards his fellowmen and towards the Church is marked by pharisaical self-righteousness. Mr. Crouchback (and Waugh) try to make Guy see that both in his religion and in his life as a militia man, that what he has been trying to seek have been self-made ideals which are incompatible with reality. Spirituality which cannot endure the "mark of sinner" on the

Church smacks of religious romanticism, lacking in humility and love. Madame Kanyi at the novel's close completes the process of Guy's humanization what his father had begun at the beginning. In different ways, they both challenge Guy's sickly romanticism. By making Guy see the multi-dimensional character of Mystical Body of Christ Mr. Crouchback cures him of his religious romanticism which has long incapacitated him spiritually. For her part Madame Kanyi helps him to see that his romantic attitude to war has been a kind of escapism from the futility of his existence.

If (as Waugh said) *A Handful of Dust* contained all that he had to say on humanism, *Unconditional Surrender* might be said to contain Waugh's positive statement on Christian existentialism or a truly Christian humanism. Faced with the evil that the War has engendered and with ontological contradictoriness of life in general, Guy has come to realize that the only way of escape lies in making a decisive and courageous choice. What the situation demands is a positive act of commitment to the human situation. In existential phraseology, Guy, at the end of the war-trilogy is Christian *'l'homme engage,'* who is humility born of Christian wisdom begins to see that love of God ought to issue in the love of one's fellowmen. His willingness to re-marry Virginia his divorced wife in order to legitimise the child she has had through Trimmer, is Guy's first major act of sacrifice. He is motivated by the same sense of sacrifice when he tries to help the displaced refugees in the final stages of his career in army. In speaking about the war-trilogy, Waugh is reported to have said, that he did imply in the war-trilogy a moral purpose, a chance of salvation in every human life. Waugh told his interviewer: "Do you know the old protestant hymn which goes "once to every man and nation/comes the moment to decide?" Guy is offered this chance by making himself responsible for the upbringing of Trimmer's child. . . . He is essentially an unselfish character."[11]

Religion plays a profoundly significant and transforming role in Guy's life. With the intervention of Providence, his quest takes a new and totally unexpected turn. Complete self-knowledge is accomplished once the protagonist recognises the need to reorder his life according to his destiny ordered by God. Outworn ideals of personal honour and heroism yield to a newly-acquired sense of humility and compassion. As the novel draws to a close Guy's quest is charged with Biblical and theological overtones. Reconstitution of one's ideal can be accomplished only through a belief in disillusion. Guy's own disillusion results from his consent to the operation of divine grace in his life. Underpinning the entire process of the hero's maturation from ignorance to self-knowledge in Waugh's philosophy that amidst all the spiritual waste and chaos of modern life there is a divinity that shapes our ends rough-hew them how we will. It is the unshakable faith in an over-riding Providence that helps Guy (and of Pinfold in the *Ordeal*) to escape the damnation of despair and total negation.

The principle of entelechy or teleology finds its fullest expression in *Unconditional Surrender*. This principle associated with Aristotle posits an intrinsic tendency within a physical body by virtue of which it is oriented towards some goal, as for example, the perfection of an individual or of the species to which it belongs. Aristotle, with his immanent Forms, provided the Catholic Church with the doctrine that the whole physical world was intrinsically orientated towards the fulfilment of a divine plan. Guy's story of attainment of authentic selfhood is illustrative of the Catholic tenet that with the aid of supervenient grace man tends towards an ever-closer hyper-personal social unity with his fellowmen. This tendency as the Christian evolutionist Teilhard de Chardin maintains, elevated to the supernatural order by virtue of the Incarnation, will be finally perfected by the union of man with God in the mystical body of Christ. Guy at the end of *Unconditional Surrender* is a far cry from the alienated human being at the beginning of *Men at Arms* who thinks that the War will provide him an opportunity to realise his chivalric, Quixotic ideals. He has since then painfully unlearnt one set of standards and learnt their opposite.

Like his protagonist, his creator discovers his own reality and his own identity. Guy's quest which involves exploration of values of the different segments of modern society may be said to be Waugh's own evaluation of the norms or their lack of the society in which he has moved. Not only the author, but we (the readers) too, as Rutherford observes, are involved in the process of achieving new self-knowledge and growing in moral insight.[12] The moral discoveries that Guy makes in the course of his pilgrimage have without doubt, the approval of Waugh. Serious art, meant to Waugh, an affirmation of traditional values which alone could nourish the creative impulse of a writer. To some one who shared T.S. Eliot's view on the high calling of the writer, a work of art was an exploration of experience. His narrative technique which gave his works a finished and consummate artistry was a means of discovery of his own self as an artist and as an individual. Guy's growing sense of tolerance and mellowing wisdom at the end of the saga is a reflection of the author's own realistic acceptance of life. However, he like his protagonist will on no account make an Unconditional Surrender to the wicked amorality of the times. Their quests have expanded the range of their sympathies and have taught them both the virtue of accommodation.

References to the knight errantry and chivalric romances and one direct reference to T.S. Eliot's *Waste Land* are certainly meant to direct our attention to the Grail quest which had spiritual renewal as one of its central themes. While the title of the novel's third book "The Death Wish" has enormous thematic significance, it offers Waugh tremendous ironic potential. The inhabitants of Waugh's wasteland, like Eliot's with the exception of old Mr. Crouchback, are afflicted with the pernicious death-wish. Like the Cumean Sibyl in the motto of Eliot's poem, they long to die. This is one of the recurring themes which Waugh never tires of exploring. One of the consequences of the loss of the meaningful sense of the past and of the traditions in culture and religion, is spiritual death. The symbolism of the Holy Grail in the Arthurian myth served an excellent correlative for serious writers of the twentieth century to give literary expression to the spiritual sickness of their times.

What the death wish or death instinct (as Freud termed it) signified was a general instinct of denial, rejection and annihilation which led people away from full expression and pleasure towards death. Such constriction meant inevitably a loss of one's identity and sense of purpose, and was in direct opposition to 'life instinct' which included tendencies that strove towards the integration of living substance into a larger whole. Theologically, such an instinct implied the second 'intensified' death which was the ultimate doom of those who were deliberately Godless and rejected Grace. This has been the theme of *The Loved One*, the novel that Waugh wrote four years before the war-trilogy. Aimee, the central female character, the beautiful cosmetician in the Californian mortuary who commits suicide, is given the significant surname of Thanatogenos; "Thanatos" is Greek for "death." *The Loved One*, an apparently light-hearted satire on the Californian funeral habits is in reality a profound moral statement on the true meaning and nature of death. As a practising Christian, Waugh held that death was the most significant event of life. His view of death is similar to that of high-ranking Christian philosophers to whom death meant a return from the alienated multiplicity of the spatio-temporal world to the "interiorized unity of the spirit."[13] One's existence ought to be an "existence towards death," by which is meant going home to God, as Kierkegaard intended and not a tumble into nothingness, which was the view of Jean-Paul Sartre. "Living and partly living," these victims of war have no time for any kind of spiritual quest. Even if they dared such an undertaking, it would be highly doubtful whether their quest would be termed a truly achieved one. Implicitly, Waugh is pointing to the inadequacy of romanticism which regards death as "easeful" and utterly devoid of pain. This is an untenable position from the Christian perspective which sees death as a painful separation of the body from the soul. All the misery and anguish of our age stems from our hopelessly secular attitude to death.

Guy himself has to triumph over his death-wish before he can ever hope to achieve his goal. In the first novels of the trilogy his quest has been a romantic chivalric one directed towards personal glory and adventure. His whole perspective undergoes a change in the concluding instalment of the trilogy where he undertakes the mission of compassionate self-sacrifice of his own honour and pride of family. It is not the easy death in a battlefield but one which calls for tremendous courage and a sense of mission. Guy's quest exemplifies the timeless significance of man's need for rebirth which is central to the myth of the Holy Grail. So long as they entertain the romantic notion of the pagan poets that the human soul went directly after death to the land of the blessed – a lotos land of ease and comfort – they can never hope to go to the City of God. The birth of a child at the close of the trilogy is symbolic of spiritual regeneration. Death wish is turned into new life. Guy's decision to save the soul of an unborn child of Virginia by Trimmer signals his salvation. What would have seemed repugnant now seems the most welcome thing.

Book One entitled "State Sword" sets the tone of the dark world of *Unconditional Surrender* in which Guy has to move in order to achieve self-realisation. Hints of the disenchantment that he experiences before the trilogy is complete have already been given in the Russian invasion of Poland in *Men at Arms* and in the disgraceful Cretan disaster in *Officers and Gentlemen*. His original beglamoured vision of war as a pilgrimage of chivalry has been rudely shattered. The knight's sword of the prologue to *Men at Arms* has been symbolically replaced by the Sword of Stalingrad at the opening of the trilogy's final instalment. Waugh makes no secret of his derision of the sword which stands for the inversion of values of war-time Britain whose alliance with atheistic Russian strikes Guy as being evil and cruel. The sword represents the new age which has forsaken religion and honour, an ethos alien to Guy who has sustained himself on dreams of national valour. It is now perfectly clear to him that chivalric quest is no longer possible in a society which runs after strange gods and bizarre cults.

The sword of Stalingrad which is displayed in Westminster Abbey for people to queue up and venerate is a parody of the sword of Sir Roger of Waybroke in the Church of Santa Dulcina in *Men at Arms*. Waugh's title to the rescension of the three war novels, *Sword of Honour* is meant to emphasise this contrast between the two swords. The exhibition of the state sword in the historical abbey provides Waugh with opportunities to play variations on the motif, a characteristic literary device of Waugh. Attitudes of marked contrast towards the sword underline the difference in perceptions of the characters. To Guy for instance the fervour of the drab queues of people who have thronged to pay homage signals the dishonour and degradation of public morality of his country. Ludovic on the other hand who muscles his way through the throngs to derive inspiration for his sonnet is a representative of the decline and fall of a civilization.

The sword, as David Wykes has argued, has several satiric and ironic functions.[14] The association of the sword with Trimmer, the bogus "war-hero" immediately reveals its negative significance. Ian Kilbannock, the journalist-peer and one of the amoral toadies in the novel tells his wife: "By the way, do you realise it was Trimmer who gave the monarch the idea for this Sword of Stalingrad? Indirectly, of course. . . . Well, you know how sharp the royal eye is for any details of equipment. He was given a preview of the Trimmer film and spotted the dagger at once . . . the royal mind brooded a bit and the final result was that thing in the Abbey. An odd item of contemporary history." (44) Exposed for worship close to the shrine of St. Edward the Confessor, the state sword stands in hideous contrast to the ideals of religion and royalty that the Confessor has always come to represent. The sword of St. Edward was the true sword of honour with which the reigning monarch of England sought symbolically to do justice and stem the growth of iniquity. There is a further contrast implied in the opening paragraph of the book with the sword of Captain Montagu who had fought against the aesthetical foe. The sword of Stalingrad was a reversal of this, since it was a symbol of British alliance with a revolutionary and Godless state.

Terms ordinarily associated with chivalry and religion are employed in references to State Sword. It "stood upright between two candles on a table counterfeiting an altar." The American Lieutenant Padfield, "Loot" for his friends, a lawyer in the years of peace refers to the "escutcheon," "scabbard" and "baldric" of the sword. Guy's romantic illusion of war has long since vanished and he does not want to be numbered among the throngs who were "suffused with gratitude to their remote allies and . . . venerated the sword as the symbol of their own generous and spontaneous emotion." The idolatry and sacrilege of the mob exhibited by their eagerness to see the "shoddy improvisation" of a senile craftsman fills him with disgust. 'Joe' Stalin is yet another 'uncle' like Apthorpe for whom he had little love. Guy is seen hurrying past the line of devotees on that day to be as far away from as he can manage in order to quietly celebrate his fortieth birthday and have lunch with his friend Jumbo Trotter. Waugh's identification with his protagonist and the values he stands for is absolute. "In this year of sten gun" he writes grimly "it was a notable weapon." The self-regarding and self-deceiving people who have come to the Abbey on that day (29 October 1943) are so undiscriminating in their judgement that they cannot distinguish between a sten gun and a true sword of honour such as the one that Captain Montagu wielded in his war against barbaric atheism.

In running away from the Abbey to Ruben's restaurant, that "rare candle in a dark and naughty world," Guy is making a symbolic escape from the literary and cultural decay of the time which the sword so resonantly represents. The Churchillian renascence which the war seemed to embody once has lost its hold on Guy's imagination. It is no longer a world fit for heroes but only for hollow men such as Ludovic, Padfield, Sir Ralph Brompton and Ian Kilbannock to live and thrive. These men are what Alexander Pope would have termed "dull." Men like Sir Ralph (the crypto-homosexual and crypto-communist) are the architects of the dismemberment of Christendom. His protege Major Ludovic, the war hero who has won the Military Medal for saving Guy in Crete, author of *Pensees* and later of the best-selling *Death Instinct* is the dominating figure in the literary world which is tainted with corrupt taste. "Loot" Padfield's discovery of the error in the design of the sword is Waugh's own comment on the flawed nature of British society. That the discovery should be made by an American, an outsider is part of the novelistic technique characteristic of the author. Guy can no longer have spiritual kinship with these "Trimmers," the custodians of an upstart culture. Everard Spruce is most ironically the founder and editor of the literary magazine called *Survival* when in fact it is men such as Spruce who have killed off all vestiges of decency in the cultural life of the nation.

The mention of Lady Perdita and of her galmorous wedding years ago at which Ludovic met his future patron further explores the theme of the death of chivalry. Unlike her counterpart in Shakespeare, Perdita of the degenerate modern age, is "lost" to all sense of virtue. When Ludovic reminds her of the arch of swords under which she passed with the bridegroom at her first wedding, her response is one of frank boredom. It is this prosaic world of cultural decay with which Guy has to come to terms. The Electronic Personnel Selector at HOO HQ from which Mr. Oates picks out a card at random is the presiding symbol of chance which governs the world of Lady Perdita and the universe of eternal mismanagement of war. Guy has to learn at once to adjust to such a world of quantification and mischance and to distance himself from the values that it represents. This implies education which will help the protagonist to discriminate between chance and Providence. As a Christian and a Catholic, Guy has to recognize that Providence is the name given to the activity of God whereby He directs creatures to their appointed ends, as opposed to chance or Fate which means in effect the removal of human freedom.

Old Mr. Crouchback warns his son of the dangers of value-system of a world in which quantity reigns supreme. He detects in Guy a tone of un-christian despair and spiritual sloth in his non-committal attitude to the war and in the letter he writes to him soon afterwards points out the gravity of his son's situation: "When you spoke of the Lateran Treaty did you consider how many souls may have been reconciled and have died at peace as the result of it? How many children may have been brought up in the faith who might have lived in ignorance. Quantitative judgments don't apply. If only one soul was saved that is full compensation for any amount of loss of 'face.'" (16-17)

Waugh makes the connection between the "sword" and Mr. Crouchback's warning about "quantitative judgments" in Book II of the novel: "There was a congress at Teheran at the time entirely occupied with quantitative judgments." (128) The Teheran conference referred to in the novel was an actual historical happening which took place in late November 1943 when Winston Churchill presented the Sword of Honour to Stalin. Churchill used the phrase the "Sword of Honour" in his speech on that memorable occasion: "Marshal Stalin – I have the command of His Majesty, King George VI, to present to you for transmission to the city of Stalingrad the *Sword of Honour* of which His Majesty himself has approved the design."[15]

Ironic references to the "sphinx," the "two puissant old gentlemen (Churchill and Roosevelt) circumambulating the "Colossus" in Waugh's narrative make it plain the low estimate that he had of the entire proceeding. Qualitatively the sword exhibited in Abbey was negligent. As David Wykes remarks Waugh intends that Mr. Crouchback's warning about quantitative judgements should apply to all the experience his novel depicts.[16] The insistent recurrence of the sentence about quantitative judgements from Mr. Crouchback's letter on the narrative surface, like a melodic phrase in a symphonic composition, underlines one of the novel's prominent philosophical themes. It is one of Waugh's profoundly charged statements on the nature of the human condition of contemporary civilization. The lives of the wastelanders in the novel ominously lack the qualitative dimension which alone can give value and purpose to their existence. The flawed sword of Stalingrad reflects the perverted judgements of the characters. Virginia's licentious opportunism, Ian Kilbannock's total lack of principles, the death wish of Ludovic and Guy, Spruce's faith in the chaos of human destiny, and the unabashedly shabby morals of Sir Ralph and "Loot" – all these are symptoms of the deeply embedded spiritual sickness of a society which, in its obsessive quantitativeness, cannot distinguish between appearance and reality. Guy's father wants him to beware of that despair that human beings without commitment easily fall into and which will inevitably entail unconditional surrender to the forces of dullness and cultural decay. Old Mr. Crouchback's timely warning, with the simple directness characteristic of the man, reverberates, almost haunts Guy the rest of his life and takes on an added solemnity after the old man's death. The advice not only saves Guy from the Christian sin of nihilistic despair but helps him to see the error of his perceptions. His ideas of quest undergo a complete transformation.

The sudden and peaceful death of Mr. Crouchback which occurs in the early part of the novel is significant both thematically and structurally. Waugh's controlled and solemn prose in the description of Guy's father is indicative of Mr. Crouchback's purpose in the novel, which was "to keep audible a steady undertone of the decencies and true purpose of life behind the chaos of events and fantastic characters."[17] His death symbolises the passing away of an old, aristocratic order which stood against the barbarous hordes pushing outside the wall. The heraldic terms in the description place the dear departed in line with Sir Roger of Waybroke to whom at the beginning of the trilogy, Guy is seen praying for his "endangered country." Waugh's ceremonial description of the entire funeral rites is befitting the man who is as dignified in his death as he has been all his life. Counterpointed against the vulgar worship of the sword at Westminster Abbey, the august grandeur of Crouchback's funeral is immediately striking. The catafalque lying at the chapel at Broome, with the tall unbleached candles burning beside it offers a staid and solemn contrast to the sword at the Abbey which the crowds come to worship "as though they were approaching a corpse lying in state." (22)

Waugh provides an appropriate setting for the funeral at Broome which has been a predominately Catholic village. Numbered among the crowd of mourners are the remote cousins of Guy with recusant names, thus suggesting that Broome is the last outpost and citadel of faith in an anarchic world. The satiric irony of the Westminster scene has given place to a scene of elegiac grandeur, recalling the Sculptured Deposition in the description of the dead soldier in *Officers and Gentlemen*. Like the unknown soldier, Mr. Crouchback is a martyr, a figure of Christ. It is the most moving moment in Guy's life, for it is while praying at the funeral that he receives his crucial insight into the meaning of his own existence. The meaning of his father's advice on the inapplicability of quantitative judgement come sharply home to him. Mr. Crouchback's death has an electrifying effect on his son. As the nuns sing *Dies Irae* with all its ancient deprecations of divine wealth, Guy knows that his father is not long for purgatory. It is a truly mystical moment when like his father, Guy has a vision of the blinding, ineffable goodness of God. To Guy his father "was the best man, the only entirely good man he had ever known" who by all the formularies of his faith should be confident of salvation, but who as a man of prayer saw himself as totally unworthy of divine notice.

Guy has arrived at a most decisive moment in his life's mission. From this point on, he is to inherit his father's robust faith in God and in human nature. For the first time in many long years, he feels himself released from the crushing sense of apathy, as his prayer amply testifies. His father seems even now sitting in God's presence among His angels and saints: "He did not expect a heroic destiny. Quantitative judgements did not apply. All that mattered was to recognize the chance when it was offered. Perhaps his father was at that moment clearing the way for him. 'Show me what to do and help me to do it,' he prayed." (66) This is the turning point; Guy will now inherit his father's tradition which will invest his life with meaning and purpose. In the mention of the "Lesser House" opposite the Catholic Church, "a stucco facade and porch," Waugh hints at the achieved quest of his hero that is in store for him. "It was here his father had suggested that Guy should end his days." (68) The social integration that Guy achieves at the end is foreshadowed in the long-forgotten image of his father which Guy conjures up at the Requiem and to which he directs his prayer:

> He had lost the solid image of his father as a man of possessions and authority (for even in his declining fortunes, up to the day of leaving Broome, Mr. Crouchback had faithfully borne all his responsibilities, sitting on the bench and the country council, visiting persons and hospitals and lunatic asylums, acting as president to numerous societies, as a governor of schools and charitable trusts, opening shows and bazaars and returning home after a full day to a home that usually abounded with guests) . . . It was to that image he had prayed that morning. (72)

His father who in his life achieved the rare fusion of pragmatism with conformity to the laws of the supernatural Order, provides Guy with a saner and safer model than Sir Roger of Waybroke. Guy realises that his private cause can no longer be divorced from the rest of the world. In an active involvement in the affairs of men, not an obsessive isolation from them, lies his salvation. The ideals Sir Roger embodied, highly commendable in themselves, are unsuited to the age in which Guy lived. Adjustment to the mores of his times, not aloofness and alienation that was called for. Guy is grateful to his father for curing him of his futile obsession with knight-errantry which sought personal honour and glory at the cost of public suffering. Thanks largely to his father, Guy succeeds at the end in reunifying his dissociated sensibilities and achieving a mediating vision of "real reality." In his very last meeting with his father, the latter chided him for his selfish indifference to the outcome of the war. If he was not interested in victory, his father told him, he had no business to be a soldier. Guy now realises with acute pain that his father was dead right. His father's philosophy that if only one soul is saved is "full compensation for any amount of loss of 'face'," begins to redirect Guy's quest on humbler and more realistic lines. Guy steps off the pinnacle of idealistic emulation of the causes of an outworn age embodied in Sir Roger to the humble service of a humdrum world. Underlying the process of the protagonist's transformation and of his quest is the belief central to the Christian faith, namely, that the moment of grace comes to an individual when he empties himself of his egotism on behalf on the unmerited need of his fellow beings. Guy's acts of kindness and of love are motivated by religion.

Two opportunities of 'self-sacrifice' present themselves to Guy before long. The first of these is his remarriage to his divorced wife Virginia and the second is his involvement with the displaced Jews in Yugoslavia. Waugh's ironic realism is at work in his description of those two episodes. Guy performs the two duties like a knight-errant in pursuit of a personal quest but in terms very different from the purely ideological heroism of his earlier days. Unscrupulous Ian Kilbannock, the journalist-peer engineers Virginia's remarriage with Guy. Virginia is down and out, having been divorced by her last husband Troy without alimony. Her affair with Trimmer, the people's hero, of operation pop-gun fame, has left her pregnant. Once Kilbannock knows that Guy has come into a substantial inheritance he suggests that Virginia went back to Guy who, immobilized by an injured knee following an accident in parachute training, is now lying in bed at Uncle Peregrine's flat in London. He consents to take her back as his wife, prompted by his new-born sense of charity. Ian's wife, Kersite whose granite "Scotch Propriety" has not been entirely atrophied by her life with her unprincipled husband is outraged at Guy's sense of chivalry. To her angry remonstrance that he is being foolishly chivalrous about Virginia, Guy replies that she is in distress and that tough women like Virginia suffer more than the tender:

> 'Of course Virgnia is tough. She would have survived somehow. I shan't be changing her by what I'm doing. I know all that. But you see there's another—' he was going to say 'soul'; then realized that this word would mean little to Kerstie for all her granite propriety—'there's another life to consider. What sort of life do you

think her child would have, born unwanted in 1944?'
'It's no business of yours.'
'It was made my business by being offered.' (151)

When Kerstie protests that half the population of Europe are homeless and one more child will not make a difference, Guy tells her with calm assurance that this is just one case where he can help. He is Virginia's last resort. To one who has come to distrust the quantitative judgements of a crass agnostic world, the answer would seem, as it does indeed to Kerstie, insane. Guy performs this service to Virginia in the true spirit of knight-errantry, looking upon her as a damsel in distress, but it is a chivalric code with a difference. It is an act, motivated not by an ego-centric love of personal glory but by a profound religious sense.

His friends (or adversaries) who mock him about being a Medieval knight-errant do not see that Guy's acceptance of sacrifice belongs to a higher qualitative order of values. Whereas Guy himself ceased to be a knight-errant, his critics have begun to see him a middle-aged pseudo-knight who is looking for damsels in distress in order to satisfy his ego-centric thirst for glory and honour. Here is irony, in the Kierkegaardian sense of being the confine between the calls of the aesthetic and ethical stages of life. Guy's decision to remarry Virginia may be from his friends' perspective a total loss of face provides a clue to the stage of life that he has arrived. In contrast to his friends who represent (to adopt Kierkegaard's categories) the life, that is the romantic level of existence, Guy has reached a far higher level, namely the ethical plane of existence which tends to establish a sense of matured responsibility in one's attitude to life's problems. Guy's behaviour is comparable, as Jeffrey Heath has remarked, to the "self-effacing behaviour of the Church in the matter of Lateran Treaty."[18] Like the Holy Catholic Church of which he is now a vital part, Guy has counted the cost in material terms his action has involved him. But by remarrying Virginia not only has he saved Virginia and her child but himself. This decision is bound to have very far-reaching consequences. Virginia is converted to the Catholic faith and little Trimmer (who is to be baptised as Gervase) will become heir to the Crouchback fortune and inherit the Lesser House at Broome. In making the decision, Guy has responded to the call of Jesus which the young man in the story rejects and the refusal costs him his salvation and the meaning of life which he thinks he had. Guy accepts the "comic irony" involved in Jesus's challenge and as a desirable consequence of such humorous acceptance, experiences new life in contrast to the rich young man who emerges at the end of the story a sadder and lesser man. The "comic shame"[19] which accompanies Guy's acceptance of the new life enables him to realise the romantic nature of his quest so far. All his earlier plans invested with personal interest, had in reality been brittle and fragile.

Guy's growth in spiritual stature is particularly contrasted with Ludovic's growing sense of romanticism which ultimately issues in nihilism. Ludovic plays a role somewhat similar to Apthorpe in *Men at Arms*. Dopplegangers, both of them, their lives are parodic parallels of Guy's. But the rise in the protagonist's fortunes is marked by a parallel decline of these doubles. Even as Guy in *Unconditional Surrender* is gradually purged of his "death-wish" engendered by specious idealism, Ludovic deteriorates further and further until at last he imprisons himself in the fabulous but false Italian castle which Guy abandoned a long time ago. It is Ludovic who is drifting into insanity and not Guy (as alleged by Ian Kilbannock and his wife Kerstie). In fact Guy has shown remarkable signs of recovery from apathy since his experience recorded in *Officers and Gentlemen* and his gallant willingness to take Virginia back as his wife is a definite indication in the novel's rhetoric that he has already grown into a whole man. Guy's injury in the parachute training ends all sense of spurious romantic ecstasy:

> He experienced rapture, something as near as his earthbound soul could reach to a foretaste of paradise, *locum refrigerii, lucis et pacis*. The aeroplane seemed as far distant as will, at the moment of death the spinning earth. As though he had cast the constraining bonds of flesh and muscle and nerve, he found himself floating free; the harness that had so irked him in the narrow, dusky, resounding carriage now almost imperceptibly supported him. He was a free spirit in an element as fresh as on the day of its creation.
>
> All too soon the moment of ecstasy ceased. He was not suspended motionless; he was falling fast. . . . At one moment he had the whole wide sky as his province; at the next the ground sprang to meet him as though he were being thrown by a horse. . . . He attempted to stand, suffered a sharp pain in his knee and toppled once more to the ground. . . .
>
> It was the same knee he had twisted on guest night at the Halberdier barracks. (102-3)

This mishap, within the religious perspective of the novel, is Providential in providing Guy with an opportunity to offer refuge to his ex-wife. His charitable gesture turns the entire course of his quest.

In a style that approaches burlesque Waugh traces the corresponding decline of Ludovic. Author of the *Pensees* and of *Death Wish*, he is referred as "Major Dracula": and in mock-Biblical phrase of the "angel of death." Mistakenly believing that Guy knows that he has committed the deaths of "Fido" Hound and the Sapper (implicitly hinted at in *Officers and Gentlemen* and more explicitly in the "Synopsis" in *Unconditional Surrender*), Ludovic flees Guy's presence, as though he were pursued by the Furies of classical mythology. Guy meets Ludovic a long time after the Cretan episode at the literary soiree of Everard Spruce, after turning away in distaste from the State Sword at the Westminster Abbey. When Guy, with genial frankness, goes up to Ludovic to express his gratitude for saving his life in Crete, the six-footed "Zombie" betrays an emotion of guilty fear. "It was as though Banquo had turned host." His hasty departure which surprises everybody is the symbolic beginning of his retreat from life and hope. As Guy achieves freedom through meaningful sacrifice, Ludovic's increasing isolation from human society spells spiritual death and despair. While with the one, the emphasis is on light and freedom born out of a faith in a higher order, the other expounds with discordant clangour the 'value' of live's emptiness.

Ludovic negates all the values implied by the term "Quest" as we have defined in the present book, namely a positive and qualitative response to the doubt and destructiveness of the modern world predicated upon a steady growth in maturity and wisdom of the individual. Ludovic, like the inverted Sword at the novel's beginning, represents the novel's reversal of all positive values. In spite of (or more truly, as a consequence of) the series of misfortunes that befall him – divorce, demotion in the army, physical injury, misunderstandings – Guy achieves meaningful relationship with his fellow beings at the end of the epic saga. His life has been an evolution, a progression towards actuality. Ludovic's career, in contrast, has been one of depressing regression and is an illustration of one of Waugh's cardinal theses as a Christian writer that human beings by refusing to accept their creatureliness and rebel against their proper place in God's creation will ultimately regress into animals. The recurrent animal imagery in Waugh's novels points to the secularity of man who is hopelessly trapped within his own subjectivity, without God's grace. Ludovic "de-evolves" into a beast and goes down into an order of being lower than that of a human, as his baby-talk to his Pekinese pet (aptly named "Fido") and his imitation of that little animal indicate:

> The floor of Ludovic's room was covered with saucers containing milk, gravy, spam, biscuits, Woolton Sausage and other items of diet, some rationed, some on points, some free to the full purse. Here and there the food had been rudely split; none of it seemed to have appealed to the appetite of the Pekinese supply which crouched under Ludovic's bed in a nest of shredded paper. It was a

> pretty animal with eyes as prominent as Ludovic's own. Ludovic was on all fours making the noises which had been audible outside; . . . Then falling into a fruity and, to Captain Fremantle, blood-curdling tone of infatuation, he addressed himself to the puppy; 'What'll kind staff-captain-man say if you won't eat his nice grub, eh? What'll kind editor-man say if you eat his clever paper?' (114)

Having won a military cross for rescuing Guy in their escape from Crete, Ludovic is made a Major and is in charge of a parachute school where Guy comes for training. When Guy fails, Ludovic plots his liquidation by recommending him for active service even though he has not successfully completed the course. Ludovic's moral deterioration finds its correlative in his deterioration as a man of letters. His *Pensees*, a collection of aphorisms on a wide variety of themes, often absurd in their triviality, are yet in places strikingly apt and written in the most polished style, succinct and economical, a result of great labour, the manner of writing that Waugh himself commended and practised. During the composition of his book of pithy maxims, like a true artist, he is wholly preoccupied with words. Often consulting Fowler and not disdaining Roger, he takes the most loving care in the construction of the sentences, truly characteristic of a writer of classical style.

But few readers of Ludovic's *Pensees* would have discerned that their author was an incurable romantic at heart, as his later novel which he titles *The Death Wish*, symbolising ironically the universal desire for anomic suicide of the modern age. The old mode of writing is abandoned:

> Since the middle of December he had without remission written 3,000 words a day; more than hundred thousand words. His manner of composition was quite changed. . . . He felt no need to find the right word. All words were right. They poured from his pen in disordered confusion. He never paused; he never revised. He barely applied his mind to his task. . . . He just wrote. His book grew as little Trimmer grew in Virginia's womb without her conscious collaboration. (160)

The product of such romantic extravagance is predictably garish and flamboyant. *The Death Wish* is a gorgeous, gaudy tale of romance. With a Shakespearean plot full of elaborate improbabilities, its characters and their equipment were far removed from reality. But for all its glitter, it is a most melancholy book. Unlike Guy who seeks absolution through confession to a servant of God of the last traces of death wish lodged within him, Ludovic parades his innermost feelings of death and destruction in the manner of a confessional romantic. At the end of *Officers and Gentlemen* Ludovic with the strength of a horse and considerable physical prowess easily overshadows Guy. The latter's comatose exhaustion is, in the novel's rhetoric, the result of his sickly romanticism. In *Unconditional Surrender* however, the roles seem reversed. As Guy grows stronger spiritually as well as physically, Ludovic decreases in importance. The altered outlooks of the two characters are reflected in their respective careers. At the end of the novel, Guy has achieved self-knowledge in full measure, as his contented life with rustic Dominica on the farm amply testifies. The Italian Castello at the beginning of *Men at Arms* where he spent eight long years of apathy was his spiritual dungeon, freedom from which has meant travail, frustration and disgrace. Ludovic's decision to buy Guy's Castello and to live there with the pansy "Loot" dramatise his spiritual annihilation.

Guy's second opportunity for selfless action (small service to which he is alone, theologically speaking, uniquely qualified) comes when he is in Yugoslavia where he tries to aid a group of Jewish refugees who having escaped from the Nazis have fallen into the worse hands of the Communists. Ludovic's sinister plans to have Guy killed in action are frustrated by the merciful Providence which in answer to his prayer at his father's funeral, intervenes in the shape of the inept Colonel Grace-Groundling-Marchpole who sees Guy as a security risk in Italy. He is to be sent instead to Yugoslavia. It is somewhere in the complicated terrain in the map that Major Cattermole has spread before him lies his mission of self-sacrifice. Waugh's deep distaste at the ideal of the British officers working in the spiritually arid terrain of the Yugoslavia of the partisans finds expression in Joe Cattermole's description of the young girls who fight for the partisans:

> 'Officers and Men,' he proclaimed exultantly, 'share the same rations and quarters. And the women too. You may be surprised to find girls serving in the ranks beside their male comrades. Lying together, sometimes, for warmth, under the same blanket, but in absolute celibacy. Patriotic passion has entirely extruded sex. The girl partisans are something you will never have seen before. In fact, one of the medical officers told me that many of them had ceased to menstruate. Some were barely more than school children when they ran away to the mountains leaving their bourgeois families to collaborate with the enemy. I have seen spectacles of courage of which I should have been sceptical in the best authenticated classical text. Even when we have anaesthetics the girls often refuse to take them. . . . Well, you will see for yourself. It is a transforming experience.

(165)

To Guy it is going to be a "transforming experience" in an altogether different sense, an experience in which his perspectives are altered and his original vision of the knightly crusade yields place to a vision of a moral reality in which compassionate involvement counts for more than ideals of personal honour. Biblical echoes in the author's description of the episode signal an entirely changed ethos. Guy has no longer any use for bungling knights of the middle ages such as Sir Roger. He would now begin to model himself on one of the well-known patriarchs of the Old Testament: "It seemed to Guy, in the fanciful mood that his lonely state engendered, that he was playing an ancient, historic role as he went with Bakic to inform the Jews of their approaching exodus. He was Moses leading a people out of captivity." (226)

Guy's mission of mercy in which he achieves only a limited success is fraught with setbacks and frustrations of purpose. Like Moses he looks upon himself as set apart by divine design for a not wholly unworthy cause. His conviction that he is exclusively set apart for something for which he turns away from the State Sword to which the London mobs throng to pay homage. His isolation from the other military events, of which the attack on the Block House, stems from the same indifference to the value-systems of the degenerate times. In working for the hundred odd Jews in Yugoslavia, he has unshakable confidence in the rightness of the cause. That Guy's undertaking is no less heroic than that of Moses, the archetypical deliverer, is suggested in the description of the homeless Jews at Guy's first meeting with them: "There were some children in the crowd, but most seemed old, too old to be parents, for they were unnaturally aged by their condition. Everyone in Begoy, except the peasant women, was in rags." (175)

Mme. Kanyi, the electrician's wife and their most articulate spokeswoman, gives succinct account of their sufferings under different oppressive dispensations. The people outside Guy's office are survivors of an Italian concentration camp on the island of Rab. Most of these are Yugoslav nationals but some like herself are refugees from Central Europe. She and her husband were on the way to Brisbane in Australia in 1939 to work there but had been caught by war. When the king fled, the Ustachi began massacring the Jews. The Italians rounded them up and took them to the Adriatic. When Italy surrendered, the partisans brought them to the main land where they conscribed the able-bodied Jews while the rest were imprisoned. Then the Germans moved in; the partisans fled taking the Jews with them. So now here they are in Begoy half-starved and with no hope for the future. The plight of the Jews not only moves him to compassion but helps him gain access into the nature of evil in the world. He commits himself whole-heartedly to helping them: "he felt compassion; something less than he had felt for Virginia and her child but a similar sense that here again, in a world of hate and waste, he was being offered the chance of doing a single small act to redeem the times." (192) Despite the odds, he manfully persists in representing their cause with the UNRRA and ultimately succeeds in sending two nervous Jews as representatives to Bari. The thought that he has had some measure of success with the Jewish problem signified by the departure of the two representatives so elates him that the news of Virginia's death in a bombing raid in London does not affect him greatly. But the evacuation of the hundred Jews will have to wait until spring. Although a special flight of four Dakotas has been ordered by the authorities the planes are unable to land in the thick autumn fog. When the aircraft fails to land three times in a row, Guy experiences a chilling sense of frustrated hopes: "But there was no divine intervention to help the Jews of Begoy, no opening of the sea, no inundation of chariots." (326)

The refugees with scant baggage had marched out of their ghetto along the road to the air field. One or two had somehow borrowed peasants' handcarts in which the oldest and feeblest rode. Most went on foot bowed under their shabby little bundles. So inured are they to hardship that they set off again on their way back, when they realise that they will not be able to leave yet. The drop of relief supplies that follows soon after proves a worse disaster, deepening Guy's distress. The anti-fascist youth who retrieve the free-drops load them onto carts to be taken away to a barn near the General's headquarters where they will be formally impounded.

Before leaving Yugoslavia in mid-winter Guy visits Mme. Kanyi, who unsuspected by Guy, is already a persona non grata with the partisans, thanks to her brief acquaintance with a "British Liaison Officer." He assures her of his continued help to the Jews. It is when he returns to Italy that he learns the horrible truth that while all the other Jews have been evacuated from Yugoslavia, the Kanyi couple have been executed by the partisans for treason—the husband for "sabotaging" the electricity plant and the wife for "having been Guy's mistress." The ironic realism of the trilogy is strenuously sustained to the very end. Insensitive critics who, like Box-Bender at the novel's close, see that it is the story of virtue rewarded entirely miss the point. Waugh the Christian artist recognizes the compatibility between the salvation of soul and the apparent triumph of evil over good. Guy's new strength that is born of his faith in the higher order of things cannot stem the flood of evil that compasses him. As in the beginning of the story, his good intentions are perverted and misunderstood and all that he can do is to seethe in impotent rage and carry on his life's mission. Waugh, with his ironic perception of the timeless and insoluble problem of evil would have whole-heartedly endorsed the views of the late Pope Paul VI. Pope Paul VI describes evil as "not merely a lack of something, but an effective agent, a living, spiritual being, perverted and perverting."[20] A terrible reality. Mysterious and frightening. Insofar as Guy has learnt to face this reality of evil unflinchingly, and learnt to accommodate it within the scheme of things, his quest has been unmistakably achieved one.

The Kanyi episode in *Unconditional Surrender* is based on a short story that Waugh wrote in 1949 (three years before *Men at Arms*) which Waugh called "Compassion," a theme which is at the core of the final instalment of the trilogy. In taking back Virginia, as his wife and in working for the welfare of the displaced Jews, Guy is motivated by a genuine feeling of compassion. To Major Gordon who is numbed with shock by the miscarriage of justice in Waugh short-story, the Chaplain offers the warning on judging by appearance, very similar to that of old Crouchback's advice to Guy on the dangers of quantitative judgements. The Chaplain's assertion born of profound optimism, that "no suffering need ever be wasted" harks back to Cordelia's dictum in *Brideshead Revisited* that no one can be holy without suffering. Mme. Kanyi in *Unconditional Surrender* confronts Guy with a similar theological dilemma:

> 'Is there any place that is free from evil? It is too simple to say that only the Nazis wanted war. These communist wanted it too. It was the only way in which they could come to power. Many of my people wanted it, to be revenged on the Germans, to hasten the creation of the national state. It seems to me there was will to war, a death wish, everywhere. Even good men thought their private honour would be satisfied by war. They could assert their manhood by killing and being killed. They would accept hardships in recompense for having been selfish and lazy. Danger justified privilege. I knew Italians – not very many perhaps – who felt this. Were there none in England?'
>
> 'God forgive me,' said Guy. 'I was one of them.' (231-32)

Mme. Kanyi is presented as one endowed with extra-ordinary moral insight into the human situation, and as one, in Guy's estimation, who makes the most sense. Her declamation on the ubiquitous ambiguous nature of evil lies at the heart of Christian theology. It is ultimately Mme. Kanyi who enables Guy gain access into the mystery of evil – that it proceeds from man's prideful will and includes that area where ugliness, pain and death spread despoliation beyond the reach of man's mastery. On the contrary, it provides a disciplinary function. One learns obedience to God's Providence through suffering which acquaintance with evil entails. Thus like the category of "love," "evil" retains its full dimension of mystery. Itself beyond explanation, it yet endows certain other areas of life with meaning, if the reality of evil is looked into with due philosophical seriousness. Guy's admission that he was once paralysed in will by a "death wish" demonstrates his new awareness of the nature of evil and his ability to cope with it.

This recognition that evil can and sometimes does provide the occasion for endurance and the conviction that good takes its meaning only in relation to evil mark the end of Guy's quest. There is an air of finality in the opening of the section which immediately follows the Kanyi episode. "Guy had come to the end of the crusade to which he had devoted himself on the tomb of Sir Roger. His life as a Halberdier was over. . . . His last act was to send by the hand of his orderly the pile of illustrated magazines to Madame Kanyi. He gave the widows such remains of his stores as the Squadron Leader did not require. The widows wept." (232)

Guy's service to the Jewish refugees has not been fruitless; on reaching Italy he is told of the escape of the Jews of Begoy. The overriding Providence of God is borne in upon him: "It was indeed as though the Red Sea had miraculously drawn asunder and left a dry passage between walls of water." (233) The realisation that no good comes from public causes but that it comes only from private cause of the soul marks Guy's maturation as a human being. He comes to understand that in imagining that he might restore his personal honour by entering the War he has been absolutely wrong. Such a quest would have meant death, not life. Even "one frustrated act of mercy" is worth all the battles won and lost. It is not through personal heroism in the battlefields but letting divine grace operate upon their wills that Charles Ryder in *Brideshead Revisited* and Guy Crouchback in the war-trilogy realize themselves fully. To such alone will the Red Sea miraculously draw open leaving a "dry passage between walls of water."

Far from sounding a note of despair, as some critics have maintained, the conclusion of the war-trilogy sounds a resounding note of hope. Stripped of all fanciful notions of chivalry Guy now looks upon the world with clear-eyed wisdom which is compounded of new-found compassion for human nature. No price will be considered too high for the peace and contentment that he is seen to enjoy at the end. Married to Dominica, aged twenty-five, the daughter of an old Catholic family like his own and like him has failed in a vocation for which she is manifestly unsuited. Guy has re-established himself in the Lesser House at Broome. The figure of Dominica, "boisterous, treasured and muddied and full of the rough jargon of the stock-yard" is the figure of robust realism triumphing over maudlin, whimpering romance. She manages the home and bears him a son. Waugh, however, corrected the detail about Guy's children in the latter one-column edition of the trilogy. In the rescension Guy has no children of his own. From thematic standpoint this is a significant change for it emphasises the nature of Guy's self-sacrifice. Long after Virginia has died, Guy has given a noble pedigree to Trimmer's bastard child. Like Leonard Bast's child in E.M. Forster's *Howards End* and little Chrissie Tietjen in Ford Madox Ford's *Parade's End,* little Trimmer, the child of an unlawful union is to inherit the title and estate of one of the ancient houses in England. In adopting the orphan in the teeth of his friends' ridicule Guy has not only demonstrated exceptional moral courage but has also dispelled Miss Vavasour's fear that Guy was to be the "fin de ligne."

The apparently farcical episode of the attack on the block house designed to impress American opinion is yet thematically significant and has a bearing on question of "death-wish" that Mme. Kanyi raises in her conversation with Guy. Like 'Operation Pop Gun' in *Officers and Gentlemen* from which Trimmer emerges a hero and which proves Ian Kilbannock's mettle as a seasoned journalist, the specious battle staged by the allies and the partisans in Begoy. The Communist partisans come off badly in this display of "heroics." For all their bluster, they prove themselves blundering cowards. But the episode has another more important function in the novel's structure. Ritchie-Hook, Guy's old hero unexpectedly appears on the scene. He is greatly altered since we last saw him. Senile and physically worn out, he has accompanied the part to act as an observer. The decrepit soldier cannot resist the opportunity of "biffing" and he gets killed during the shameful operation. His servant Dawkins who is himself blistered in the mishap sums up his master with uncommon acumen: "He's led me into some sticky places . . . these last three years. . . . As you will remember . . . he always spoke very straight and more than once he's said to me right out: 'Dawkins. I wish those bastards would shoot better. I don't want to go home.'" (223) Ritchie-Hook's decline and inglorious death perform a cathartic function on Guy who is exorcised of his death-wish symptomatic of deep-seated romanticism.

In moral terms Guy at the end of the epic, has achieved the synthesis out of the "antithesis between sacrifice and the will to win" over which he brooded when he was lying in bed at Uncle Peregrine's flat in the days following the parachute accident. Since then he has made at least two outstanding acts of self-sacrifice. His father's timely advice has helped him to see that a life of sacrifice alone is the eminently proper way to redeem oneself. Guy has no longer any illusions about the war and his participation in it. In the brief sojourn in Italy on his way to Yugoslavia the reality of his situation strikes him with perfect lucidity:

> In this limbo Guy fretted for more than a week while February blossomed into March. He had left Italy four and a half years ago. He had then taken leave of the crusader whom the people called 'il santo inglese.' He had laid his hand on the sword that had never struck the infidel. He wore the medal which had hung round the neck of his brother, Gervase, when the sniper had picked him off on his way up to the line in Flanders. In this heart he felt stirring the despair in which his brother Ivo had starved himself to death. Half an hour's scramble on the beach near Dakar; an ignominious rout in Crete. That had been his war. (168-69)

The evil without him has forced Guy to recognize his own shortcomings and overcome them. In a world of grotesques who have wilfully turned away from Christ, the true centre of existence, Guy's story demonstrates that it is still possible with the aid of divine grace, to achieve one's quest in a meaningful way. His quest has involved literally and metaphorically a long and painful journey. He heeds the promptings of grace in contrast to the other wastelanders and as a consequence achieves total self-awareness. Providence in the guise of his saintly father pulls Guy away from the wrong path and sets him on the proper course. The "operation of divine grace" which Waugh claimed was the theme of his *Brideshead Revisited* is equally at the thematic core of the war-trilogy. Guy's active response to grace determines his quest. He achieves his quest for redemption precisely because out of his own volition he opts to co-operate with what is divinely offered. *Unconditional Surrender,* in words of Carens, is an account of Guy's spiritual "return to life after disillusionment [and] descent into hell."[21]

NOTES

1. Evelyn Waugh, *Unconditional Surrender* (Penguin, 1965, rpt. 1988).
2. Quoted by William J. Cook, Jr., p. 331.
3. *Ibid*., p. 330.
4. Vincent B. Sherry, Jr., "Literary Effects of World War II," p. 623.

5. Isaac Sequeira, *The Theme of Initiation in Modern American Fiction* (Mysore: Geetha, 1975), p. 10.
6. Catherine Roberts, "The Three Faces of Humanism and Their Relation to Problems of Science and Education," *Education and Values*, ed. Douglas Sloan (NY: Columbia University, 1980), pp. 169-90.
7. Joseph Campbell, *The Hero with a Thousand Faces* (New York: Pantheon, 1949). Quoted in Isaac Sequeira, p. 18,
8. Karl Rahner, "The Church of Sinners," *Cross Currents* (New York: Kraus, 1969), pp. 64-74.
9. *Ibid.*
10. *Ibid.*
11. Quoted in Andrew Rutherford, *The Literature of War*, p. 113.
12. *Ibid.*, p. 131.
13. *Philosophical Dictionary,* ed. Kenneth Baker (Washington: Gonzago University Press, 1974), p. 86.
14. David Wykes, "Evelyn Waugh's Sword of Volgograd," *Dutch Quarterly Review*, no. 7, 1977.
15. Quoted in B.W. Wilson, "*Sword of Honour:* The Last Crusade," p. 90.
16. David Wykes, p. 97.
17. Quoted in Màrston La France "*Sword of Honour.* The Ironist Placatus," p. 48.
18. *The Picturesque Prison*, p. 255.
19. Jeffrey G. Sabosan, "Irony and the Unexpected," p. 433.
20. Quoted in Andrew M. Greeley, "The Devil, You Say," *The New York Times Magazine*, 4 Feb. 1973, p. 26.
21. Quoted in William J. Cook, Jr., p. 335.

Conclusion

This book has attempted to show that a chronological study of Waugh's major works reveals that the quest for meaning and order in the chaotic flux of life becomes a readily discernible, almost consistent pattern. Waugh's protagonists ranging from innocent and inarticulate young men to sensitive, deeply introverted individuals reveal varying religious attitudes. The movement from *Decline and Fall* to *Unconditional Surrender* is a movement from a state of *angst*, of passive alienation from experience towards a state of reconciliation. The quest-motif of the Grail runs through the whole fictional oeuvre, a quest for rebirth after spiritual death. Through the skilful use of imagery, Waugh conveys in his early novels the sense of a life governed by blind chance, a fragmentary experience ultimately without aim or meaning. Even from the very start, Waugh's perspective was that of a moralist, of a Christian or we might even say of a Catholic (although his actual conversion to Roman Catholicism took place two years after his first celebrated novel *Decline and Fall*). With their oblique modes of irony and allusiveness, Waugh's early works were announcements of a quest out of darkness. The grail symbolism and references to the rituals of rebirth are explicit in *A Handful of Dust* but the quest element is latent in the satires preceding it.

Critics such as R.M. Davis and Jeffrey Heath have argued that we cannot divide Waugh of the thirties from the Waugh of the forties. A similar view has been taken throughout the present work which insists on the wholeness of Waugh's oeuvre implying that the later works were systematically planned to complete the theme of the quest adumbrated in the earlier ones. The theme of discovery of the exploration of self which culminates in its union with humanity and discovery of humanity and eternity gives coherence to the whole Waugh corpus. Epiphany or spiritual manifestation is denied to the early questers for they ignore the promptings of grace but is the reward of those who accept that travail and suffering are essential prerequisites of salvation and spiritual illumination. Waugh posits that transfiguration of the human being is possible if he earnestly strives to search for his soul. A search for one's soul presupposes release from the bondage of time and finitude and an experience of timeless reality. Waugh's later realistic novels are thus seen to be in direct line of succession of the early satires. The early "entertainments" are written from an ultimate moral position even as the later religious works are informed by a satiric sense. Beginning with blistering satirical denunciation of the contemporary moral collapse, Waugh's works end on a serene note of compassion and wisdom sustained by a maturing moral vision. The novels that we have chosen for study belong to three clearly defined categories corresponding to the three distinct stages of the quest. Out of the fragmentariness of experience and spiritual nullity of the first group to which belong *Decline and Fall, Vile Bodies* and *Black Mischief* the pilgrimage passes through the crucial stage of despair leading to death of *A Handful of Dust* of the middle group before reaching the third stage of resolution and synthesis of *Brideshead Revisited, Helena* and the war-trilogy. As early as *Decline and Fall* Waugh reaches out, albeit negatively, for an experience of totality. Waugh's quotation from Mary Queen of Scots, in his essay *St. Helena Empress,* "In my end is my beginning" may be applied with equal relevance to his own fictional career, suggesting as it does the extent of the progress achieved at the final stage of the spiritual journey of Waugh the novelist as well as that of his characters. The direction that the quest takes, of which early indications are given, insists on orthodox Christian solutions. Along with the deference to the pristine ideals embodied in the Church comes the insistence on the need for self-effacing humility which allows the operation of divine grace in the lives of the individuals.

An interpretation of Waugh's novels in terms of the quest-motif has enabled us to distinguish between the point of view of the author and that of his characters. Such an approach has underlined one of the persistent dichotomies in his fiction – the dichotomy between the evil and deceptive City of Man and the enduring values of the City of God. The characters of *Decline and Fall, Vile Bodies* and *Black Mischief* are grotesque caricatures whose quest for false sanctuaries and idols betrays their immaturity and godlessness. The same may be said of the more rounded characters in the later fiction but the difference is that the latter show an awareness of their unactualised potentialities. Waugh's Christian belief, far from being an impediment to an appreciation of his art aids us in perceiving the fundamental difference between the world of greed, violence and grotesquerie of his characters and Waugh's own moral vision. The tension created by two opposed points of view heightens the dramatic nature of the stories. Implied throughout is the need for self-transcendence of the characters which alone can endow their lives with a sense of uniqueness. It is indeed his Catholicism that causes Waugh to see the characters as grotesques who refuse to recognise the need for redemption and the need for the search of their souls. Waugh might have made his defence of his devoutness in much the same way as Flannery O'Connor: "When people have told me that because I am a Catholic, I cannot be an artist, I have had to reply, ruefully, that because I am a Catholic, I cannot be less than an artist."[1]

Our approach to Waugh's novels through a study of the quest-motif makes us perceive with clarity the author's deep religious commitment and the perspective from which he viewed his grotesques. Furthermore the approach helps us to gain access to the mystery of evil which is at the heart of Christianity. The heroes in quest narratives had to contend with the forces of evil personified by monsters. In Waugh's novels in the place of actual dragons are the seductions of the world which are sometimes made to appear nightmarish and in which either the protagonists tamely acquiesce or with the assistance of the supernatural strength of religion they subdue them. In any event, confrontation with evil is an essential condition for the characters' initiation. However frivolous, irreligious and absurd the ethos of the early novels may appear, it still performs a religious function. The early novels with their themes of alienation and break-down of human communication are yet concerned with the fundamental problems of life, namely man's need to search for durable pockets of sanity. Like the medieval mystery plays Waugh's satires are intent on making the readers aware of man's precarious and mysterious position in the universe. With the baroque allegories the early novels share the deeply religious concern with the ultimate realities and a cosmic system of values from which the characters are totally divorced. Having lost touch with the living ritual of their religion which once made people part of a real community, these characters are just atoms in an atomized society and fall easy prey to the dragon, ready to devour the unwary traveller. The picaresque form in the early novels offers the writer the advantage of portraying the search of the protagonist for comfortable illusions which prove inadequate in the end.

Waugh's later novels indicate that what matters for him is the redemptive grace of God in which resides the ultimate truth and meaning of existence. Only when he is assisted by grace will man be able to return to the primordial reality which seems irrecoverably lost through pride. Waugh posits in his Catholic novels that grace is to be thought of in personal categories that affect the whole man; it cannot be quantified in the same way as material possessions and worldly successes are reduced to categories of quantity. Illumination through grace breaks the narrow and empirical calculus of the ever-growing scientific outlook of our society. A recognition by the later protagonists of the fact that the Church provides the only continuity with the necessary emotional equipment to face intellectual chaos of the world. Grace endows the protagonists with intellectual humility which admits that all judgements by their nature are partial and clouded by fallen nature of humanity.

Decline and Fall, the first of the novels portrays a world of false values and erratic discipline in which any attempt at self-discovery is bound to fail. Highly derivative as Waugh admitted to his biographer Christopher Sykes,[2] the novel is written in a style of wide-ranging allusions. Lacking a stable ethical or religious centre, several of the characters including the protagonist undergo a quick succession of identities. Several recurring images flesh out this theme of identity. Unlike the great missionary-apostle of the first century whose name he bears, Paul experiences no mystical experience or epiphany which transforms the inner nature. "Immortal" Grimes who survives a sequence of deaths personifies the Dionysiac energy and the chaos of the novel's setting. Written two years before Waugh's reception into the Roman Catholic Church, the novel contains one of Waugh's severest verdicts on the state of religion in his country. Anglicanism is just another of many religious heresies of disorder. Prendergast, the "Modern Churchman" represents the religious perversion to which can be traced several of the social ills in the novel. King's Thursday, one of the two houses owned by Margot Beste-Chetwynde, the "Great Whore," represents the spiritual poverty and inertia of the modern day. The house which dates back to the Tudor times is now been hideously remodelled; reflecting the state of degeneracy of the novels and religion. Professor Otto Silenus, the authority on architecture with his highly individualistic notions of "vile becoming" is another product of the sterile freedom on which the age prides itself. Living in an ethos of such spiritual undernourishment, Paul Pennyfeather's quest is a gross parody of the classical quest in which the heroes fought great battles and proved their valour. At the novel's closure Paul disguises himself as his own cousin and is seen pursuing the course in theology at his old college in Oxford from where he was sent down not long ago for indecent behaviour. Paul's fate is that of an innocent who in consequence of a lack of knowledge of evil abandons himself to the absurdities of the modern age. His life and career, to echo Professor Silenus's philosophical categories, is one of sterile "stasis" and regression. Waugh argues that a denial of the unifying idea of God leads to a disjointed view of the world in which each individual wishes to exist in a separate reality of his own. There can be no true quest without a recognition of the need of God and of His mercy and grace.

Vile Bodies the second novel continues the attack on the decay of civilisation. In the absence of a meaning-giving faith, the characters, the "vile bodies" drift along aimlessly. Their only quest, if it can be dignified by that title, is for money and the comfort that they believe that money brings with it. Adam Fenwick, the "hero" and the only character who shows some degree of discrimination uses marriage, traditionally a sacrament, as a pretext for his gross pursuit of fortune. As in *Decline and Fall* the protagonist suffers from a lack of personal identity, doomed as he is from the opening pages of the novel to sterile anonymity. The readiness with which he agrees to pass off as Nina's husband reflects the fragmentation of the self in a world of spiritual bankruptcy and total reliance on Dame Fortune, chief of whose minions is the drunken Agatha Runcible who like the car in which she races to death lacks essential identity. Perversion of religious faith is embodied in Mrs. Ape, the evangelist with a shabby troop of "Angels," who uses religion for making monetary gains. The novel's characters with their spiritual blindness parody the questers in the legends of Holy Grail who by their purity of lives and spiritual insight achieve wholeness. Their moral blindness prevents them from making an honest evaluation of their true nature and from seeing themselves as "vile bodies" which are incapable of the glorious transformation that awaits the faithful after the death of their bodies. Their life like the huge cheque that Adam receives from the major at the end of the novel is "worth nothing." Although Waugh himself spoke deprecatingly about the book years later, *Vile Bodies* demonstrates Waugh's growing mastery of fictional technique and allusive style. Images that are the outward projection of the states of mind, fear and conflict within the characters are used with telling effect. The image of "the edge of the canal" on which stands the disreputable Royal George where the Bright Young Things take their lodgings before the car race, connects the novel to the Kingfisher image in T.S. Eliot's *Waste Land*. All is sordid outside the hotel. The factory, the scrap iron and bottles floating on the shallow canal and a derelict perambulator heightens the wasteland bleakness. Adam, Nina, Agatha Runcible, Colonel Blount, Prime Minister Outrage, Simon Balcairn, grotesques all, in their daily lives confront a world that has split up into a series of disconnected fragments and lost its purpose but are tragically unaware of the disintegrating effect that such a world has on their personality.

With its double focus on barbarism and the so-called civilisation whose guardian the West prides itself to be, *Black Mischief* explores the nature of the personal quest which is pursued in total exclusion of spirituality. Two lonely figures—Basil Seal from England and Seth the young idealist emperor of Azania—search for meaning and identity. But in moving from England which he finds intolerably futile to Azania where history is being made, Basil Seal is merely running from one kind of barbarism to another, quite as bad, if not worse. Seth likewise, Oxford-educated and a visionary fails to realise his grandiose dreams because his quest lacks a proper spiritual goal. Basil Seal and Emperor Seth are a couple of misfits who are ignorant of the mysteries of the universe in which they move and have their being. Seal's journey is not a journey towards blessedness but turns out, in the end, to be one of escapism; Seth's exuberance stems from "hubris," from an overweening sense of personal glory. Waugh's main point in the novel is that despite the surface dissimilarities, the England of Basil and Azania of Seth are alike in savagery. The anarchy that the reader witnesses in Azania is only an externalisation of the insidious evil that is inside the individual which he hardly knows how to overcome or come to terms with. A civilisation like post-Reformation England without spiritual values is little better than Azania where perversion and inversion of values reign supreme. The return of the seasons which in the vegetation myths bring rebirth, the cycle of seasons with the return of rain bring spiritual death and cannibal savagery in Waugh's *Black Mischief*.

The protagonist of the next novel *A Handful of Dust* bears a close resemblance to the quester in T.S. Eliot's poem from which Waugh has borrowed his title. Tony Last is a distorted parody of the questing knight in the Grail legends, who goes to the "Chapel perilous" and after killing the dragon lifts the curse of the Land of the Fisherking and restores it to former fertility. Tony's quest differs from the archetypal quest in one very important respect: it is not guided by faith. His motivation is far from pure. After being cuckolded Tony, to avenge his disgraceful humiliation goes in search of the City in the mapless terrain of the South American jungles full of swamps, stony ground, red pebbles, dry grass and rushing rapids. Unlike the Grail knight, Tony cannot ask right questions at the end of the journey, for he is not spiritually equipped. Rather than releasing the maimed Fisherking, he himself becomes a prisoner of a half-caste madman to whom he has to read Dickens over and over again. Waugh implies that this is the fate of the modern wastelander who rejects true faith and seeks the consolations of Victorian humanism whose chief exponent was Charles Dickens. Tony's fate like that of Cumean Sibyl in the epigraph to Eliot's poem, who grows older day after day but has no hope of release from the tyranny of time which death alone can give. Tony's City is the boring City of Man, full of grossness and evil.

Regarded by many as Waugh's masterpiece *A Handful of Dust* is a carefully constructed novel in which the idea of quest is the basic component and is thus linked more closely than the other Waugh novels with the Arthurian cycle and *The Waste Land.* Tony's predicament exemplifies the all-encompassing chaos of modern life which is the theme of Eliot's poem. Rejecting the call of tradition sanctified by the Church and choosing the wrong guide, Tony the quester goes in the wrong direction. In fleeing to the unknown City in Brazil, to avoid Death he finds that that is the place where his spiritual Death awaits him. In both Eliot and Waugh the wound of the "Fisher King" that the quester sets out to heal is less physical than spiritual, which only belief in God and transcendental values can cure. Whereas in Eliot, the quester at least hears "what the thunder said," Waugh's hero is denied even that. Imbued with an incurable sense of nostalgia, Tony tries to rediscover the past, to realise that he has a future which alone can be his past. The novel ends on a most pessimistic note and Waugh offers no apology to it. There is no poetic justice in the gruesome incarceration of a decent and upright man by a maniac. But Waugh maintains that that is the price one has to pay for refusing to grow and attain spiritual maturation. For a more affirmative statement we have to turn to *Brideshead, Helena* and the war-trilogy which together may be termed his religious novels.

The questing action becomes more complex and religious in the novels beginning with *Brideshead Revisited.* Themes connected with the quest such as alienation, self-definition and the individual's need for search for wholeness find dramatic expression in these explicitly Christian books. Avowedly Christian in tone these novels may be, but yet they tackle existential problems of identity, the nature of good and evil, the possibility of fulfilment in society and the effects of solipsistic actions on the individual concerns which are common to serious writers of fiction on both sides of the Atlantic. The difference lies in the specifically Christian solutions that Waugh offers to these problems. These novels exemplify Waugh's repudiation of the philosophy of art for its own sake which in Waugh's opinion, leads to a dissociation of art from its human roots, a domination of the artist by the art and a perversion of transcendental truth and beauty. In its highest sense, art to Waugh was Christian art which while not absolving the artist from experiencing all the painful stages of the artistic process, reveals to the artist, the beauty of interior reflection of divine grace.

Brideshead Revisited is an outstanding religious novel of our century, which dramatises the conflict between man and God and the ultimate victory of the latter. Charles Ryder, the protagonist moves from being a youthful romantic to a cynical adult to a mature human being capable of understanding the nature of God's love. Such a theme gives the novel its extraordinary metaphysical dimension. Waugh posits that the process of questing which leads to man's self-enlightenment and an awareness of his ontological condition, ought, by its very nature, be a process of religious conversion. The primary thrust of Ryder's adventure is towards a Christian growth which implies self-knowledge and self-control emphasised by the novel's deeply moving conclusion. Man is no longer regarded as a victim of a cosmic joke; he is a free moral agent with the potential of reclaiming his lost dignity. If the test of authenticity of an aesthetic experience is to involve the reader in the experience of the "shock of being" then *Brideshead Revisited* is assuredly an authentic work of art having for its theme the transformation of man's nature by the power of divine grace. A reconciliation between heavenly absolutes and relativistic earthly standards is masterfully achieved in the novel.

Helena, which in the opinion of most critics is too doctrinaire in tone and uncompromisingly propagandist in intention, is yet of value because of its complex structural design and its theme of quest. Helena, it might be said, alone among Waugh's protagonists has a unique sense of mission which was one of the reasons why the book remained the author's firm favourite. She is perhaps the one protagonist in Waugh's entire oeuvre who is aware of the blessedness ahead of her quest. Whole-heartedly accepting the will of God she undertakes the long and arduous journey, shirking the comforts to which has hung humanity's destiny. Waugh has insisted all along that Providence fulfils its design in each of its creatures in strange and extraordinary ways. The quest of Helena exemplifies the mysterious operation of grace. *Helena* is a simple but forceful tale of a woman whose unquestioning response to God's call determines the outcome of her quest. Her mystical vision gives her the physical courage to overcome the shoddy values and bulwarks of the City of Man that hinder the deeper apprehension of reality.

Waugh's concern for the spiritual sterility and emptiness of the modern age finds its fullest expression in his war-trilogy extending over a period of ten years. Complex moral issues such as the alienation of a hyper-sensitive individual in the face of lax morals which are the direct consequence of the war and the absurdities that such an individual has to come to terms are handled with superb artistry. The quest which plays a crucial role in the structure and metaphysical composition of the trilogy emerges as the author's most potent literary weapon in the relentless probing of the ills of a society sorely out of joint. Twentieth-century alienation has its root in the self-consciousness that was portrayed variously by the poets of the nineteenth-century romanticism. Separated from the religious and metaphysical roots and traditional values modern man is isolated not only from God but from humanity. Patterned throughout on the motif of the quest of the Crusade, the trilogy makes a discovery of the pain and evil of a world which is totally irrational and is devoid of the ideals of purity and purpose. The quest and goal patterns are shown to be present in the trilogy in various recurrent images.

The central figure in the trilogy is a modern English Don Quixote who sees life's issues in black and white with no shadings in between. Like Sir Roger Waybroke, the Knight of the Second Crusade, with whom he feels kinship, Guy Crouchback sets out on a great journey with grandiose illusions about himself and the world he has no doubt of conquering. Waybroke and Crouchback are imperfect men whose spiritual blindness prevents them from seeing themselves for what they really are. Roger Waybroke's journey remained incomplete and his great vow unfulfilled since he was killed early on in the expedition in disreputable circumstances. Guy's crusade in the modern world would have met with a similar fate had it not been for the fact that he realised before it was too late of his own moral and spiritual inadequacy. Like Ryder in *Brideshead Revisited* Guy is stripped of his romantic delusions in the course of his quest for glory. In Guy Waugh has created a fully rounded character who has the potential for spiritual growth. As in *Brideshead Revisited* Guy's response to the divine grace leads his soul out of the spiritual wasteland in which he has been long languishing.

Waugh's Catholicism provides him with a definite standard against which to measure and evaluate his character's actions. Guy likewise who, despite the meaninglessness and absurdity of life that confronts has retained his Catholicism, invariably examines his problems and failures in the light of his faith in which he has been reared. He has inherited from his father that it is the mysterious or mystical part of his religion that will enable him ultimately to retain his integrity and humanity. His Catholic values indeed are part of his self-awareness. Waugh uses the liturgical calendar, which is the Church, whose teachings, Waugh implies, the Protestants have distorted by de-emphasising its rituals. By retaining his adherence to the Church, Guy perceives the true nature of reality and learns to accommodate himself to it.

The three instalments of the trilogy mark the three distinct stages in the quest of the protagonist. *Men at Arms* presents Guy Crouchback as a self-contained, self-alienated individual who despairs of any constructive effort in what seems a meaningless void. Severely alienated, he is unable to maintain any meaningful contact with the real world. The dragon that he has to contend against is both within himself and without. He has to wage a fierce battle with his "double" whose function is to reveal the hero's true nature. Apthorpe, after whom each of the novel's three books takes its motto is a duplication of Guy's own irreligious vanity and inner emptiness. Guy's acquaintance with Apthorpe is metaphorically his first initiation into a vision of evil. The comic downfall of the over-techni coloured plebeian from his "throne" in the thunderbox prefigures the collapse of Guy's ideals. Apthorpe's death at the novel's closure of which Guy is an innocent cause dramatically externalises the ultimate overthrow of the dragon by the quester.

The inversion of the Grail quest in the opening book of *Officers and Gentlemen* emphasises the false notions of military grandeur of which the protagonist has yet to be stripped. The setting in the island of Mugg, of the dark tower of the castle with the "infernal" dogs guarding the gates is a Gothic evocation of the nether world. Allusions to the mythological heroes complete the parody. The entire episode is a foretaste of the disaster of the battle of the Crete which is going to shock Guy out of his romantic complacency. Events in the novel bring Guy face to face with evil in the shape of cowardice and betrayal among men whom he once lionized. The irrational world of battle governed by incompetent officers who are not gentlemen apparently represents the fallen order of nature from which one must struggle to escape and seek redemption. Julia Stitch, Ivor Claire, Trimmer and Fido Hound embody the values or dis-values of a godless society which seduce the soul and lead it to perdition.

Unconditional Surrender records the reclamation of the hero from the depths of despair into which he was shown as having fallen in the second volume of the trilogy, to an awareness that human affairs deserve to be judged qualitatively. Guy has passed through the three stages in Frye's paradigm: after a perilous journey in which the quester's soul is beset with dangers, he is engaged in a combat with the forces of evil in which he comes of with credit and is in the end exalted for his daring. At the end of *Unconditional Surrender* Guy is seen reaching the final stage of the quest, namely *anagnorisis* or discovery of himself. He has proved himself a hero who has survived the conflict unscathed. In mythical terms, Guy is associated with spiritual vigour and revival while the evil forces which he has subdued are those of moribund life and negativity.

Guy's gains have to be judged from a moral perspective and not according to the quantitative norms of an acquisitive and amoral society. On acting on the principle of his father on the importance of saving even one single human soul, he has won a truly moral victory. In taking back his promiscuous wife who has been left pregnant by a worthless man Guy has performed an uncommonly unselfish and magnanimous action. His concern for the Jewish refugees in Yugoslavia falls in the same category of humanitarianism which stems from a sense of God. But this sense of God is predicated upon a recognition of evil and an acknowledgement of the fact that evil is a potent force which can never be wholly overcome even if goodness is possible of achievement.

Writing to his daughter Margaret in 1957, Waugh said that "the whole of our life is a test and preparation for heaven—most of it irksome. So each part of our life is an irksome test and preparation for something better."[3] These words give a clue to the nature of Waugh the man as well as

Waugh the writer. The entire work of Waugh can be seen as a search for the reality beneath life's surface. An elucidation of his major works in terms of quest illustrates the seriousness of purpose in his art. Among the writers of the present century who have explored the Grail impulse as the quest for self-realisation Waugh's position is secure. An examination of the quest-motif in his writings has also exemplified Waugh's development as a novelist. The differences and similarities between the early heroes and the later ones demonstrate the basic concern of Waugh as a novelist, namely the necessity of man's realisation of the role assigned to the human spirit in the great drama of existence.

NOTES

1. Mattie Daniels Thomas, "The Quest Motif in Flannery O'Connor's Short Stories," Diss., Purdue, 1982, p. 2.
2. Christopher Sykes, *Evelyn Waugh*, p. 87.
3. *Letters*, p. 490.

Bibliography

Primary Sources

A Handful of Dust. UK: Penguin, 1987.
A Little Learning. Boston: Little, Brown. 1964.
A Tourist in Africa. London: Chapman and Hall, 1960.
Black Mischief. Boston: Little, Brown. 1946.
Brideshead Revisited. Penguin, 1945.
Decline and Fall. London: Heinemann Educational Books, 1966.
Edmund Campion. London: Cassell, 1935.
Helena. UK: Penguin, 1963.
Labels: A Mediterranean Journal. UK: Penguin, 1985.
Love Among the Ruins. UK: Penguin, 1962.
Men at Arms. UK: Penguin, 1965.
Ninety Two Days. The Account of a Tropical Journey through British Guiana and Part of Brazil. London: Duckworth, 1934.
Officers and Gentlemen. UK: Penguin, 1965.
Put Out More Flags. London: Chapman and Hall, 1942.
Remote People. UK: Penguin, 1985.
Robbery under Law, the Mexian Object-Lesson. London: Chapman and Hall, 1939.
Rossetti, His Life and Works. London: Duckworth, 1928.
Scoop. Boston: Little, Brown, 1949.
Scott-King's Modern Europe. UK: Penguin, 1951.
Sword of Honour. Boston: Little, Brown, 1961.
Tactical Exercise. Boston: Little, Brown, 1954.
The Holy Places. London: Queen Anne, 1952.
The Life of the Right Reverend Ronald Knox. London: Chapman and Hall, 1959.
The Loved One. Boston: Little, Brown, 1948.
The Ordeal of Gilbert Pinfold. UK: Penguin, 1962.
Unconditional Surrender. UK: Penguin, 1964.
Vile Bodies. Boston: Little, Brown, 1930.
Waugh in Abyssinia. UK: Penguin, 1951.
Work Suspended and Other Stories including Charles Ryder's School Days. UK: Penguin, 1967.
Evelyn Waugh: A Little Order, ed. Donat Gallagher. London: Eyre Methuen, 1977.
The Diaries of Evelyn Waugh, ed. Michael Davie. UK: Penguin, 1979.
The Essays, Articles and Reviews of Evelyn Waugh, ed. Donat Gallagher. London: Methuen, 1983.
The Letters of Evelyn Waugh, ed. Mark Amory. UK: Penguin, 1982.

Secondary Sources

A Dictionary of Symbols, ed. J.E. Cirlot, trans. London: Routledge and Kegan Paul, 1971.

Auty, Susan Garis. "Language and Charm in *Brideshead Revisited.*" *DQR*, 6 (Winter 1976), 291-303.

Bender, Elaine. "Sour Grapes." *Evelyn Waugh Newsletter*, 2 (Autumn 1968), 4-6. Hereinafter cited as *EWN.*

Benedict, Stewart H. "The Candide Figure in the Novels of Waugh." *Papers of Michigan Academy of Sciences, Arts and Letters,* 48, 1963

Bergonzi, Bernard. "Evelyn Waugh's Gentlemen." *Critical Quarterly, 5* (Spring 1963).

_____. *The Situation of the Novel.* London: Macmillan, 1971, 104-18.

Betjeman, John. "Evelyn Waugh" in *Living Writers,* ed. G. Phelps. London: Sylvan Press, 137-50.

Booth, Wayne C. *The Rhetoric of Fiction.* Chicago: Univ. Press, 1961.

Brady, Charles A. "Contemporary Catholic Authors: Evelyn Waugh: Shrove Thursday Motley and Lenten Sackcloth." *Catholic Library World*, 16 (March 1945), 163-77, 189.

Bradbury, Malcolm. *Evelyn Waugh*. London: Oliver and Boyd, 1964.

_____. *Possibilities: Essays on the State of the Novel.* London. OUP, 1973.

Bredvold, Louis I. "A Note in Defense in Satire." *A Journal of English Literary History*, 77 (December 1910), 252-64.

Brailow, G. David. "'My theme is memory': The Narrative Stucture of *Brideshead Revisited.*" *EWN*, I41 (Winter 1980), 1-4.

Braybooke, Neville. "Evelyn Waugh en uniforme." *La Vie Intellectuelle*, 27 (27 April 1956), 135-40

Campbell, Joseph. *The Hero with a Thousand Faces.* New York: Pantheon, 1949.

Carens, James F. *The Satiric Art of Evelyn Waugh*. Seattle: University of Washington Press, 1966.

Cecchin Giovanni. "Echi di T.S. Eliot Nei Romanzi di Evelyn Waugh." *EM*, 14, 1963, 239-75.

Charlesworth, Max. "The Meaning of Existentialism." *The Thomis*, 16, October 1953, 473-95.

Cook, William J. Jr. *Masks, Models and Morals: The Art of Evelyn Waugh.* Cranbury, N.J., Fairleigh Dickinson University Press, 1971.

Corr, Patricia. "Waugh, Sanity and Catholicism." *Studies*, 51 (Autumn 1962), 388-99

Cosman, Max. "The Nature and Work of Evelyn Waugh." *Colorado Quarterly,* 4 (Spring 1956), 428-41.

Costello, P. "An Idea and Waugh's *Sword of Honour.*" *Kansas Quarterly,*1 1969, 41-50.

Churchill, Thomas P. *The House of Waugh: A Critical Study. Evelyn Waugh's Major Novels.* Diss. Washington University, 1963.

_____. "The Trouble with *Brideshead Revisited.*" *Modern Language Quarterly,* 28 (June 1967), 213-28.

Costello, Harry P. *The Mature Novels of Evelyn Waugh: A Study in Structure, Imagery, and Theme*. Diss. Loyola University of Chicago, 1969.

Critical Theory since Plato, ed. Hazard Adams. San Diego: Harcourt Brace Jovanovich, 1971.

Davis, Robert Murray. "Evelyn's Juvenalia." *EWN,*10 (Winter 1976), 1-7.

_____. "Evelyn Waugh's Early Works: The Formation of a Method, *Texas Studies in Literature and Language,* 7 (Spring), 97-108.

_____. "Title, Theme and Structure in *Vile Bodies*." *SHR,* 11 (Winter 1977), 21-27

_____. "Title and Theme of *A Handful of Dust*." *EWN,* 6 (Autumn 1972), 1.

_____. *A Catalogue of the Evelyn Waugh Collection at the Humanities Research Center.* The University of Texas at Austin Troy, N.Y: Whitson, 1981.

Delbaere-Grant, J. "'Who shall Inherit England?' a Comparison between *Howards End*, *Parade's End* and *Unconditional Surrender*." *English Studies,* 50, 1969, 101-5.

DeVitis, A.A. *Roman Holiday: The Catholic Novels of Evelyn Waugh.* NY: Bookman Associates, 1956.

Delasanta, Rodney and Mario D'avanzo. "Truth and Beauty in *Brideshead Revisited,*" *Modern Fiction Studies*, 11 (Summer 1965), 140-52.

Dennis, Nigel. "Evelyn Waugh and the Churchillian Renaissance." *Partisan Review* (Summer 1948).

Dictionary of Literary Biography. No.15, British Novelists 1930-1959. Part II. M-Z, ed. Bernard Oldsey. Detroit: Gale Research, 1983.

Didion Joan. "Gentlemen in Battle," *National Review*, 12 (March 27, 1962), 215-17.

Donaldson, Frances. *Evelyn Waugh: Portrait of a Country Neighbour.* London: Weidenfeld and Nicolson, 1967.

Doyle, Paul A. "*Decline and Fall:* Two Versions." *EWN,* 1, no. 2 (Autumn 1967), 4-5.

_____. *Evelyn Waugh.* Grand Rapids, Mich.: Eerdmans, 1969.

Dulles, Avery S.J. "The Essence of Catholicism: Protestant and Catholic Perspectives." *The Thomist,* 4, no. 5, 1984, 607-33.

Duran, Manuel. *Cervantes*. Boston: Twayne, 1974.

Duer, Harriet W. *All Us Exiles: The Novels of Evelyn Waugh*. Diss. University of Connecticut, 1970.

Dyson, A.E. "Evelyn Waugh and the Mysteriously Disappearing Hero." *The Crazy Fabric: Essays in Irony*. NY: St. Martins Press, 1965, 187-96. Also in *Critical Quarterly*, 2 (Spring 1960), 72-79.

Eighteenth Century English Literature, ed. Gefforey Tillotson et al. NY: Harcourt Brace Jovanovich, 1969.

Eliot, T.S. *The Complete Poems and Plays.* London: Faber and Faber, 1968.

Esslin, Martin. *The Theatre of the Absurd.* 3rd ed. Great Britain: Penguin, 1980.

Evelyn Waugh Newsletter 1967 onwards.

Evelyn Waugh: The Critical Heritage, ed. Martin Stannard. London and Boston: Routledge and Kegan Paul, 1984.

Farr, Paul D. "The Edwardian Golden Age and Nostalgic Truth." *DR,* 50 (Autumn 1970), 378-93

_____. "The Success and Failure of *Decline and Fall.*" *EA,* 24 (April- June 1971), 257-70

_____. "Waugh's Conservative Stance: Defending 'The Standards of Civilization.'" *Philological Quarterly,* 51 (April 1972), 471-84.

_____. "Waugh: Tradition and a Modern Talent." *South Atlantic Quarterly,* 68, 1969, 506-19

_____. "The Novelist's Coup: Style as Satiric Norm in *Scoop.*" *Connecticut*

Review, 8 (April 1975), 42-54.

Firchow, Peter E. "In Search of a Handful of Dust: The Literary Background of Evelyn Waugh's Novel." *JML*, 2 (Winter 1971), 406-16.

Forster, E.M. *Aspects of the Novel.* NY: Harcourt, Brace and World, 1927.

Frye, Northrop. *Anatomy of Criticism.* Princeton University Press, 1957.

Friedmann, Thomas. "*Decline and Fall* and the Satirist's Responsibility." *EWN,*6 (Autumn 1972), 3-8

Gindin, James. *Post-War British Fiction: New Accents and New Attitudes.* Univer-sity of California, 1962.

Gnerro, Mark L. "Echoes of the Anima Christi in a Pivotal Paragraph of Evelyn Waugh's *Men at Arms.*" *EWN* (Winter 1986), 3-6.

Great Writers of the English Language; Novelists and Prose Writers, ed. James Vin-son. NY: St. Martins Press, 1979.

Greenblatt, Stephen J. *Three Modern Satirists; Waugh, Orwell, and Huxley* New Haven: Yale University Press, 1965.

Greeley, Andrew M. "The Devil You Say." *The New York Times Magazine,* 4 Feb. 1973, 26.

Green, Martin. *Children of the Sun.* New York: Basic, 1976.

Green, Peter. "Du Cote de chez Waugh." *Review of English Literature* (Leeds), 2 (April 1961).

Gribble, Thomas A. "The Nature of a Trimmer." *EWN* (Autumn 1981), 1-3.

Hall, James. "Stylized Rebellion." *The Tragic Comedians.* Bloomington: Indiana University Press, 1963, 45-65.

______. "The Other Post-War Rebellion: Evelyn Waugh Twenty-Five Years After." *EWH,* 28 (June 1961).

Hardin, Richard F. "'Ritual' in Recent Criticism: The Elusive Sense of Com-munity." *PMLA,* October 1978, 846-62.

Hardy, John E. "*Brideshead Revisited*: God, Man and Others." *Man in the Modern Novel.* Seattle: University of Washington Press, 1964, 159-74.

Hart, Jeffrey. "A Touch of Chrism." *Triumph,* 5 (June 1970), 28-30

Harty, E.K "*Brideshead* Re-Read: A Discussion of Some of the Themes of Waugh's *Brideshead Revisited.*" *Unisa English Studies,* 3 (September 1967), 66-74

Heath Jeffrey. "The Private Language of Evelyn Waugh." *English Studies in Canada,* 2 (Fall 1976), 329-38.

______. "*Vile Bodies*: A Revolution in Film Art." *EWN,* 8 (Winter 1974), 2-7

______. *The Picturesque Prison: Evelyn Waugh and His Writing.* Kingston and Montreal: McGill-Queen's University Press, 1982.

Heck, Francis S. "Brideshead or Proust and Gide Revisited." *EWN,*9 (Autumn 1975), 293-310.

Hinchcliffe, Peter. "Fathers and Children in the Novels of Waugh." *UTQ,*35, 1966, 293-310.

Hines, Leo. "Waugh and His Critics." *Commonweal*, 13 (April 1962), 60-63.

Hollis, Christopher. *Evelyn Waugh*. London: Published for the British Council and the National Book League by Longmans, Green, 1966.

Hopley, Claire. "The Significance of Exhilaration and Silence in *Put Out More Flags.*" *MFS,*30 (Spring 1984), 83-97

Hopper, Stanley R. "Irony—the Pathos of the Middle." *Cross Currents,*12, 1969, 31-40

Howarth, Herbert. "Quelling the Riot: Waugh's Progress" in *The Shapeless God:*

Essays in Modern Fiction, ed. H.J. Mooney and T.F Staley, Pittsburgh, 1968, 67-88.

______. "The Character and Language in *Decline and Fall*." *EWN*, 11 (Spring 1977), 8-9

Hunter, Jeanne Clayton. "Uneventful Order: The End of *Decline and Fall*." *EWN*, 12 (Autumn 1978), 7-8

Hutton-Brown, Charles. "Sebastian as Saint: The Hagiographical Sources of Sebastian Flyte." *EWN*, 11 (Winter 1977), 1-7.

Introduction to Satire; Modern Essays, ed. Ronald Paulson. Englewood Cliffs, N.J.: Prentice Hall, 1971.

Jamkhandi, Sudhakar Ratnakar. *The Rhetoric of Waugh; An Evaluation of Evelyn Waugh's Military Novels*. Diss. Texas, 1980.

Jebb, Julian. "Evelyn Waugh: An Interview." *Paris Review*, VIII (1963), 73-95

Jervis, Steven A. "Waugh's *Vile Bodies* and the Younger Generation." *South Atlantic Quarterly*, 66 (Summer 1967), 440-48.

Johnson, J.J "Counterparts: The Classic and the Modern 'Previgilium Veneris'." *EWN*, 8 (Winter 1974), 7-8

Joost, Nicholas. "*A Handful of Dust*: Evelyn Waugh and the Novel of Manners." *Papers on Language and Literature*, 12 (Spring 1976), 177-96.

Kaplan, Stanley R. "Circularity and Futility in *Black Mischief*." *EWN*,15 (Winter 1981), 1-4.

Karl, Frederick R. "The World of Evelyn Waugh; The Normally Insane." *The Contemporary English Novel*. NY: Farrar, Straus and Cudahy, 1962. 167-82.

Kellog, Gene. "The Catholic Novel in Convergence." *Thought*, 45 (Summer 1970), 265-69.

Kernan, Alvin B. *The Plot of Satire*. New Haven: Yale University Press, 1965.

______. "A Theory of Satire," *Modern Satire*, ed. Alvin B. Kernan. NY: Harcourt Brace, 1962, 164-79.

______. "'The Wall and the Jungle' The Early Novels of Evelyn Waugh," *Yale Review*, 53 (Winter 1963), 164-79.

Kermode, Frank. "Mr. Waugh's Cities" in *Puzzles and Epiphanies*. London: Routledge, 1962, 164-75.

Kierkegaard, Soren. *The Concept of Irony*. Lee M. Capel, trans. London: William Collins, 1966.

Kiley, Robert. "The Craft of Despondency—the Traditional Novelists." *Daedalus* (Spring 1963), 220-37

Knight, Gareth, *The Secret Tradition in Arthurian Legend*. Northamptonshire: The Aquarian Press, 1957.

LaFrance, Marston. "Context and Structure of Evelyn Waugh's *Brideshead Revisited*," *Twentieth Century Literature*, 10 (April 1964), 12-18.

Lane, Calvin W. *Evelyn Waugh*. Twayne's English Authors Series. Boston: G.K. Hall, 1981.

Lewis, R.W.B. *The American Adam: Innocence, Tragedy and Tradition in the Nineteenth Century*. Chicago: The University of Chicago Press, 1955.

Linck, Charles E. *The Development of Evelyn Waugh's Career*. Diss. University of Kansas, 1962.

______, Jr. and Robert Murray Davis. "The Bright Young People in *Vile Bodies*." *PLL*, 5 (Winter 1969), 80-90

Linklater, Eric. "Evelyn Waugh," *The Art of Adventure*. London, 1947.

Littlewood, Ian. *The Writings of Evelyn Waugh*. Oxford: Basil Blackwell, 1983.

Lodge, David. *Evelyn Waugh.* Columbia Essays on Modern Writers. New York and London: Columbia University Press, 1971.

Loe, Keith D. *Evelyn Waugh: Man Against History.* Diss. Stanford University, 1969.

Long, Richard A. and Iva G. Jones. "Towards a Definition of the Decadent Novel." *College English,* 22 (January 1961), 245-49.

Macaulay, Rose. "The Best and the Worst II—Evelyn Waugh." *Horizon,* XIV (December 1946). Rep. in *Writers of Today*, 2nd series, ed. D.V. Baker. London, 1948.

Mack, Maynard. "The Muse of Satire," *Studies in the Literature of the Augustan Age,* ed. Richard. C. Boy, 219-31. Also in *Yale Review,* 41 (1951), 80-92.

Manning, Gerald F. *Christianity and Change; The Pattern of Development in Evelyn Waugh's Fiction.* Diss. Queen's University, 1969.

Marcus, Steven. "Evelyn Waugh and the Art of Entertainment." *Partisan Review,* XXIII (Summer 1956).

Martin, Graham. "Novelists of Three Decades; Evelyn Waugh, Graham Greene, C.P. Snow." *The Pelican Guide to English Literature,* 7. Baltimore: Penguin, 1963.

McAleer, Edward C. "*Decline and Fall* as Imitation." *EWN,* 7 (Winter 1973), 1-4

McCartney, George P. *Confused Roaring; Evelyn Waugh and the Modernist Tradition.* Diss. City University, NY, 1980.

McDonnel, Jacqueline. *Evelyn Waugh.* London: MacMillan, 1988.

Meckier, Jermone. "Cycle, Symbol and Parody in Evelyn Waugh's *Decline and Fall.*" *Contemporary Literature,* 20 (Winter 1979), 51-75.

_____. "Evelyn Waugh." *Contemporary Literature*, 18 (Winter 1977), 98-109.

Merton, Thomas. *The Ascent to Truth*. New York: Harcourt, Brace, 1951.

Mikes, George. *Eight Humorists*. London: Allan Wingate, 1954.

Morriss, Margaret and D.J. Dooley. *Evelyn Waugh: A Reference Guide.* Boston: G.K. Hall, 1984.

Myers, William. "Potential Recruits: Evelyn Waugh and the Reader of *Black Mischief,*" *RMS,* 21 (Special Number), 1977, 40-51

Nardin, Jane. "The Myth of Decline in *A Handful of Dust*." *MQ*, 18, (Winter 1977), 119-30

Nemoianu, Virgil. "Evelyn Waugh and The Motley Society." *Clio,* 12, no. 3 (Spring 1983), 233-43

Nichols, James W. "Romantic and Realistic: The Tone of Evelyn Waugh's Early Novels." *College English,* 24 (October 1962), 46-56.

O'Donnell, Donat. *Maria Cross, Imaginative Patterns in a Group of Modern Catholic Writers.* New York: Oxford University Press; rpt. London: Burns and Oates, 1963.

O'Donnovan, Patrick, "Evelyn Waugh's Opus of Disgust." *The New Republic* (February 12, 1962), 21-22.

O'Faolain, Sean. *The Vanishing Hero: Studies in Novelists of the Twenties.* London: Eyre and Spottiswoode, 1956.

Pandeya, S.M. "The Satiric Technique of Evelyn Waugh." *Criticism and Research* (Banaras Hindu University), 1964, 107-23.

Paul, Martin T. *The Comic-Romantic Hero in Eight Novels of Evelyn Waugh.* Diss. University of Wisconsin, 1968.

Phillips, Gene. D. *The Christian Vision of Evelyn Waugh.* Diss. Fordham University, 1970.

_____. *Evelyn Waugh's Officers, Gentlemen and Rogues*. Chicago: Nelson-Hall, 1975.

Philosophical Dictionary, ed. Kenneth Baker. Washington: Gonzago University Press, 1974.

Poems of Tennyson, ed. Christopher Ricks. London: Longman, 1969.

Pryce-Jones, David, ed. *Evelyn Waugh and His World*. Boston: Little, Brown, 1975.

Rahner, Karl. "The Church of Sinners." *Cross Currents,* 1969, 64-74.

Reinhardt, Kurt F. "Waugh; Christian Gentlemen" in his *Theological Novel of Modern Europe.* New York: Frederick Ungar, 203-16.

Revell, Peter. *Quest in Modern American Poetry.* U.S.A.: Vision and Barnes and Noble, 1981.

Robert, Catherne. "Three Phases of Humanism and Their Relations to Problems of Science and Education." *Education and Values,* ed. Douglas Sloan. NY: Columbia University. 1980, 169-80.

Rolo, Charles J. *The World of Evelyn Waugh*. Boston: Little Brown, 1958.

Ruff, Lawrence, A. "Comments on the 'Decadent.'" *College English,* 23 (October 1961), 113-34.

Rutherford, Andrew. "Waugh's *Sword of Honour*" in *The Literature of War.* London: Macmillan, 1978, 113-34.

Sabosan, Jeffrey G. "Irony and the Unexpected." *Cross Currents,* 12, 1969, 429-34.

Savage, D.S. "The Innocence of Evelyn Waugh" in *The Novelist as Thinker (Focus Four),* ed. B. Rajan. London: Dobson, 1947, 34- 46

Sayers, Dorothy L. *The Mind of the Maker.* Connecticut: Greenwood, 1941.

Schorer, Mark. "Technique as Discovery," *Twentieth Century Literary Criticism; A Reader*, ed. David Lodge. USA: Longman, 1972.

Semple, H.E. "Waugh's Modern Crusade." *English Studies in Africa*, 11, 1968, 47-59.

Sequeira, Isaac. *The Theme of Initiation in Modern American Fiction.* Mysore: Geetha, 1975.

Sinha, B.K. "The Sword of Honour." *Indian Journal of English Studies,* XXI, 1981-82, 87-95.

Slater, Ann Pasternak. "Waugh's *A Handful of Dust*: Right Things in Wrong Places." *Essays in Criticism*, 32 (January 1982), 48- 68

Spears, Monroe K. *Dionysus and the City: Modernism in Twentieth Century Poetry.* New York, 1970.

Spender, Setphen. *The Creative Element.* NY: British Book Centre, 1954.

Stannard, Martin. *Evelyn Waugh: 1903-39. The Early Years.* London: Dent, 1987.

_____. "*Work Suspended*: Waugh's Climacteric." *Essays in Criticism,* vol. 28, 1-4, 1978, 302-20.

Stopp, Frederick J. *Evelyn Waugh; Portrait of an Artist.* London: Chapman and Hall, 1958.

_____. "Apology and Explanation." *Renascence,* 10 (Winter 1957-58), 94-99.

_____. "End of an Illusion." *Renascence*, 9 (Winter 1956), 59-67, 76.

_____. "Grace in Reins." *The Month,* 196 (August 1953), 69-84.

_____. "The Circle and the Tangent." *The Month,* 198 (July 1954), 18-34.

Surmelian, Leon. *Techniques of Fiction Writing: Measure and Madness.* New York: Doubleday, 1969.

Sykes, Christopher. *Evelyn Waugh: A Biography.* London: Collins, 1977.

Taylor, Beverley and Elisabeth Brewer. *The Return of King Arthur.* UK: Barnes and Noble, 1983.

Tosser, Yvon. "Le sens de l'absurde dans l'oeuvre d'Evelyn Waugh." Lille: Atelier Universite de lillle; Paris: Champion, 1977.

T.S. Eliot, ed. Hugh Kenner. Englewood Cliffs, N.J.: Prentice Hall, 1962.

The Climate of Faith in Modern Literature, ed. Nathan A. Scott Jr. New York: The Sudbury Press, 1964.

Thomas, Mattie Daniels. *The Quest Motif in Flannery O'Connor's Short Stories.* Diss. Purdue, 1982.

Towards a Poetics of Fiction, ed. Mark Spilka. Indiana University Press, 1977.

Voorhees, Richard J. "Evelyn Waugh's War Novels: A Toast to Lost Causes." *Queen's Quarterly,* 65 (Spring 1958), 53-63.

______. "Evelyn Waugh's Travel Books." *Dalhousie Review* (Summer 1978), 240-48.

______. "Evelyn Waugh Revisited." *South Atlantic Quarterly,* 48 (April 1949), 270-80.

Wallis, David H. "A Reading of Evelyn Waugh's *Brideshead Revisited*: A Critical Survey and Thematic Analysis. II." Diss. Tulsa University, 1968.

Wasson, Richard. "*A Handful of Dust*: Critique of Victorianism." *Modern Fiction Studies*, 7 (Winter 1961-62), 327-37.

Waugh, Evelyn. "Fan-Fare." *Life* (April 1946), 53-60.

______. "Felix Culpa?" *Commonweal,* 18 (July 1948), 322-25.

Waugh, Alec. *My Brother Evelyn and Other Profiles.* London: Cassell, 1968.

Webster, Harvey Curtis. "Evelyn Waugh: Catholic Aristocrat," *After the Trauma: Representative British Novelists since 1920.* Lexington: University of Kentucky Press, 1970, 72-92

Weston, Jessie L. *From Ritual to Romance.* New York: Doubleday, 1957.

Wiley, P.W "Evelyn Waugh." *Contemporary Literature*, 9, 1968, 261-64

Wijesinha, Rajiva. "The Vile Bodies (Evelyn Waugh Memorial) Society." *EWN*, 17, 3, 1983, 6-7

Wilson, Edmund. "Never Apologise, Never Explain: The Art of Evelyn Waugh" in his *Classics and Commercials.* New York: Farrar, Straus, 1950, 140-46

______. "Splendours and Miseries of Evelyn Waugh" in his *Classics and Commericals,* 298-305

Wooton, Carl. *Responses to the Modern World. A Study of Evelyn Waugh's Novels.* Diss. Oregan University, 1967.

______. "Waugh's *Brideshead Revisited*: War and Limited Hope." *Midwest Quarterly,* 10, 1969, 359-75

Wright, Andrew H. "Irony and Fiction." *Journal of Aesthetics and Art Criticism,* 12 (Sep. 1953), 111-18.

Wykes, David. "Evelyn Waugh's Sword of Volvograd." *DQR,* 7, 1977.

Index